PRAISE FOR THE BOOK

I have never sat down to read a book in one sitting before, but I simply could not put *Bassie – My Journey of Hope* down. Bassie's memoir, written so that her children and grandchildren will know her truth, makes every reader privy to an extraordinary life, lived in the full glare of the public and under the intense scrutiny of the media.

Bassie writes in a chatty, engaging style that is no different from an intimate face-to-face chat. She introduces the pivotal people in her life and, with her characteristic generosity, acknowledges 'the village' that raised her. While her journey is deeply personal, she shares universal truths and life lessons from which everyone can benefit, regardless of the stage of their journey.

Hers is a story of 'great wins and spectacular losses' underpinned by her strong faith that centres her in times of triumph and sustains her in times of trial. *Bassie – My Journey of Hope* will leave you feeling like an insider, invested in her success as she continues on her stellar journey. Above all, it will encourage you and leave you smiling, assured in the knowledge that it is possible to achieve way beyond your wildest dreams.

– **Doreen Morris, producer**

Bassie's life is testimony to the fact that it is possible to have everything and achieve everything while at the same time retaining your core values of respect, integrity and service. In her memoir, Bassie teaches us that dreams only become reality when you work hard at them and that they are just the beginning. Her humility, authenticity and generosity of spirit are inked onto every page.

– **Zelda la Grange, author of** *Good Morning, Mr Mandela*

My wife Zelda and I have known Bassie for many years and it warms our hearts to see how she has emerged as a woman of God. Since being crowned Miss South Africa, she has been a formidable force and so much has happened in her life. With every chapter, she has grown and excelled. It makes us incredibly proud when we see her accomplishments, but what makes us most proud is that she has always honoured

God and remained faithful to Him. Bassie has been a member of our church for over thirty-five years and we are privileged to have her.

We have watched Bassie face struggles and opposition with bravery and seen her emerge victorious. She always gets up, grows and reinvents herself. There is no such thing as 'standing still' for her. Her energy and passion is contagious, so you will often see her simultaneously empower and take others along with her.

Bassie is an inspiration to women. I often ask my congregation: 'Do you wear Jesus well?' Bassie definitely does. She is a wonderful wife, mother, daughter, sister, businesswoman, philanthropist and producer, an inspirational speaker and a child of God – she fulfils each role with excellence.

This book will inspire and encourage you, because it comes from real experiences and a true heart. We hope you will enjoy reading it as much as we have enjoyed observing Bassie's exciting journey thus far.

– **Pastor Ray and Zelda McCauley,**
Rhema Bible Church North, South Africa

Bassie's indomitable spirit, fierce loyalty and strength of character, in addition to her grace, beauty and creative intellect, have found a home in me as a 'daughter of my heart'. Her journey has proved that there is no dream too big, no path too rocky and no obstacle insurmountable. This is a book that I hope will inspire a new generation of female entrepreneurs, women leaders and black girl-children to realise that no matter where they were born or their background, their dreams are valid, and to not allow the circumstances of their past to define and determine their destiny and future.

– **Graça Machel, humanitarian and founder of the Graça Machel Trust**

BASSIE

BASSIE
My Journey of Hope

BASETSANA KUMALO

PENGUIN BOOKS

Bassie – My Journey of Hope
Published by Penguin Books
an imprint of Penguin Random House South Africa (Pty) Ltd
Reg. No. 1953/000441/07
The Estuaries No. 4, Oxbow Crescent, Century Avenue, Century City, 7441
PO Box 1144, Cape Town, 8000, South Africa
www.penguinrandomhouse.co.za

Penguin
Random House
South Africa

First published 2019

1 3 5 7 9 10 8 6 4 2

PUBLISHER: Marlene Fryer
MANAGING EDITOR: Ronel Richter-Herbert
EDITOR: Bronwen Maynier
PROOFREADER: Dane Wallace
COVER DESIGNER: Monique Cleghorn
TEXT DESIGNER: Ryan Africa
TYPESETTER: Monique van den Berg

Set in 11.5 pt on 15 pt Adobe Caslon

Printed by **novus print**, a Novus Holdings company

	MIX
FSC www.fsc.org	Paper from responsible sources
	FSC® C022948

Penguin Random House is committed to
a sustainable future for our business, our readers
and our planet. This book is made from Forest
Stewardship Council® certified paper.

ISBN 978 1 77609 481 3 (print)
ISBN 978 1 77609 482 0 (ePub)

Disclaimer
Every effort has been made to accredit the copyright holders of the images
used in this book. In the case of an omission, please contact the publisher
in order for the correct attribution to be made in event of a reprint.

To my #Heartbeat, Nkosinathi Gabriel, uShaka Kgositsile Emmanuel and Bontle ba Morena Jasmine, I wrote this book for you, to know my truth, to hear my story, in my own voice. I love you to infinity.

To my husband, Romeo, thank you for the journey and thank you for your love. Doing life with you is a blessing.

To my parents, Phillip and Nomazizi Makgalemele, I hope I did you proud. Thank you for everything.

To my siblings, Lerato, Johanna and Mojalefa, you make life beautiful.

To the sisterhood, indeed I stand on the shoulders of great and formidable women. My gratitude to you. You know your fine selves by name. Love you, my girls.

CONTENTS

MY JOURNEY OF HOPE

FOREWORD

ADVOCATE THULI MADONSELA

Crowned Miss South Africa at a time when the main achievement of beauty queens was marrying the most eligible bachelor and thereafter pursuing philanthropy courses, Basetsana Kumalo, née Makgalemele, took a road unimagined. As M. Scott Peck once said, that made all the difference.

Bassie, as she is affectionately called, leveraged every opportunity presented by her title to establish herself as a formidable business-woman. How did she do it and, above all, what has been the key to her career sustainability?

In her memoir, *Bassie – My Journey of Hope*, Bassie answers these and many other questions about her career, her epic success, transcending humble beginnings and keeping her feet on the ground. In this book, which reads like a playbook on living a *carpe diem* life, the super beauti-ful Bassie outlines her entrepreneurial journey.

Bassie credits her business acumen and ethical values to her parents. Hers is a classic case of the African saying that it takes a village to raise a child. She also attributes her epic journey to relatives, particularly her grandparents and uncle.

Her teachers also get a positive mention and so do a number of strangers who touched her life positively. Among those strangers who contributed to the trajectory of her journey is Nelson Mandela. She credits Madiba, as we affectionately know him, with appreciating the importance of education.

Life has not been a walk in the park for Bassie. The narrative of her journey includes unimaginable heartache, including stalking and being the target of a smear campaign. She says that it was hope that got her through it all, hence the title of the book. We may also add spiritual intelligence, as her story has dimensions of a classic case of faith like a mustard seed.

Unashamedly honest about having leant on others in times of turbulence, Bassie is committed to making it a little easier for those who come after her, particularly in the areas of entrepreneurship and media. When I spontaneously asked for her to contribute to a course on transcending poverty and underdevelopment through enterprising minds as part of our Enterprising Communities Initiative, she instantly offered to travel all the way to KwaMzimela Traditional Authority near Empangeni to empower young people directly. Raising young entrepreneurs, she says, is her way of passing it on.

She has known pain, she has tasted ecstasy, and she has weaved it all to make a life of purpose and joy. Bassie's story offers great lessons for us all. But it is a particularly instructive story for young girls about stumbling on opportunities and making the most of them. It's also about staring adversity in the face, and kicking its behind while retaining your joy, humility and sense of wonder.

I can't imagine a better timing for Bassie's story of hope. As our country and the world go through turbulence, it's easy to lose hope, yet it's hope-anchored leadership that we need to reset us on a winning streak.

A copy of this book is undoubtedly a worthy investment regardless of the stage of your career. My greatest hope is that young people, particularly women and girls, will organise circles of hope to discuss Bassie's journey and extract lessons for their own healing and advancement, and pass it on.

Advocate Thuli Madonsela
August 2019

FOREWORD

DR PHUMZILE MLAMBO-NGCUKA

With her memoir, *Bassie – My Journey of Hope*, Basetsana Kumalo has gifted the world with a fast-paced page-turner filled with enriching life lessons. Reading her story was wonderful and effortless; at the end of each chapter, I was always hungry for more.

Readers will learn of Bassie's many triumphs, told with endearing humility, along with the inevitable trying moments, told without grudge or bitterness. This has to be one of the essential takeaways from the book: the importance of winning and losing gracefully.

As we often think of celebrities as people who mistake social media friends for their 'besties', it is wonderful to see how Bassie still cherishes real kinship, family, her siblings and everyday friends – real people you can truly confide in, touch and feel.

She highlights her family moments much more than her interactions with famous people. This makes her relatable as *umtanasekhaya*. Of course, she does start by letting us know that she is writing this book for her family and children.

This memoir shows that fame comes with unique challenges and privileges. Privileges – such as quality time with Madiba and Oprah, and travels to the best places in the world – must co-exist with the dangers of stalkers and invasions of privacy. Bassie shows us what it's like to fly high and keep your feet on the ground at the same time.

She courageously takes us into her personal space, including dark places, notably the abuse by Dingaan Thobela. She powerfully shares her #metoo moment, which I hope will give courage to other women to walk away from abusive relationships.

All of her readers will be proud of her and her decision to choose Romeo, who brought happiness to her life, and may she give hope to other women that a bright future can follow a trauma.

Readers will experience a valuable teaching moment through the description of how Bassie went about building her business empire, and how she learnt to use her connections, hard work and perseverance to become a brand. Hers is a story of beauty with brains.

Most endearing to me in this book is the generous affirmation heaped on others, especially women, whom Bassie has met along her journey. Those of us included in her memoir cannot help but be humbled by the kind mention.

Dr Phumzile Mlambo-Ngcuka
Under-Secretary-General
Executive Director of UN Women

PROLOGUE

For the better part of my adult life, I have kept a journal and recorded thoughts and recollections on my dictaphone. The plan was always to one day sit down and write my memoir, to tell my story in my own words, share my thoughts and feelings, and relate the hard-won lessons. But I have a busy life – my three children and my full-time career take up pretty much all the hours in the day – and I never quite got around to the sitting down and writing part as a working mom.

I've been in the public eye for twenty-five years, and in that time so many untruths have been written about me that I generally don't pay them too much attention. I am sure we can all agree that people need to be declared man and wife before they can be reduced to plaintiff and defendant in a divorce proceeding, but when Romeo and I got married, sources were reporting our divorce before we'd even made it down the aisle. The desperately painful miscarriages that I endured as we struggled for a family, my weight gain during that difficult time, my business problems, just about anything you can imagine – my struggles, real and invented, have been tabloid fodder.

I learnt to let people talk and I just got on with my life. I generally have a happy disposition. I forgive quickly, I laugh often and I don't take myself too seriously. I know who I am, and I have never needed the opinion of others to help me with that. I don't go rushing to the newspapers with my side of the story. When you know something to be true in your very core, there is no need to shout it from the rooftops.

Lately, though, I have started asking myself some serious questions

1

about the legacy I have created. I do not regret my decision not to engage in rumours and gossip-mongering, but unfortunately, that choice has resulted in some untruths being told about me in the public domain. Unfortunately, as the saying goes, 'A lie told into history lives as truth.' I won't allow that.

I asked myself, what if my grandchildren were to wonder who I was and where I came from, what inspired me, what I believed in, what brought me joy, what gave me hope, and I realised I would want to tell them in my own voice. Many beautiful South Africans have embraced me and supported me over the years, and I want them, too, to know me, the essence of me, not from a magazine cover story, or a television or radio interview, but in my own words.

There were other factors that pointed to this being the moment to write my memoir. The year 2019 marks twenty-five years since I was crowned Miss South Africa, twenty-five years of being a television producer, twenty-five years of being an entrepreneur, twenty-five years of my walk with Christ, twenty-five years of democracy in this country and, of course, my forty-fifth birthday!

I was also drawn to reflect on the zeitgeist of 1994. It was an extra-ordinary year for South Africa and for me personally. The main theme of that year, for me, was hope. That message of hope is something we all still need to embrace today, a quarter of a century later. I want my voice and my story to help recall that sense of hope.

This is a story of possibilities, of what a black girl-child could achieve back in 1994, and of what women can achieve today, regardless of their background or their race. My hope is that my story will inspire a whole new generation of young entrepreneurs and achievers.

When I actually sat down to work on this book, I was able to feel a deep sense of gratitude for the good fortune I have had to live this full and beautiful life. I wanted to pay homage to my mother the school teacher and my father the bus driver, people whose influence still lives within all who knew them. I turned my mind to my childhood in Soweto, growing up with my amazing sisters Johanna and Lerato, and my brother Mojalefa, and the early beauty-pageant days that brought me to the Sun City Superbowl and the Miss South Africa crown. And that was just the beginning.

I've lived a charmed life. Yes, I have been truly blessed and I count my blessings each and every day, but there have also been many barriers to overcome and battles to fight. I wanted to share those stories too. I wanted to pay tribute to the many people who sheltered me, loved me and forced me to get out of bed when I was so broken I didn't even have the courage to do that.

A lot of South Africans know a little bit about my story. They may know me as the former young Miss South Africa or the *Top Billing* presenter. Some may recall my fairytale wedding to Romeo, the man of my dreams who serenaded me on our wedding day, or my relationship with uTata Madiba, my mentor, father figure and guiding light. Others may be familiar with my business interests. This book weaves all these little strands into the tapestry of my life.

My father used to say, 'Baby girl, keep the faith and don't lose hope.' May *My Journey of Hope* inspire you to do the same.

Love, light and gratitude,

Basetsana

PART I

THE EARLY YEARS

ONE

The year was 1980 and I was a six-year-old girl growing up in Soweto, a township located in the south-west of Johannesburg, South Africa. Soweto was created in the 1930s when the government of the day started separating people according to race, thereby creating 'black' townships. They did this by applying different iterations of the now infamous Group Areas Act, which was officially promulgated in 1950. The effect of the Act was to assign different residential and business sections in urban areas to different racial groups, and in so doing, to exclude non-whites from living in the most developed areas.

My family and I lived in a township called Killarney, just next to Mzimhlophe. Like any other residential area in Soweto, Killarney consisted of row upon row of identical four-roomed houses. People often refer to the dusty streets of Soweto, but to a child born into that environment, there is nothing dusty about it. There is only the familiarity of a close-knit community made up of family, neighbours and friends.

In the winter, we warmed our houses with coal stoves – people even wrote songs about those 'Welcome Dover' stoves. The tiny kitchens were the heart of the home, and those stoves were where meals were prepared every day. Each house had two small bedrooms, and so the children often slept together in one room. The toilets were outside and there were no bathrooms, so we would boil water on the stove and wash in metal basins.

It seems that I was destined to be an entrepreneur from the word go.

One of my earliest memories is of standing in Mama's kitchen, making sandwiches to sell. It was a production line: Mama cutting the bread, my big sister Lerato and second-eldest sister Johanna slicing French polony or grating cheese, and me, so small I had to stand on an upturned bucket to reach the counter, adding a lettuce leaf or a slice of tomato to each sandwich. At the end of the line was Papa, wrapping the finished products in cling wrap.

We sold those sandwiches outside Orlando Stadium before soccer matches. The crowd would gather, and my sisters and I would take up position at the stadium's doors. Our dad made us these special boxes with a ribbon that you put around your neck to put the sandwiches in. If it was a big game, Mama would also make a huge pot of *pap* and Papa would braai *nyama*. So we were busy!

Back then, Orlando Stadium was the Mecca of soccer culture in South Africa, regularly attracting thousands of fans to its doors as they came to witness their beloved teams fight it out on the field. The atmosphere in the township before a big game was palpable, especially if it was a game between Kaizer Chiefs and Orlando Pirates (Amakhosi and Amabhakabhaka), and the festivities started way before kick-off. From early in the morning, you would see fans dressed from head to toe in their regalia greeting their neighbours and friends with excitement and anticipation. Local shebeens would host those who had not managed to buy a ticket to the game, and loud cheering would erupt onto the street whenever a goal was scored.

The streets leading to the stadium would be lined with people who wanted to be there early so that they could partake in the pre-match festivities. Those who were more interested in making a quick buck could be seen trying to sell their tickets to others for a tidy sum. They would haggle about the price in *tsotsitaal*, a dialect spoken only in Soweto, until an agreement was reached, one departing from the stadium a little richer and the other relieved to have secured his way in.

As the afternoon wore on and the game drew nearer, vendors like my family would appear, peddling food, drinks, branded T-shirts and caps. A market of sorts welcomed fans as the powerful sound of vuvuzelas (made out of metal back then) filled the air, adding to the urgency of the moment. There was no mistaking the chatter and cheering as people took their places and waited for the players to take to the field. The atmosphere was electric.

I saw all of this as I stood at the stadium doors selling sandwiches. Thinking about it now, although I was very small and the crowd was huge, I never for a moment felt unsafe. Quite the opposite, actually, because our communities were so tight. In those days, the adage 'it takes a village to raise a child' was real and true. Things in Soweto have definitely changed since then.

On the face of it, my parents were not entrepreneurs. When they first met, my mom, Beatrice Nomazizi, was a schoolteacher. She led the school choir, and one of the things they would do was visit the patients at Baragwanath Hospital and sing for them. On one of those visits, she met a good-looking young clerk named Phillip Makgalemele. The way my mom told it, those nurses were not at all happy to have her come and claim this eligible bachelor. Dad was quite the catch, and more than a few of the nurses had their eye on him. But he only had eyes for my mom.

Their love blossomed, and they were soon married and living in Soweto. Before long, Papa left Bara to become a bus driver – I think Mama was keen to get him away from those nurses – and they started a family. Papa had been married before, to Mma Sarah, and had three sons, Brian (now deceased), Harrison and Botsang, my brothers, whom I love dearly.

When I came along, neatly spaced four years behind Johanna, who was four years behind Lerato, my parents named me Basetsana, which means 'girls' in Setswana. (My second name is Julia, after Koko Julia, one of my dad's relatives in Botswana.) They say in our culture that if you have a lot of girls and you want a boy, you name the girl Basetsana or Ntombizodwa and that somehow closes off the netball team of girls and the next child will be a boy. The same if you have many boys; you name the boy Bafana, which means 'boys', and the next child will be a girl. I am not quite sure about this logic, but who am I to argue? A year and a half later my brother was born! He was named Mojalefa, which means 'the heir to the throne', as befits the first son. His second name is Abbegarcia, after our maternal grandfather.

My parents told me that I was impossible when my brother was born. I was too young, he came too close and I was not at all happy. There's a picture of my mom, my brother and me standing outside the gate, all dressed in our Sunday best. My mother's looking spiffy, holding the baby. I'm in my church dress and white socks, and I'm howling, absolutely howling, looking at this dude who's just decided to come and usurp my place. Like, where did you come from? The long-awaited son had arrived and was taking my shine! Actually, in most pictures from our childhood, I am crying, especially if my brother is being held.

It didn't help that he was a beautiful baby. He had a very fair complexion and his nickname was Tshehla, which is Setswana for 'the fair one'. I still call him that. When he got older, being the only boy, he was mollycoddled and got away with not doing very much, unlike us girls, who were hard at work on our chores every day. Ooh, I tell you, that would really rub me up the wrong way. 'Why is Tshehla not washing the dishes? Why doesn't he have to do this or that?' So I can't say I was always happy with him, but he was and is a beautiful, kind and gentle soul.

By the time I was four or five, I was desperate to go to school. My older sisters were already at school, and I was always on my mother's case, begging to be allowed to go. The classroom environment had always intrigued me. My mom even brought a chalkboard and some chalk home, and I started to play teacher-teacher. Mama didn't like us to go out and play in the streets, but she welcomed kids to our house, and when they came, we would play teacher-teacher. I was the teacher, of course, and I was strict! Best you do your homework right or you'll get a hiding.

Eventually Mama decided to take me with her to the school where she taught, Thabisang Primary School in Phefeni, for part of the week. I was too little to be in the formal school programme, but at least I was there, where I wanted to be. And seeing as I was there, Mama figured I might as well be useful. During break, she would give me a bag of little lollipops to sell to the other kids for a few cents each. I loved it. Just loved it! It made me important. I may have been the littlest kid at the school, but I was the one you went to for a lollipop.

School finished at 2 p.m., but we were still hustling. My mom had us selling hard-boiled eggs around the neighbourhood. We would get

home and she would hand us a tray of eggs and say, 'Right, eggs, go ...'
I learnt some business lessons that way, I can tell you.

There was an old lady, Ma-Rooi, who would always take my eggs
on credit and say, 'Tell your mother I'll pay her next time.' When I got
home, my mom would count the eggs left in the tray, and count the
money I brought back, and of course my loot would not add up. I'd
have to tell Moeder – that's what we called her; it's the Afrikaans word
for 'mother' – that it was because of Ma-Rooi. One day I came home
with the same story – 'Moeder, Ma-Rooi says she'll pay you next
time' – and Mama said, 'No, I'm done with Ma-Rooi.' She got up,
wrapped her little *ibhayi* (blankie) around her waist, and off she went
to Ma-Rooi's house. What happened in that house remains a mystery
to this day. All I know is that Mama came back with her money. And
from then on, Ma-Rooi paid up. You didn't mess with my mother!

I can't tell you that I was delighted to be out there selling. To be
honest, I often felt quite resentful. It was unfair! While other kids
were having a good time playing in the streets, we were only allowed
to go out on the streets if it was to hustle for the family. Why did
we have to work so hard? And there was no incentive. We didn't get to
keep a cut or anything like that. You just did what was expected of you.
It all went into the pot, and of course we always had food on the table,
clothes on our backs and a roof over our heads.

As we all know, hindsight is the best science, and I know now that
what I picked up and learnt from my mother was the best informal
education and training I could ever have received. No Ivy League institution could have taught me what I learnt in my mother's house, in the
sandwich production line, or in the hustle of the streets doing my part
to help supplement the family income.

My mother learnt her business skills from her father, uTat' Mkhulu
Abbegarcia, who started a printing business called Zam-Zam Printers
at no. 10 Good Street, Sophiatown, in 1937, the year my mother was
born. The business flourished. By day, they printed the regular sort
of things for businesses and the public – advertising fliers, wedding
invitations, calendars and what have you – but at night, when the
doors closed, they began to print African National Congress (ANC)
pamphlets and paraphernalia.

For a black family with little to no access to skills and funding, to be able to run a successful business was unheard of in the townships back then. There were so many structural barriers to overcome in a country that sought to control and suppress black people. The segregated education system was not designed to help them expand their horizons in any way, and the Bantu Education Act of 1953 directly affected the lives of their children.

The apartheid government strove to ensure that Africans received an inferior education to whites. Matriculants of Bantu Education, if they were able to cope with the challenges of actually attending school, therefore had little exposure to the English language and very limited knowledge of the world. Most dreamt of becoming civil servants such as nurses and teachers, because that was all they knew. It was exactly what the state wanted: an entire racial group that sought nothing more than to do as they were told.

My grandfather showed great courage in the face of real and present danger, and he did so because he wanted something better for his children and grandchildren. It was this sense of defiance that ensured his descendants believed in their own abilities and talents.

My uncle, Malume Seiiso, tells me that my grandfather was a real community builder and somebody who was very much loved. Kofifi (as Sophiatown was known) had its share of gangs in those days – there were the Vultures and the Russians – and Malume says they all loved my grandfather and watched out for him and his business. When the police were on their way and it looked like a raid was coming, the gangs would tip him off with a whistle or someone would come and tell him, '*Nanka amabhunu Mkhulu*.' (The white policemen are coming.)

The apartheid system eventually chased Zam-Zam Printers, along with many black families, out of Sophiatown. Thanks to the Group Areas Act of 1950, over 60 000 black inhabitants were forcibly removed from the suburb. By this stage, my grandfather's business was well established. He had imported top-of-the-range printing machines from England – if you want the names, ask my uncle, he knows them all! – but when the shop was raided and they had to move, the best of those machines were taken. When they relocated to Meadowlands, Zone 4, 510f Mziki Street, they were left with just the basics. Entire communities of people lost all their worldly possessions in the displacements. I imagine they felt gutted, violated and lost, but, most of all, afraid. If the government could do this to them once, who was to say it could not happen again? It was a show of power, a way for the state to spread the message that it was in control.

It seems impossible that people like my grandparents had the fortitude to begin all over again, but that is exactly what they did. The hope they carried in their hearts could not be forcibly removed. My grandfather reopened the business in their home, but had to buy the equipment again and rebuild. My mom's youngest sister, Auntie Thozama, still runs that printing business in Meadowlands to this day.

Malume Seiiso was a salesman par excellence. He sold furniture for the Goldbergs and later the Savells. He was one of those dynamic uncles with a fantastic sense of humour. He helped train us girls. I remember when we were selling ice creams – oh yes, another of Moeder's schemes – he showed us how to market them. 'Now, girls, you must be very clear when you ring that bell,' he said, 'and you must shout, "I scream for ice cream, I scream for ice cream", and then you will move that stock.' He always says that one of his great regrets in life is that he never got the opportunity to go to university, but Uncle knew what he was talking about. We sold those ice creams, all right!

Malume Seiiso and I remain very close. When I need guidance, whether it's about my marriage or life in general, I call him, and he is always ready to share a cup of tea and have a heart-to-heart. That man has my heart, I tell you. He is my only surviving uncle, and he's a father figure to me. I feel truly blessed that he is still with us. When the going gets tough, I go to him; his wisdom guides me and my truth. He offers counsel, never judges and always believes the best of you. I love him so deeply. Even my friends know him and reach out to him for guidance. Okay, he is 'open' for sale ... ha ha ha, just kidding.

As well as being a good businessman, Malume Seiiso is a community leader and involved in local politics. If there is a big cultural or traditional event, Malume is the person who comes to speak to the cow that will be slaughtered. If there are problems in the neighbourhood or within families, he's the one to whom people turn to resolve matters.

Of course, a salesman like that never really stops selling. Even though he is in his late seventies now, he is still in business, running a trading store from the front of his home. And that stock is still moving fast! Now you come for your goods, plus prayer and advice. I adore him.

One thing I know for sure is that I come from a family of people who truly believed that they could make a difference. People who did not allow fear to get in the way of their aspirations. They did not have money or power, but their faith gave them the resilience they needed to keep moving forward.

TWO

The 1970s and 1980s were marked by violence in South Africa. On the morning of 16 June 1976, thousands of black students planned a protest march that would start at their respective schools and end at Orlando Stadium. They were protesting the fact that Afrikaans had been made compulsory in township schools throughout the country.

What was meant to be a peaceful rally to implore the government to hear the students' concerns turned violent when the police were called in to disperse the crowds. Riots broke out and hundreds of students were killed as a result. Among the victims was twelve-year-old Hector Pieterson, whose lifeless body was captured in an iconic image that made it into newspapers around the world. In the photograph, fellow student Mbuyisa Makhubu is seen carrying Hector's body as the boy's distraught sister, Antoinette Sithole, runs next to them.

The violence continued into the 1980s, as masses of ordinary South Africans took to the streets to protest against the apartheid regime, and the government responded with extreme brutality and repression. In 1983, under Prime Minister (and later President) P.W. Botha, a tricameral (three-chamber) parliament was created, which included limited representation for coloureds and Indians but excluded black people. This was meant as a concession on the part of the government, but most people knew that was a lie. By now, blacks only had political rights in the so-called homelands, which were established to prevent them from living in urban areas. In the late seventies and early eighties, several homelands were granted 'independence', with the aim of eventually stripping black people of their South African citizenship, and any accompanying protections and rights.

By 1985, the apartheid time bomb was ready to explode. In July of that year, Botha declared a state of emergency in thirty-six of the country's 260 magisterial districts in response to the civil unrest that had rocked the country for months. Within the first six months of this state of emergency, more than 500 people were killed in political violence, mostly at the hands of the South African Police. Between 1985 and 1989, the government used states of emergency to change restrictions at will. It was estimated that by February 1988, more than 20 000 people had been detained under emergency regulations.

Through all of this, life in the townships carried on, and it was in this context that I came of age on Msitshana Street, Soweto. My siblings and I were oblivious to the political turmoil, shielded by our parents from the harsh reality surrounding us.

Mama and Papa made a formidable team as business partners and parents, not least because they were complete opposites.

My mom was a strong-willed woman who didn't suffer fools. We were petrified of Moeder. She was the one who administered corporal punishment. If you did anything wrong, at home or at school, don't you worry your fine self, that shoe would come at you. If you were out of line, don't you worry, that wooden spoon with which she made *pap* would land on your bum – *thwack!* My mom was very clear as a disciplinarian. This was what she expected, this was how she was going to raise her kids, and it was her way or the highway. I know we think about these things differently today, but my generation of women who were raised by disciplinarians didn't turn out too badly, to be frank.

Her influence extended beyond our house, into the neighbourhood. If a parent thought their child was becoming a delinquent, my mom was the one who was called upon to address the child. In fact, she was sometimes used as a threat: 'If you carry on like that, I will get Mma Makgalemele to come and sort you out ...'

Very occasionally, we would disobey our mother. She didn't like us to leave the property unless we were at school or church, or out working for the family, but sometimes we would venture out. When we did go out in the street, there would always be a lookout and the other kids would shout, 'She's coming! She's coming! Moeder is on her way!' It was nerve-racking!

Zwipi is a two-player game using a single coin. Each player places a bet as to how the coin will land (heads or tails), and then one of them spins it as fast as they can. Whoever predicted correctly wins the bet. Johanna has always been good with money, and her fearless nature inclined her to play these kinds of games, even though she was technically gambling. She believed she was going to win, and she often did. She would go out to play *zwipi* with other kids in the street. The deal was that I would do her chores and she would split her winnings with me. One time Johanna got into trouble with her coin game. There was this guy called Peter, who was quite the little thug, and one day he robbed Johanna of her winnings, which were probably all of a few cents. Lerato, who had never hurt a fly, went to sort Peter out. Word soon got around: 'Lerato, the quiet one, you don't want to be messing with her, or her siblings. She beat up Peter.' That was also the last day that anyone was scared of Peter.

Luckily, Mama never found out about Johanna's street antics or Lerato's brawling with the neighbourhood thug. It wouldn't have ended well, I can tell you. When we did get into trouble, we went to Papa, because we knew that we would have a better, softer landing. He wasn't a disciplinarian at all.

Let me tell you about my dad. My father's family was originally from Botswana. My paternal grandfather, Reverend Johannes Makgalemele, was one of five brothers, of whom two were businessmen and three were clerics in the Anglican Church. My dad's mom, Maria Frentie – we called her Mawe – was blessed with four children. Mawe is the only grandparent I got to meet. My other grandparents were already deceased by the time I was born. When I was a child, we regularly visited Mawe in Orlando East. She didn't speak much. I do remember two things about her very clearly. One was that she loved the Lord. The other was that she baked the best muffins. She made these banana muffins with fish oil instead of butter, and they were the bomb! I always wanted to go to Orlando East because I knew Mawe was going to make those muffins.

My father was heavily influenced by his Christian upbringing. At suppertime, we would say grace: 'For the food we are about to receive, we thank the Lord, amen.' And after dinner we would gather round as a family and Papa would read the Bible. He would always elaborate, extrapolate and philosophise, so if we were reading about Paul on the road to Damascus, he would explain what Paul did and then go and find a book about Paul and what his journey meant. These lessons ended with us praying individually and then collectively, saying the Lord's Prayer.

Papa got matric, called a junior certificate, or JC, in those days. He never went to college – he always said he went to the University of Life – but he had a real love of books and he was a philosopher at heart. He showed a deep thoughtfulness and understanding of who we are and why we are here on this earth. He encouraged us to see the bigger picture and to think about a greater calling in our lives.

People in the township loved to hear Bra Phil philosophise. He was great at it, and he brought so many others along on the journey of figuring out what life is all about. He had a penchant for using 'bombastic' words. He would then say, 'Go and check in your Oxford dictionary what that word means.' To be literate was a big deal in the township, and it was a point of pride for my father. Not only did he have a large vocabulary, he was also an avid reader who collected books. He passed his love of reading onto us, and it is one of the ways that his legacy lives on.

Papa was so funny. He loved life and enjoyed people and the conviviality of gathering people around him. At family events, he was the one who would be asked to make the speech. When he laughed, he literally laughed with his entire body! He enjoyed his shot of brandy with his mates, who called him by his township swag name, Phil Jones. My dad showed up for life. Even when he was retired, he would dress sharply in his three-piece suit every day, with his Dobbs hat and Florsheim shoes. I think it inspired his children to show up for life too, and to make their mark.

Having him for a father was like having your own personal motivational speaker in the house. We were raised in an environment where we were affirmed every day and never belittled. He would say, 'Yes, baby girl, you are great. You can be whatever you want to be. If you work hard in life, there's nothing you can't do.' Or he would say, 'You look so pretty today, my darling.' Especially as girl-children, I think this attitude of his was very significant in our lives. We didn't have to look outside for validation. We grew up with confidence, believing that we were worthy and were enough.

Papa was incredibly positive. He thought positively and spoke positivity into our lives every day. When I was thirteen, he gave me the book *The Power of Positive Thinking* by Norman Vincent Peale. At that age, okay, it was quite interesting, but when I was in my early twenties I went back to it and reflected on it. It was only then that I really started to understand what Papa was trying to teach me – that your thoughts are so important in creating your universe and your reality. I still revisit that book. It's interesting how, as you go through life, you see and understand different things when you are ready for them, and they get illuminated in your spirit in a profound way.

Papa worked for the Public Utility Transport Corporation (PUTCO), which had been established in 1945. During the apartheid era, PUTCO was the main 'blacks-only' bus company. Still in operation today, it has grown into the biggest commuter bus operator in the country and is the only public passenger company previously listed on the Johannesburg Stock Exchange (JSE). When I was quite young, Papa had an accident. His bus collided with another bus and he injured his shoulder quite badly. He was in hospital for some weeks, and when he came out, he wasn't able to continue full time as a bus driver. He was laid off from PUTCO and decided to take early retirement. He then put all of his effort into the family businesses.

One of his tasks was to drive us to school in his second-hand yellow Peugeot 404. My parents always purchased their cars second-hand, and they would go hunting for bargains. The Peugeot was one such find, but unfortunately for my father, it was difficult to get it to start, especially during the winter months. He would have to wake up very early so that he could pour hot water over the engine before turning the key to get the ignition system going. He'd then have to leave it idling for half an hour to 'warm' up. I remember watching him go through this tedious process every single morning. I remember the sounds the car would make, the cold winter air surrounding him and the diligence with which he performed the task. It was the kind of thing that would have been discouraging to many others, but my father did it with pride, because to him it represented his ability to take care of his family and to get them to where they needed to be.

My mother never learnt to drive and had always been dependent on my dad to drop her and fetch her at work, and take her on errands, like going to some factory for discounted goods or anything to do with their businesses. That frustrated my mom, and she always said to us, 'My children, learn how to drive. That's your independence. Make sure you learn how to drive.' Occasionally, Papa, bless his heart, would be late to pick Mama up from school. School finished at two o'clock and Papa would sometimes get there at three o'clock, and my mom would lose it. 'Why did you make me wait?' she'd demand.

At around this time, my mother went to bricklaying school and learnt how to make and lay bricks. I'm sure she must have been one of the first black women to do such a thing – as I've said, my mom was a force! She and my dad went into the brick-making business. Using the money that we'd made as a family with all of our hustles, they bought a little site nearby and started to make and sell bricks there.

Building was big business. In the township in those days, most people started off with the basic four-roomed house. Not a four-*bedroomed* house: a four-*roomed* house! That's what we had – a kitchen, a sitting room, a bedroom for us kids and a bedroom for our parents. When you made some money and you wanted to extend your house, the first things you'd build were usually an additional two rooms and a garage at the back of the property, either for the family or to rent out for additional income. All the houses had wire fences to start with, so when you made a bit more money, you'd build a brick wall – what we in the township called a 'stop nonsense'.

And once you made a bit *more* money, you would extend your house by adding an additional two rooms to the structure of the main house and replacing the original small windows with big windows. Big windows were a big deal in those days. When you got to the point of having big windows, you had really made it! Often, when people were looking for a particular house in the neighbourhood, the response would be, 'It's that house with the big windows.'

I often wonder why the apartheid government built those four-roomed houses with such tiny windows, and why they were one of the first things the inhabitants of those homes wanted to change. Was it because they wanted to see more of what was happening outside in the street? Or was it because they recognised that bigger windows would let in more light and warmth? Perhaps there was something in their subconscious telling them that they were not that powerless after all, that they could do something about their surroundings, starting with their windows. Those small home improvements represented resilience and hope. The system tried to break us, but we found strength in ourselves and in our communities. We built homes, we started businesses, we still dared to dream.

With all this building going on, there was a good market for my parents' face bricks. Then my mom decided, well, why stop at supplying bricks? We should actually be the ones building for people in the neighbourhood. And that was how the construction company, named Zam-Zam Construction, after my grandfather's printing business, was born.

My dad bought a red Datsun van (second-hand, of course) to deliver the bricks, and they employed a lovely man called Uncle Joe, from Hammanskraal, as the foreman. He had a team and my dad had a team, and soon they were building all over Soweto.

So you see, I grew up in a hive of entrepreneurial prowess and activity. I think my parents were ahead of their time in so many ways. They wanted to write a better future for their kids, and they did just about everything possible to give us a decent and dignified life. At the same time, they set a good example for their children, which I think we've all followed in our own different and unique ways.

THREE

_____ THE EARLY YEARS _____

I was born on 29 March 1974, a month before a general election in
which black people were not allowed to vote because they did not
have any political rights. The government had decided to hold the
election a year earlier than required by law because, as Prime Minister
B.J. Vorster explained, they wanted to ensure that a strong government
was in power to meet the domestic and international crises that were
facing South Africa. Since the previous year, workers all around the
country had been downing tools in protest over poor wages, and the
police were retaliating with maximum force.

In the Makgalemele household, my arrival must have been a dis-
traction from the tensions on the streets. My mother had to go back to
work ten days after I was born, and my sisters were already at school
by then, so my parents went to QwaQwa to find someone to take care
of me. They would travel to QwaQwa every month-end to sell curtains
that my mother made at night on her black-and-gold Singer sewing
machine. I can distinctly remember the sound of that machine as my
dear mother toiled away during the night.

They found this angel of a woman – Agnes Mofokeng, whom we
call Rakgadi. I can't talk about my childhood without mentioning
Rakgadi. She has just the sweetest and gentlest nature and is compassionate, honest and loyal to the bone. Rakgadi has been the greatest
gift and blessing to my family, and has looked after me since I was ten
days old. She has been in my life ever since. When I was Miss South
Africa, she moved into the two-bedroomed Rosebank apartment that

I was given as part of my prize. She and I lived there in the northern suburbs, just the two of us. She was and still is this kind, constant and loving presence, and I honestly don't know what I would do without her. She is my mother and my protector. Forty-five years later, she is raising my own children. They call Rakgadi 'Mama' and me 'Mommy'.

Rakgadi never once raised a hand to any of us children. I have only one memory of her getting properly cross. One night, she had bathed all four of us and cleaned us up very nicely for dinner and bed. My brother and I decided to go and play *black mampatile*, and I went to hide in the coal box. We came out from our hiding places and I was pitch-black, covered in coal dust. Rakgadi went to Papa and said, 'Papa, look at Basetsana. I just bathed her and look at her!' Now my dad is supposed to deal with this, but he's as much of a softie as Rakgadi, and he doesn't know what to do. He said something like, 'Baby girl, this is not a good thing!' and gave me this little tap, not even a smack, just so that Rakgadi could see he was doing something. He is calling this naughty kid to order! His treat for us was Toff-o-Luxe, and the next day, don't you worry, I got my Toff-o-Luxe. 'Just don't tell anyone,' Papa said.

Toff-o-Luxe was a brand of toffee sweets that came in a cylindrical paper tube, much like Rolos. They were soft, chewy and oh-so deliciously creamy. I seem to remember that the wrapper was bright red with gold foil on the inside, and there were about ten toffees in each tube. My father would always have enough sweets for me and my siblings, as well as any other kids who came over to play. One such regular visitor to our house was a girl called Zodwa Kekana. She lived nearby, and she was my very first friend outside of my siblings. My mother didn't believe we needed friends, and she would often tell us to just play with one another. Zodwa, however, grew on her and over the years became part of the family. Zodwa was strongly built and definitely not afraid of a fight – unlike me, who would run for the hills if challenged. We formed a natural alliance that saw us play together almost every day.

The reality of township life was that money was scarce. My parents had four children to feed on their meagre salaries. It was no easy task, and it was why they needed to think entrepreneurially. They never spent money on anything other than necessities such as food and clothing.

Toys were just not on the shopping list, and so we found ways to make magic from garbage. We would scrounge around in rubbish bins for items that we could bring to life with our imagination. Tin cans were used to play street games involving tennis balls and lots of running, and, with a bit of ingenuity, empty bottles of fabric softener were transformed into dolls. Mama would give us her old towels and dishcloths and we would carefully place our 'baby dolls' on our backs and secure them with safety pins, just like real mothers.

One day – it was month-end – Moeder came home with two little real-life dolls, white Barbie-type dolls with long blonde hair and an outfit for each, which she had bought from OK Bazaars. I remember vividly my first real doll after playing with the Sta-Soft bottle for so long. We were engrossed and enchanted by these two dolls. I loved that Moeder bought a doll for Zodwa too. That was very generous. As you can imagine, Moeder did not spend money easily. Even when we were young, she taught us about being wise and financially savvy. One of the things she would tell us was, when you get a bit of money, don't squander it, don't buy cars. Invest in property. Always property. I heard that many times.

Looking at how many dolls my daughter Bontle has now, I realise how far we have come. She has tea sets and a toy kitchen with appliances to keep her occupied, and where my brother would push me around in an old cardboard box, my youngest son has an actual miniature car he can drive around the yard. Of course, we did not know we were poor; all we knew was that we were safe and loved.

When we weren't playing with dolls, there were all the old-fashioned games that kids used to play in the street in those days – although we mostly played them in the driveway, because of my mother's rule against playing in the street. There was *umgusha*, the one where you take an old stocking and cut it into strips and knot the strips to make a loop of elastic. One girl stands on one side, another stands opposite her, both inside the elastic, stretching it between them, and a third player jumps in and around the elastic. There was a game called *bathi*, also a three-player game, but this one involved a tennis ball. And another one called *three toti*. For that one, you would stack empty old tins in a particular order – a Ricoffy tin on the bottom, followed by a Bull Brand tin, then a Glenryck tin, and so on (basically whatever you could find in the dustbin) – in a pyramid shape. And then, from a distance, you would try to demolish the pyramid with a tennis ball. There was also *diketo*, a game played with stones. You'd draw a circle on the ground and put the stones in the middle, and then throw the biggest stone in the air while trying to grab as many stones out of the circle as possible, before catching the big one again.

Here's the truth: I was terrible at sports, actually quite useless. I had no coordination, and no one wanted me in their team, for they were guaranteed to lose. So I would be picked as an 'all over', meaning I played for both teams, as everyone knew there would be no scoring from me. Nevertheless, thinking back on those childhood games evokes so many pleasant memories. I can hear the thwack of that tennis ball and the sound of girls' laughter in the streets. Growing up in Soweto, in that community, in that family – it was a happy childhood, and although sheltered in a lot of ways, it felt very secure. We grew up knowing that we were loved, and that we mattered and were wanted.

As a teacher, my mother was well aware of the number of young schoolgirls in our neighbourhood who fell pregnant. She was determined that this wouldn't happen to any of her daughters, and so she was extremely protective. She was at her most comfortable when she could see us and so, yes, we led sheltered lives. It might have felt restrictive at times, but now I know that my parents were doing their best to protect our innocence. When girls fell pregnant in the township, they were shamed by the community. They would not be able to go to school any more, and some never made it back, even after the baby was born. They were often sent away to live with family members in the rural areas until they gave birth. While some families accepted the children, others rejected them. In certain instances, the baby would be raised as its mother's sibling in order to protect the family's reputation. The child could go years without knowing the truth.

The school my mom taught at was only a junior primary, so for senior primary I went to Immaculata Secondary School, a Catholic school in Diepkloof. I was there from Standard 3 to Standard 5 (Grades 5 to 7). The intention was for me to stay at Immaculata, but that changed with the unrest of 1986. The police came to the school one day; at the time, I was not sure why, I just knew that there was teargas. The school was double-storey, and I was so frightened that I jumped from the second floor to get out of the building and landed on a cactus, which made me bleed and cry hysterically.

And that was that. My parents decided to take me out of Immaculata and move me to a school in Lenasia, Trinity Secondary School. It was a completely different world. I was one of only six black children at that otherwise entirely Indian, predominantly Muslim, school. It wasn't easy to make friends, but I connected with a lovely girl called Fatima Bulbulia.

Mostly, my school days were uneventful. I was a quiet kid and an obedient student. I didn't shoot the lights out academically, but I did well in maths and science, and fine overall. Maybe that's why I don't like putting my own kids under pressure. I'm not one of those parents who demands perfect grades or asks, 'Why aren't you in the first team?' As far as I'm concerned, that kind of thing doesn't determine your outcome in life. Just go to school and do what you need to do, be the best person you can be: be kind, be considerate, be compassionate, be true, and don't forget to have fun in the process.

Another thing that really anchored my childhood was my family's faith. My mother grew up in the Methodist Church, but in our culture, the children are raised in the father's faith. My father was a server in the Anglican Church, and so we were raised as Anglican. I was confirmed at the age of thirteen at St Augustine's Anglican Church in Mzimhlophe.

My mother's best friend when I was in my early teens was a woman called Mam Gwen Jele. She was the principal at Thabisang Primary School, where my mother taught, and she was like our second mother. Mam Jele invited my mom to go with her to Rhema, a charismatic Bible church in Randburg, where she worshipped. So one Sunday, Moeder took us children. There was a free bus that went around Soweto picking up worshippers who wanted to go to Rhema in Randburg. The bus ride from Soweto to Randburg was quite the eye-opener. I had not really travelled much outside of the township, and I remember looking out of the window as Soweto disappeared and made way for a whole new world. A world where people drove fancy cars and lived in huge houses. I could not believe how big the driveways were; they seemed to go on forever. Most amazing was the fact that many of these people had their own swimming pool in their backyard. In Soweto, all we had was the communal Orlando swimming pool, where throngs of people would go to swim. That bus trip was an adventure in itself, as far as I was concerned.

Then I walked into the church, and, oh man, I could not believe it! There was a live band. There were guitars, drums, pianos ... it was going down, big time. Honey, the party was *on*. There were all kinds of people there. Young and old. People wearing jeans! And people clapping and singing *loud*. Now I was an impressionable teen, and remember, we didn't go to clubs or discos, we didn't go anywhere like this at all, and I'm thinking, this place is soooo cool. I just felt such resonance there, from the moment I walked in.

'We're going to go back to that other church, right?' I remember saying to Moeder the following week. So that's how I started going to Rhema with my mom and siblings. It wasn't easy for Papa, us moving to a different church. He took time to process it, but he finally realised that he wanted to go to fellowship with his family on a Sunday, wherever that might be. So he started going to Rhema too. It's been an amazing journey for me to serve the Lord in the house of Rhema for the past twenty-five years under Pastor Ray McCauley. Now that is one man I absolutely love. Such a beautiful being, he's been my spiritual father for over two decades.

There's a sad note to this story. Mam Jele was brutally murdered not long after she introduced us to her church. If you remember, in those days school fees were paid in cash at the school and were kept in some silly moneybox. One day, robbers walked into the Thabisang school office and started shooting, and she was gunned down. My mother arrived just after the thugs had fled, and she held her friend and watched her slip away. Moeder was never the same after that. It changed her, losing her dear friend in such an awful way.

I will always be grateful to Mam Jele for introducing us to her sanctuary. I am the woman I am today because of my faith. My faith has sustained me through the most difficult and painful times of my life. If I didn't have my faith, I don't think I would be here to tell this story. It's been an extraordinary journey, serving the Lord. The

Lord has been so good to me, and His grace is sufficient and His mercies are new every day. I love the Lord. I am a child of God. That I know for sure.

PART II

DREAM REALISED

FOUR

The year 1990 was a very exciting time for South Africa, because it was when the process of ending apartheid officially began. The then president of the country, F.W. de Klerk, made the decision to unban organisations such as the ANC and the South African Communist Party, which had been operating underground for many years. The ANC's armed wing, Umkhonto we Sizwe, suspended its activities and political prisoners, including our beloved Nelson Rolihlahla Mandela, were finally released.

I remember seeing the footage of Madiba walking out of prison hand in hand with his wife, Mama Winnie Madikizela-Mandela, while the crowds gathered around them. He held up his right hand in a clenched fist and she did the same with her left hand. As long as I live, that moment will be etched in my memory. It was not just Mandela who walked out of jail and claimed his freedom that day; it was all the people of South Africa.

While things were changing in the country, our household was its usual hive of activity. My mom firmly believed that idle time was a very dangerous thing for a young person. In her mind, that's how girls ended up pregnant, with no education, no future, and no ambition to do better and be better. She would have none of that for her three daughters. She decided that the best way to keep us off the streets and out of trouble was to keep us busy, and so she got us involved in youth clubs, church choirs, Sunday school … and beauty pageants. Along with boxing and soccer, township beauty pageants were a big deal at the time. There were many in Soweto, such as Miss Ellerines and Miss King Kong. Even shoe stores had pageants. People came out in droves to support the contestants. The crowd would cheer and whistle and rumble when their favourite girl took to the stage, and one could often predict the winner based on audience participation. The winner would get a prize, usually appliances or furniture, as well as the attention and admiration of her community.

My mom made it her business to enter us in every pageant that came along. I still remember the excitement when Lerato won Miss King Kong. She won a fridge! We had an old, battered Kelvinator that could hardly close, and now here was this fancy new double-door fridge with a freezer section, baby. And then Johanna won Miss Ellerines. Her prize was a combo: a two-plate stove and a kettle. She went on to win Miss Inter-University when she was studying for her BCom degree at Rhodes, and won her first car, a red Uno. We had arrived. We were *mobile*.

To be honest, I was never really keen on participating in pageants, but I was not one to defy Mother's orders. There was not much else to keep township children off the streets, and since I couldn't play soccer or take part in boxing, I was going to do beauty pageants.

My first pageant was Miss Helio, which was sponsored by a shoe shop of the same name. The venue was the Diepkloof Community Hall. I was thirteen and at Immaculata Secondary School. I felt so awkward standing there, being stared at by strangers. And even though I won, it didn't get any easier. Overall, I was really not keen on the competition process. The preparations would start the night before, with my mother straightening my hair with her hot comb – that was no walk in the park either. I would be seated on the floor in front of her and she would use her legs to keep me still as she literally burnt my hair straight, using our Primus stove to heat the iron comb. I remember it like it was yesterday. I would cry, and it still gives me chills to think about it, but hey, the standard of beauty demanded straight hair.

I was introverted, which meant I was very self-conscious, and I really didn't believe there was anything special about my looks. I would be generally filled with dread as my sisters did my make-up backstage. Walking up and down that ramp, I would try to remember all the tips my sisters had shared with me. I would smile at the judges as I did my half-turn, and hope my feet would not buckle under me or that I wouldn't trip and fall on the full turn. I would hear my father's voice telling me that I was worthy and beautiful and talented, that I could do anything I put my mind to. Each and every pageant was a huge learning curve. They forced me to come out of my shell and to show up for myself. My family was always there to support me, and if my courage failed me, I would just look for their smiling faces in the crowd and do it for them.

When I entered and won Miss Phefeni in 1990, I qualified to compete in Miss Soweto. Miss Soweto was huge. The township was abuzz when the Miss Soweto competition was happening, and it was the talk of the town. The *Sowetan* newspaper was full of reportage on the semi-finals and finals. It was one of those pageants that everyone in the township wanted to be a part of, even if it was just to watch. But, my goodness, if you made it to the finals, you were *the* kid on the block. It was like 'that girl, she's representing'.

In the lead-up to the Miss Soweto finals, some of the other participants voiced their discontent about allegations that I was, in fact, not black but coloured. They wanted me disqualified on the basis that I didn't really live in Soweto and that I had lied about my race. You can imagine how strange this news was for me and for my family, and how uncomfortable we felt when the pageant promoters visited our home to meet my parents and verify that they were actually both black. They also interviewed me to make sure that I spoke one of the African languages. (By virtue of growing up with different people from different cultures and backgrounds in the township, I ended up speaking many languages.)

Through this experience, colourism made its way into my consciousness in a very real way. I had never once thought of myself as fair or light in complexion, but the other girls in the competition clearly felt that I was, and to them this represented an unfair advantage. Unfortunately, that was the status quo among black people; having lighter skin was seen as more desirable than having dark skin. One could argue that this kind of thinking was brought about by the racial policies of the day. Young women who were born with light skin were often given nicknames like 'Pinky', and there were even wedding songs that celebrated the fact that the bride looked like a coloured person.

Maybe I was too young to realise that I looked a little different, or maybe my parents just didn't subscribe to that kind of thinking for it to have become an issue in my life.

Regardless, once that had been cleared up, we got down to the business of preparing for the event, which was to be held at Highgate Shopping Centre. I was still not keen on being paraded in a swimsuit, and once again I had to steel my nerves in order to make it through. No one wants to be subjected to that kind of objectification, but the fact is, there is so much to be gained by using these pageants as a platform for your future. As with many things in life, I could not get one without the other, so I put my hand up and I did what I had to do. I walked up and down that ramp with determination, and I did my family proud.

In June 1990, when I was in Standard 9 (Grade 11) at Trinity Secondary School in Lenasia, I was crowned Miss Soweto. I was so young – just sixteen – and all of a sudden I was in the newspapers, and being interviewed on radio and TV. Everyone was talking about the pageant and about me. My family's name was suddenly well known, and even people who hardly knew me would whisper: 'That's the Makgalemele daughter, she won the pageant!' In December, all the provinces and Miss Soweto sent their winners to the main national pageant, Miss Black South Africa. As Miss Soweto, I competed and won.

I'll never forget the prize – I furnished my mother's house with that prize. It was a dining-room suite and a black-and-white faux leather lounge suite, with a lovely coffee table and a room divider in which my mother put all her special glasses and dishes for visitors, who came once a year. I could never understand that, but I tell you, if you touched those glasses or dishes, that would be the end of you! By then my parents had built us a beautiful new home in Protea North. We had moved to the 'burbs, baby. When they designed that house – no. 2772 in Mark's Square – they added a very long passage specifically for us to use as a ramp. We'd practise our moves and deportment up and down that passage, at times with books on our heads to learn to walk upright. So you thought Malcolm Gladwell with his 10 000 hours was playing a trick on us? No! He was not.

Mr Leonard Sithole owned the Miss Soweto pageant back then, and Mr Simon Manana represented the promotions company, Pink Parrot

Promotions. The first time I met Bra Si, as I came to call him, was when he came to our home for the bizarre verification visit. He had an open disposition and came across as friendly and warm. I got to know him better in the years that followed, and he turned out to be the most colourful person I had ever met. He was blessed with such a wonderful sense of humour, and his presence drew people to him wherever he went.

After I won Miss Soweto, Pink Parrot Promotions managed all my appearances, and Bra Si quickly became a trusted family member and elder son to my parents. They knew they could trust him with my safety in their absence and he would often agree to be my chaperone. Now Simon was good friends with Zindzi Mandela, Tata Nelson and Mama Winnie's daughter. One day he came home and told my parents, 'Your daughter has been invited to meet Tata Mandela and Mama Winnie.'

Of course, I knew about Madiba – I had seen the footage of him being released in February that year. I remember we had an old picture of him, which my father kept tucked into one of his books. To this day I remember that picture of a young Madiba in a suit, his close-cropped hair with the distinctive side-parting, and I remember the smell of that book. Apartheid had tried its hardest to erase him from our memory, and at that time there were no new pictures of him in public circulation, and we didn't know what he looked like now that he was older. Some of us hadn't even been born when he was jailed for fighting for his people's liberation. He was an enigma.

Now I was going to meet this enigma, this force, this being, the leader of our people who had been incarcerated for twenty-seven years. And who wouldn't want to meet Madiba? But I was just a kid. It was all very daunting and overwhelming. I remember I wore a white suit – a little panelled skirt with a jacket. Bra Si took me to Tata and Mama Winnie's house in Orlando West, which we all referred to as Parliament (and still do today), because we believed that was the legitimate parliament of the people. I *have* to pause on this moment. To be invited to the home of two fearless leaders of the struggle, who bravely fought for our freedom and emancipation from the oppressive and inhumane apartheid system, ranks as one of the highlights of my life. I saw it, I felt it, I touched it, and, more importantly, I was embraced by it. What a lucky child I am. Truly, it cannot get better than that moment as long as I shall live. That was the beginning of my journey of hope. I remember being welcomed by Mama. 'Hello, darling,' she said, embracing me and bringing me into their home. And there he was. 'I'm very proud of you, congratulations for winning the competition,' said Tata.

I wish I could tell you everything that happened that day, what he said, what I said, but I'm sorry to say I hardly remember a thing. I don't think I was able to string two words together! It was almost like an out-of-body experience. He was larger than life in character and presence and energy and being. And his eyes showed such deep compassion. I do remember him asking me what I wanted to become, and I said I wanted to be a teacher. My frame of reference was teachers: my mother was a teacher, my uncles were teachers, and my older sister Lerato was a teacher – she still is, at Fons Luminis Diepkloof after thirty years. In my community, in my township, teachers were held in the highest regard. I wanted to be like my mom. 'That's a good thing,' he said. And by the way, I still want to be like my mom. She is not my SHERO – she is my HERO!

The rest of the visit is a complete blur. I was in awe. There I was, a sixteen-year-old, Tata had been out of prison for just a few months, and I had the great privilege to be invited to meet him and break bread with him and Mama Winnie. While I don't remember what we talked about, I do remember feeling embraced by them. Both Mama Winnie and Madiba loved me, and over the years they brought me into their home and into their hearts.

I completed my matric in 1991, and by then my sister Johanna had enrolled to study for her Bachelor of Commerce degree at Rhodes University in the Eastern Cape. Her marks at school were always very good, and because of her hard work and natural intelligence, she was able to secure donors who graciously funded her studies at a time when very few black students could even dream of attending that institution. My older sister, Lerato, had graduated from Turfloop, which is now part of the University of Limpopo. She had taken up a teaching post at a school in Diepkloof, where she still teaches. My brother Mojalefa was attending high school at Topaz Secondary School in Lenasia.

In 1992, I was admitted to study for my Bachelor of Arts in education at the University of Venda. I was all set.

FIVE

In June 1994, I was well into the third year of my four-year teaching degree at the University of Venda. I had chosen psychology and education as my majors, so I was going to become an educational psychologist. My mind was made up.

When I arrived home for the mid-year holidays, my mom said, 'Right, we're going to take pictures. You're going to enter Miss South Africa.' Of course, we all knew about Miss South Africa. At the time, our family had a big black-and-white Blaupunkt TV at home. Ours was one of the few houses that had a television set, so when Miss South Africa was on, neighbours would come round to watch. In 1992, black women were allowed to enter the competition for the first time. Previously, only white women were allowed to compete. When the lovely Jacqui Mofokeng walked away with the crown in 1993, it was a historic moment, wondrous and a true turning point for us as black people. Johanna had entered Miss South Africa in 1992, the year that Amy Kleinhans won. If you know my sister, it wouldn't surprise you to hear that she won Miss Personality. Johanna takes after my father in so many ways. She is not only beautiful and intelligent, but also possesses the kind of larger-than-life personality that cannot be ignored. When she enters the room with her powerful aura, you can feel the energy change. Unlike me, she is a total extrovert who has never had a problem putting up her hand and making her mark. I have admired her since we were children, and I still marvel at her extraordinary achievements.

So I'm back home for the holidays and my mom commissions the neighbourhood's resident photographer, an uncle who lives down the street, to take pictures. She puts me in the gold Speedo that Johanna wore the year before – they made twelve of those gold costumes especially for the twelve finalists, and you couldn't buy them in the shops – and Abuti Peter takes the snaps. Then I go back to varsity to continue my third year, and my mom fills in the forms and sends everything off for me to represent Northern Transvaal, where I'm based for my studies.

There were no cellphones at the time, but a few weeks later I got a call on the tickey-box. It was Johanna. 'Listen, girl, the Miss South Africa people are looking for you. These people are in the area and they're doing the pre-judging. The judging is today and today only. I think you'd better go.' It turned out that they'd tried my Soweto home without success (the phone bill hadn't been paid for months, so the phone wasn't working), and then recognised the gold swimsuit and my surname, and tracked me down through my sister. Can you believe the gold swimsuit was the reason they found me? It was like my mother planned the whole thing. Quite a story! But it made no difference to me. The judging was in Tzaneen. Campus was in Thohoyandou. It was a two-hour drive and I was in the middle of an exam. There was no way I was going to go. 'Girl, I'm writing an exam,' I said. 'I actually have no time for this competition thing that you and Mama are on about.'

I put down the phone and went back to my day. The phone rang again. Guess who was on the line this time? My mother.

'Basetsana.'

When my mother called you by your full name, you knew there was trouble. At home they called me Setse or Setse-girl, the middle syllables of my name. It was a fond name, a term of endearment. So when you hear Basetsana, you know it ain't pretty, honey; it's about to go down.

'Basetsana, I believe we have a problem.'

'Uh, no, Moeder, there's no problem.'

'Are we sure we don't have a problem?'

'Yes, Moeder, there is absolutely no problem.'

'I thought so.'

I literally dropped that phone like it was hot. When you are raised by someone like my mother, they don't have to be near you to tell you what to do, they are in your head. I knew my mother would have me for breakfast if I didn't get to that judging. But it wasn't going to be easy.

Of course, I didn't have money. You know what it's like as a student – your parents put fifty rand in your FNB BOB card at the beginning of the month and in two days that fifty rand is gone. I was going to have to hitchhike from campus in Thohoyandou to Tzaneen. I told my friend Maria Mudau (now Nekhudziga) that I had to go to this competition in Tzaneen, and she said, 'My friend, I'll go with you.' (Maria is a dear friend who spoke at our wedding, and I was her birth partner for two of her kids. Our friendship spans close to three decades.)

It was already after lunch. I needed to get moving! I didn't have time to change or freshen up, so, still in a T-shirt and a pair of jeans and sneakers, I set off with Maria to hitchhike to Tzaneen. Luckily for us, somebody graciously gave us a ride in his van all the way there. I got to the judging at around 4:30 p.m. and walked into a room full of the most beautifully made-up women I'd ever seen. Their hair was coiffed, their make-up just so. They looked flawless, and here's this student in a T-shirt, jeans and sneakers. But I had made it. 'Cos Mama told me I must go or else …

I was both mortified and overwhelmed, and quite frankly I felt unprepared and inadequate. No one even noticed that I was late, because they were too busy making themselves look flawless for the judges. The Northern Transvaal, which now encompasses the Limpopo province and Pretoria, was traditionally an Afrikaner stronghold, and so most of the participants were statuesque blondes. Not only was I seriously underdressed for the occasion, I felt very outclassed as well.

I remember standing there thinking, 'I can't believe this is happening to me,' and being rather upset at my mother and sister for forcing the issue. I wanted more than anything to go back to campus and continue with my life, but that was not to be. There was a big world out there, and I was destined for much, much more.

The way the judging process worked, there were around fifty contestants, and the judges had to whittle them down to twelve. Those twelve would then compete for Miss South Africa Northern Transvaal, to be held four days later. There were three segments to the pre-judging:

swimsuit, interview and cocktail attire. I had neither a swimsuit nor a cocktail dress, but the organisers kindly lent me both.

The individual interview segment was the most intimidating. I was the last girl to be interviewed – I had got there just in time. The pre-judging process was closing at five o'clock, so I basically made it by the skin of my teeth. The room was set up so that the seven judges were seated next to one another at a long table facing the contestant, who sat on a chair directly in front of them. It was like being at a job inter-view with seven people, and it didn't help that many of the contestants walked out of there in tears. I was standing in line thinking, 'Well, this is not going to go well at all.'

Finally, it was my turn to be grilled. They asked me anything and everything under the sun. My opinion on world politics, on what was happening in South Africa, on euthanasia ... they covered basically everything from local and international current affairs to my dreams and aspirations and what I thought I could bring to the pageant if I was selected. It was absolutely nerve-racking! I remember thinking, 'I've just come out of an exam room, and now I'm sitting here being grilled by these people, like really!'

Anyway, lo and behold, when it came to the announcement, my name was called eighth out of the twelve. I was dumbfounded.

There was one person who wasn't surprised – Jan Malan. Jan Malan and Jannie Pretorius worked with Doreen Morris, who owned the pageant. Doreen became my mentor and is still my dear friend today. The way Doreen tells the story, when this well-put-together and groomed girl in a T-shirt, jeans and sneakers arrived at the last minute and made it through the crazy round of questions, Jannie turned to her and said, 'You've got your queen.'

But that's a story for later. For now, I was just thrilled to have made the final twelve to compete for Miss South Africa Northern Transvaal. I went on to win that title, which meant I would represent the province at Miss South Africa on 24 September 1994.

I never made it back to campus. As it turned out, the universe had other plans for me.

SIX

In 1994, I was a twenty-year-old student at university. I had become active in campus politics and had been elected president of the Central Cultural Committee. I would say I was having a normal student life with lots of new friends and a very busy study schedule. I was definitely not concerned about the fact that Miss South Africa was a few months away.

The student body had been excited when I qualified by winning Miss Northern Transvaal, and they had absolutely claimed the title for themselves. I would often be accosted by fellow students who seemed more excited about the whole thing than I was. They would wish me luck and tell me to 'bring it home'.

There was so much happening in the country that year too. The first democratic general election was held in April 1994, and I was old enough to vote! It was one of the most emotional moments of my life. As I reached the front of the line and walked into the voting booth with my ballot paper, I thought, 'This is me, little Basetsana Makgalemele, a black child from the ghetto, and I have been given the opportunity to make my mark on the future of our country.' I walked towards the ballot box, tears streaming down my face, and paused for a moment before casting my vote. I looked at the people around me, who were also feeling the importance of this day, many of them still incredulous that they were actually able to vote in their lifetime.

In September, the ten finalists (nine provinces, plus Miss Soweto) were brought up to Johannesburg to prepare for the pageant. We each got a roomie. It felt like we were all at boarding school, a really fun boarding school with a lot of people around us who made us pretty every day and who gave us nice clothes. I was twenty years old and I'd led a very sheltered existence. My mom was very strict. Besides not allowing us to play in the streets, she was also anti friends. 'Friends will not do anything for you,' she would say. 'You've got siblings. If you want to play, go and play with them in the yard.' My mother didn't suffer fools, as I've said, and you really didn't take chances with her.

So now I was hanging out with all these really nice girls. You might think there would be jealousy and cattiness, but there was really nothing like that. They were fantastic girls. I'm still friends with some of them, and they've gone on to do some amazing things with their lives – some of them are doctors and lawyers.

All the races were represented. Before 1992, very few women of colour had successfully managed to enter Miss South Africa. News-reader Sibongile Sokhulu was among the first, and she made it to the top twelve in 1987. Other finalists before 1992 were Robyn Poole, Shawn Coutries and Sandy Ngema. Now, we came from all over the country and from different backgrounds. We were truly the rainbow nation that Madiba spoke about and wanted for his people. For the first time, I actually felt the rainbow nation, it was tangible, I experienced it first-hand, I knew what it tasted like. Yes, we came from different worlds, but at the end of the day, we all had one thing in common, the pageant. We all wanted to change our lives, and we believed that the pageant would give us that opportunity.

That time of preparation was loads of fun. The media interviewed us, we were on television, there was a Miss South Africa bus, and we were taken around to different centres and towns. Wherever we went, people would go crazy. A week before the pageant, we went to Sun City to go through all the drills and be put through our paces to prepare for the final. Sun City is a luxury hotel resort and casino situated in the North West province, about two hours' drive from Johannesburg. It was developed by hotel magnate Sol Kerzner as part of his Sun International group of leisure properties, and officially opened its doors in 1979. I had heard about it, but I had never imagined in my wildest dreams that I would stay there one day. I had no idea how spectacular it was, with its grand entrance halls and luxury furnishings. I had also never been to a casino before, so you can imagine my excitement when I first saw the bright lights and heard the loud electronic slot machines. I was totally bowled over. It was a completely new world. Finalists were closely guarded and totally secluded, with security all around. Closer to the pageant night, you were not even allowed to speak to your family.

The final was to be held in the Sun City Superbowl. The grand conference and concert venue is enormous, with seating capacity for 6 000 people. The organisers had created the most magnificent stage and the production itself was world-class. Top clothing designers like The Boys, Julian, Errol Arendz and Dicky Longhurst had been commissioned to make our garments, which were absolutely stunning. It was obvious that no expense had been spared in making the experience unforgettable.

The day of the pageant started with a communal breakfast, which was immediately followed by a final rehearsal, where each girl had to practise receiving the crown if her name was called out that night. That was followed by many hours of make-up and hair.

There was a great deal of commotion backstage as we prepared to take part in the biggest spectacle of our lives. We each had someone to help us with costume changes, and our beautiful garments were labelled in order to avoid mix-ups.

The pageant itself went by so fast. One minute we were preparing for the swimsuit segment, and the next it was time for me to change into my pink satin gown, bedecked with Swarovski crystals, and return to the stage for the moment of truth!

Then I heard my name. Basetsana Makgalemele. I was being announced as Miss South Africa 1994. I don't think it dawned on me immediately that I had actually won the crown. There was this moment of utter shock rather than disbelief. I don't think I could process it, or even understand what it all meant. And then I heard Prince singing 'The Most Beautiful Girl in the World'. Now that's the moment I will never forget.

What made it all real to me was the car. One of the big prizes for Miss South Africa was always a car. They would fix a seat on the bonnet of the car, and Miss South Africa would perch there and they'd drive it around the auditorium to a standing ovation. And now it's me, driving around the Superbowl on top of a silver Ford TX5, doing the royal wave while the music plays. If you ask me, the highlight of the evening was not hearing my name being called, it was that moment. I had grown up watching the winner being driven around the Superbowl, and now it was me! My family had never been in a position to be able to afford a brand-new car, and there I was, at only twenty years of age, with my very own car. I mean, how crazy can life get? It was totally surreal.

Every now and then I'd spot people I knew. I caught sight of my mom and dad. I saw a lot of my peers from varsity. I was very involved with student politics on campus and was president of the Central Cultural committee, and the student representative council had dispatched two buses to bring people to the finals. It was the most beautiful experience.

I've just remembered a story my mom shared about that day. Now, you must know that my mom made sure we all had chores at home, and my knees were always black from kneeling down to scrub the floors and the outside *stoep* (verandah). So Mama and Papa are watching the pageant and it's the swimsuit parade, and I'm up there, and there's a couple sitting behind them in the audience and Mama hears the woman say, '*Ag*, look at that one with the black knees – that one doesn't stand a chance.' When my mom told me later, she said, 'You know, my baby girl, it hurt me to hear that. I feel so bad, because I made you clean those floors and scrub that *stoep* until I could see myself in them.'

Even so, not long after that, we girls were all gathered at our mother's house, sitting outside talking, and she said, 'Well, what do you think? Do you think this *stoep* is going to clean itself?' And then you literally took off your fancy garb, and you were on that *stoep*, shining it with Sunbeam! Even after I won the pageant, when I went home there was no Miss What What. I was expected to do my bit, the same as always. Anyway, looking back I'm glad I was brought up like that. It certainly kept me grounded.

Back to Sun City. After the Superbowl and the car and the waving, there's a Coronation Ball, which is a huge banquet with about a thousand VIP guests. I was waiting to go in, Doreen Morris holding me by the hand to walk in with me, when I heard: 'Ladies and gentlemen, may we all rise and please put your hands together as we welcome Miss South Africa 1994.' I think the moment I walked into that room and saw all those people rising to welcome me, it hit me that my life had changed forever.

And it did, right from that very moment.

Here's an example. Before the pageant, the contestants stayed at the Cascades hotel, sharing two to a room. When I left the Coronation Ball, six bodyguards, Doreen and my sister Johanna accompanied me. It was an entourage second to none! I'm thinking, what have I got myself into? I can't walk to my room by myself without all these people following me!

I was whisked off to the Sol Kerzner Suite at the Cascades. Everyone left except Johanna, who was staying with me in the suite. We were always together; we were as thick as thieves and still are. We got to the room and opened the door, and I tell you, this suite was bigger than my mother's house. A lot bigger!

'Girl, how insane is this?' Johanna shrieked. It was like we were in Disneyland – not that we'd ever been there. There was food for us, fruit baskets, huge arrangements of flowers, bathrobes. And the bath! We couldn't believe the size of it. Jacuzzi, darling! Oh my goodness, it was all beyond. BE-yond! We were running around the suite looking at it all and laughing our heads off.

Then I said to my sister: 'Listen, girl, I need to go downstairs to my room to get the stuff I left there.'

I opened the door and there were two white men standing outside. 'Sorry, ma'am, you can't leave,' one said.

I'm like, 'Excuse me, what do you mean I can't leave?'

'No, you can't leave the suite.'

'What do you mean I can't leave the suite?' It still had not dawned on me at this point quite how much things had changed. 'I need to go and get my stuff from my room.'

'No, you can't leave. Your stuff will be brought to your room.'

I stepped back inside and closed the door. And then I cried. I was crying from being overwhelmed, because I knew my life had changed irrevocably, and I was saying to myself, 'What is happening *kanti* (now)?'

By now I was howling, and my sister, who is just hilarious – I mean literally, she's a laugh a minute – says sharply, 'Girl! Stop that crying. What's your problem? No one died. You won a pageant! You're a queen! Pull it together, girl. Everything's organised, you hear me? Just be calm.'

And then Doreen came and asked me what I wanted her to bring while they were packing up my things. 'Just bring my Bible,' I said. 'That's all I need, just bring my Bible and my toothbrush.'

SEVEN

My reign as Miss South Africa had begun. But before I go on with the story, I'd like to pay tribute to Jacqui Palesa Mofokeng, the fine young black woman who won the title in 1993. She had a really hard time. Not everyone was happy that the institution of Miss South Africa was now fully open to women of all races. There was a feeling among some people, and some in the media, that Jacqui didn't represent their definition of beauty in South Africa – their ideal being white women – and they would say things like 'She is not our queen.' The white media in particular were awful to her. She was vilified and insulted. Every horrible thing they had ever wanted to say on a public platform about a black girl – big nose, fat bum – they flung at her.

I can only speculate that the country was not ready for a black woman to be crowned Miss South Africa. For the very first time, someone with brown skin and shaped like an African woman had burst onto the scene, and they were struggling to accept her. I suppose it was strange for many people to observe this beautiful, confident black woman who was not a maid or a servant. Jacqui took all of the abuse and bravely stood on the stage and said, 'I believe I deserve to be here and to wear this crown.' She really broke down barriers and opened the door for me and so many other women who subsequently entered the pageant, but she paid a heavy price. She was horribly undermined.

I had seen how appallingly Jacqui had been treated, and the crassness and ugliness of the media. By the time I was crowned, I was nervous about how I would be received. Who was I to take on this vicious and unkind system? Me and what army? But in many ways, 1994 was a very different time to 1993. There was a new dispensation, a new government – a black government. Madiba was the leader of a new and democratic rainbow nation.

Madiba and I had a conversation around that time about how the struggle was every day and everywhere, not only in prison cells. He said something along the lines of, 'You as a black girl-child have decided to go out there and show the world a different kind of beauty, and you're going to have your own struggles to overcome. There will be words that people will hurl at you and that will hurt, but you just have to remain strong and courageous.' My favourite Madiba quote is on courage; it's actually my email signature. 'I learnt that courage was not the absence of fear, but the triumph over it,' he wrote in *Long Walk to Freedom*. 'The brave man is not he who does not feel afraid, but he who conquers that fear.'

I think it was a conscious decision by Madiba, as president, to embrace me so openly, purposefully and intentionally, and I think that's part of why South Africans rallied around me in the way that they should have rallied around Jacqui. The bile that was thrown at her was extreme and unexpected, and I think it surprised and horrified some people to the extent that, when I won in 1994, they said, 'Actually, we should do better this time.' And thankfully, they did. Tata made it his unwavering mission to always call and congratulate the winner in subsequent years, to invite her over for lunch or dinner, whether it was to the Union Buildings while he was still president or to Houghton after he had retired.

I remember the call he made to me, just days after I was crowned. The phone rang and it was Zelda la Grange, Madiba's personal assistant, saying that the president would like to speak to me. I stood up to receive that call! Madiba came on the line to congratulate me. 'Congratulations, our queen, we are very proud of you and I would like for you to come and visit,' he said.

To a large degree, by 1994 the majority of South Africans had processed where the country was going, and part of that change was the new face of the pageant. Many of the mainstream white publications embraced me as well, in a really beautiful way. I made the cover of

My father, Phillip Makgalemele, who worked as a clerk at Baragwanath Hospital for ten years

My mother, Nomazizi Mdhluli, a vibrant, stylish woman

A rare photo of my parents while courting; they were thick as thieves

My mother (far left, in black) was a member of the choir in her hometown, Meadowlands

My parents' wedding day in 1967

The first members of the Makgalemele tribe — my older sisters Lerato and Johanna

Fighting toddler jealousy as I howl in protest while Mom carries my new brother, Mojalefa. Then ...

... my mother having to carry both of us to keep the peace!

Looking fabulous on Christmas Day at my uncle's place in Daveyton

My first BFF, Zodwa Kekana

Rivals no more — bonding with my little brother

It takes a village — Mam Gwen Jele, my mother's dear friend, with me, Dad, Ms Fikile Khumalo, who was my Grade 2 teacher and taught me how to read, and my mother

Mom and Dad at one of the homes they built. They used a 'billboard' with our home telephone number to advertise Zam-Zam Construction to customers

A teenager raised in faith — my confirmation at St Augustine Anglican Church in 1987

Winning my first beauty competition, Miss Junior Helio, in 1985

The home my parents built for us in Protea North. They designed it with a long passage especially so that we could practise our moves

Winning Miss Northern Transvaal, with Doreen Morris putting the sash on me. I entered Miss South Africa that same year, as Miss Northern Transvaal

A special night with Peggy-Sue Khumalo, Simon Manana (promoter of Miss Soweto) and Dali Tambo

A happy moment with my darling dad, who attended Miss Soweto and many of my other pageants

The crowning moment

A moment I'll never forget — becoming Miss South Africa 1994

Mentor, sister and friend Doreen Morris and I entering the Coronation Ball

The morning after, all ready for my very first interview as Miss South Africa!

Reporting for duty at the Union Buildings a few days after my crowning

Soaking it all in — a moment at the Union Buildings as the newly crowned Miss South Africa, with the old guard behind me

Meeting Madiba as one of the ninety-four Miss World finalists who visited the Union Buildings

With Mama Winnie Madikizela-Mandela at the Miss World 1994 pageant, where I was crowned first princess

Cosmopolitan magazine – a first for a black person. I was also one of the first black women on the cover of *Femina, You, Huisgenoot* and later *Fairlady*. It was a very different world to the one I had been born into. So much more was possible for someone like me. In fact, *anything* was now possible for a little black girl who believed in herself. I had journeyed from the sandwich assembly line in my mom's kitchen to a place where my dreams and aspirations actually mattered and were being realised. In the first twenty years of my life, I had gone from being totally disadvantaged to literally standing in the biggest spotlight possible.

But back to Sun City and my first day as Miss South Africa, which began with a big press conference. Remember, in 1994, South Africa was big news on the world stage. That day I was interviewed by CNN and BBC, as well as local and international lifestyle, variety and entertainment shows. It was an entire day of media, and I had to change outfits for every television interview. I must have changed ten times!

At this point I started to process the fact of my win and the role I had to play. And then I started to own it. I took a moment to have a big, ugly cry – actual *snot en trane* – and then I said to myself, 'Okay, girl, you wanted to be the ambassador of a new nation and carry the hopes and dreams of this new democracy ... Well, you had better buckle up, because it's going to be quite a ride!'

Also on that first day, after the marathon of interviews, I finally got to see my parents and spend some time with them. The night before, all I could do was give them a hug, as there was just this flurry of activity to meet and greet the sponsors and take photographs with the high-profile guests, including politicians, celebrities and actors whom I grew up watching on television. *Hey beku busy nana* (it was busy).

Spending time with my parents was very special. My mom was never one for many words, but somehow in her quietness, her presence said everything. I was aware even then of how much she had wanted a better life for us, how she had envisioned this amazing future for us. She had worked hard towards making it happen. And now, to see this success in her lifetime in front of her eyes ... I think that everything was well with her soul. I don't think she ever realised how far the beauty-pageant journey would actually take me. In her silence, I could hear her telling me, '*Ngawaka o berekile*' (You have done so well, my child).

You wouldn't call my dad quiet, that's for sure. He was this larger-than-life character with a big personality. But for once, Dad was at a loss for words. He just hugged me and said, 'Baby girl. My baby girl.' Don't you worry your fine self, though. My father wasn't quiet for long! In fact, my only fight with my dad was because he would go around Soweto telling anyone who would listen, 'Did I tell you that my child is Miss South Africa?' As if they didn't know – usually because he was telling them for the umpteenth time!

As part of my prize I was given an apartment at the Courtyard Hotel in Rosebank, which I shared with Rakgadi, who you will recall was my nanny since I was ten days old, but I didn't spend much time there. I was so used to being home when I wasn't at school, and I didn't want to be apart from my family and community for too long. In the weeks after the win, there was such a jovial atmosphere in Soweto. The kids in the street would come and hang out at my parents' house, and the old ladies would come visit and we would make them tea. In my 'hood, it wasn't a case of 'Makgalemele's daughter won', it was *we* won. It was *our* victory. *Our* crown. Not so long ago we were not even allowed to enter this pageant, and now this neighbourhood girl had won. It gave a sense of hope and a face to what was possible for the black child.

It was such a busy year. Apart from my official duties, I went back to all my former schools – to my high school, my primary school, my Sunday school, even my crèche. I became a true reflection and representation of what was possible for a black girl-child, a symbol of hope. This was all my mom's doing, by the way. She insisted we go to each community and say thank you. Even though I had this wonderful lady, Natasha Wadvalla, who was responsible for my diary, my mother always managed to fit in her activities as well. 'Today we are going to church,' she'd say, and I would go to church with her to give thanks, because 'thank you' is the best prayer anyone can offer. It was a beautiful time.

I also got to spend a lot of time with my dad that year, which was extremely special. Although I had won the car, I didn't have a driver's licence yet, so Dad would drive me around the township and suburbs in my new wheels, 'Miss South Africa' blazoned on the side. Dad would also accompany me to functions as my companion. He was a sharp and fine dresser. Even in his retirement, he would look debonair in his suit and Nunn Bush shoes. 'These are can't-gets,' he'd say, 'can't *tholakala* (rare finds).' He'd phone and say, 'Baby girl, we've got this function on and we cannot be late. I'm going to pick you up at such and such a time.' It was wonderful to have his love, presence and devotion. Except, of course, when we got to the function and he'd start telling everyone, 'Do you know my daughter? She's Miss South Africa,' and I'd want to crawl under the table.

'Papa, please don't do that,' I'd say.

'Well, aren't you Miss South Africa?' he'd reply, looking all surprised.

'Yes, but—'

'So?'

You didn't often win an argument with Papa.

EIGHT

Right from the beginning, I was well aware that my reign was only for a year. The important thing was what I was going to do with my life once those twelve months were up. I had always been a firm believer in the value of journalling. In Habakkuk 2:2, the Lord speaks about writing down your vision: 'Write the vision, and make it plain upon tables, that he may run that readeth it.' So that is what I did. I was very clear on how I structured my year. I had my short-term goals, my medium-term goals and my long-term goals.

My short-term goals were as basic as getting my driver's licence. I had won a car and I needed to know how to drive it. That one was soon ticked off the list, thanks to my dad, who patiently taught me how to drive.

A medium-term goal was to travel the world. I had seen all these exotic places on television, and that had sparked my curiosity. I wanted to experience different cultures and what they had to offer. At school, we'd had a globe that we used in geography class. We learnt to name the continents and the oceans, and it had always been a dream of mine to see them for myself. The furthest I had been outside Soweto was to Durban, when I was about twelve years old. My father had packed us like sardines into his red Datsun bakkie with its mattress in the back under the canopy. My mother had made *idombolo* and *umleqwa* (dumplings and 'runaway chicken'), and we'd driven to Durban to see the sea.

Durban is located on the east coast of South Africa and it is famous for being the busiest port in the country. It is also one of the major centres of tourism because of its warm climate and extensive beaches. Most people who lived in land-locked provinces like ours would go to Durban when they wanted to experience the sea. It is about 560 kilometres from Johannesburg and the drive takes less than six hours.

The first time I laid eyes on the Indian Ocean was totally surreal. The sheer expanse of it seemed impossible to imagine, but I didn't have to imagine it, because it was right there in front of me. The waves came and went slowly, and the seagulls flew above our heads. I remember the ocean wind hitting my face as we ventured closer. Of course, none of us could swim, and because of all the horrible urban legends about people being taken by the tide, we were very cautious.

My parents had brought empty plastic bottles with them all the way from Soweto, as apparently a lot of people who visited Durban collected sea water to take home with them whenever they got the chance. It seemed strange to us, but our parents insisted, so we helped with 'Operation Ocean Water Collection'. It had been a wonderful adventure, our first road trip to uMgababa beach, but now I wanted to see what the wider world had to offer. My year as Miss South Africa delivered, and more, on my travel goal.

My long-term goal at the start of my reign was still to finish my teaching degree and eventually enter the classroom. Miss South Africa and its associated travel, however, soon opened a whole new universe to me. I realised that I enjoyed the independence of owning my time and controlling my future. The entrepreneurial blood in me had been stirred. Now I discovered that I wanted to be my own boss, and this crystallised into a new long-term goal: I wanted to run my own business, be self-employed, set my own goals and chart my own direction. I wanted to work on my own ideas and plans, and have the ability to earn more. I was open to it all.

Miss South Africa gave me a window of opportunity: I had gained a bigger platform and a bigger voice, and a better chance to achieve my dreams and realise my goals. I would meet and network with all sorts of people, and I knew that I would have access to individuals I would never otherwise get to meet. Being Miss South Africa would open doors – I could get a meeting with a CEO to pitch an idea, or a financial institution if I was trying to raise capital for a business in the future, for instance. But while the title could get me an appointment, what was ultimately more important was what I did when I stepped through that door. I knew the time was fleeting, and I could not afford to squander the privilege and let opportunities slip through my fingers.

I had to make a choice. Was I going to get on with the business of adulthood – 'adulting', as young people call it these days – and really knuckle down, work hard and take full advantage of the opportunities, or was I going to waste that time?

I chose the former. I knew I had only one shot. Sometimes I think I should have had more fun. I was a very serious young person. My peers went out clubbing, but I never got to do that. But then, think what I was doing instead! I was travelling the world; introducing Madiba, leader of the rainbow nation, as a keynote speaker at global events; delivering speeches and motivational talks; and being interviewed and photographed.

It was a dream life. It was as if a fairy godmother had come down and waved her magic wand. Johanna and I often felt like two kids in a candy store. We could not believe our lot or our luck. Overnight I had a car, beautiful clothes, an apartment in the northern suburbs, jewellery and cosmetics, and lots of shoes. I had a glam squad that came in daily to do my make-up and hair. And I was able to realise my dream of travelling the world.

The first time I went on an aeroplane, and the first time I went overseas, was to go to Spain. I went with Doreen and Carl Isaacs, the brilliant make-up artist and hair guru, on a shoot for M-Net at a resort in Málaga as one of the prizes from RCI. I had four suitcases full of the most beautiful clothes you've ever seen, specially commissioned and created by four of South Africa's top designers: The Boys, Julian, Dicky Longhurst and Errol Arendz. I can still picture some of the items. There was this gorgeous black tux with gold buttons and these big old nineties' shoulder pads, as well as couture gowns, of course, and shoes, handbags and accessories.

Unfortunately, we came back to our villa after our first shoot on location to discover that we had been robbed. They took everything, including my Miss South Africa sash. They even drilled the safe off the wall to get the cash, although they were gracious enough to leave our passports. I was traumatised! My first overseas trip and this happens. I suppose I thought things like robberies and petty theft only happened in South Africa. Clearly I was wrong, because criminals could also be found in the First World. There is something ironic about someone who lived in an allegedly dangerous township her whole life being robbed blind in Spain. Carl tried to cheer me up with his eccentric sense of humour. 'Darling,' he declared, 'the gypsies are wearing your sash in the nightclubs of Málaga.' I didn't find it funny at all. I had lost an entire collection of couture garments. The three of us curled up in one bed that night, afraid to sleep in our own rooms, Carl and me sobbing hysterically, stoic Doreen trying to calm us down. Carl had brought a stunning black Jean Paul Gaultier jacket and it was gone. He was inconsolable, as was I.

I had left with four suitcases; I arrived home with a handbag and one boot that the thieves must have dropped. When I picked it up, Doreen said to me, 'Darling, what are you going to do with one boot?' She was right, of course, but those Preview Shoes boots were the business – I just couldn't leave it there. Funnily enough, I kept that one boot for a very long time, I don't know why. So my first trip overseas was not perfect, but it definitely came close. There were too many beautiful moments to count. The people, the architecture, the food and, of course, the company. Despite the initial speed bump, Doreen and Carl really made the trip extra special by just being there with me.

If you were to ask me today if Miss South Africa did me good, I'd say it did me *real* good! It gave me experiences I would never otherwise have had, it opened previously unexplored avenues and it gave me access to business opportunities. As an employer over the last twenty-five years, I have created a few hundred jobs in my various enterprises, brought others along, and hopefully made a tangible difference in many people's lives. And I am where I am today because I was given just one opportunity, and I took it and I ran with it and I did not look back.

It wasn't always easy. The sash has its pros and cons. As much as the title opened doors for me, it also counted against me at times. As a 'beauty queen', you are often stereotyped. Yes, you're a pretty face, strutting your stuff on stage in a bathing costume, but what have you really got to offer? People can be ugly and unkind. I had to work ten times harder to prove myself and challenge the status quo to show that I was smart and determined. My title precluded me from certain transactions, because the narrative in some boardrooms was along the lines of 'What value can Miss South Africa really add?' Sadly, it was often black women who held this view.

At the end of the day, I knew I was not just a pretty face. And I was determined to prove it.

With the fanfare of my inauguration over, it was time to get to work. There were a lot of different aspects to the 'job' of being Miss South Africa. Every day there was something, and it was varied. They call you an ambassador, and that was part of it – representing the country in different ways and at different events. One night it might be a fund-raising gala dinner and the next day I would be doing a cover shoot for a magazine or visiting a children's shelter or fund-raising for the purchase of incubators for a hospital. I travelled all over the country, as well as overseas. I did radio and television interviews with various media outlets. I did a lot of shoots – so many shoots! I don't even know how many covers I was on that year – *Cosmopolitan*, *Femina*, *Fairlady*, *You*, *Huisgenoot*, *Drum*, *Tribute*, *Ebony*, *True Love*, *Soul*, *Bona*, *Pace*. The daily and weekly newspapers also covered my every move.

In the year of my reign I raised funds for the Nelson Mandela Children's Fund (NMCF). A percentage of what I earned in speaker fees, modelling assignments and so on went towards the NMCF. It was very important to me that I made my small contribution to this charitable fund, which was championed by our beloved Madiba. Its aim is to change the way society treats its children and youth, and to give voice and dignity to the African child. The fund was building a rights-based movement, and I wanted to do my part. At the end of my reign, I went to the Union Buildings to present the cheque to Madiba.

I considered inspiring a new generation an important part of my role. I did a lot of work in schools, talking to young people about achieving their hopes and dreams. I was passionate about encouraging the youth to stay in school and get educated, because you are your education.

It's funny to think that I was not all that much older than those schoolkids. I, too, was discovering who I was and trying to figure out my own identity, but I was doing so onstage, in the spotlight, in front of the cameras.

NINE

Another new development in my life around this time was that I had started dating my very first boyfriend. I had, in fact, met him the year before, while attending a function with Bra Si at the Mariston Hotel in downtown Johannesburg.

His name was Dingaan Thobela and he was a well-known professional boxer. He had gained notoriety by winning the WBO Lightweight title in 1990, and he was affectionately known as 'the Rose of Soweto'. After our initial meeting, he pursued me because he wanted us to be in a romantic relationship, but I wasn't that keen at first. I was still very young and naive, and with all the events I had to attend as Miss Soweto, I was very busy too.

Nevertheless, I slowly got to know him as someone kind and dependable. His parents lived in Chiawelo, which was very close to Protea North, where my parents had moved, and he had a house in Kelvin. When the relationship started getting serious, I introduced him to my mom and dad. I would often accompany him to social events and I even attended some of his boxing matches. He would fetch me from campus when school closed so that we could spend time together.

Everything was great at the beginning, but unfortunately that was not to last. One day, while I was at his house, his phone rang and he decided to ignore the call. He had done this before, and I had put it down to him not wanting to be disturbed in his downtime. But after a while it started to make me feel uncomfortable that he never answered his phone in my presence. I wondered if he was dating someone else and if those calls were from her. Eventually I decided to confront him about it, along with the fact that I had previously discovered women's apparel at his house that did not belong to me.

His response was to accuse me of not trusting him enough, but that also didn't sit well with me. I persisted, because I wanted to get to the bottom of the issue. He retaliated by physically assaulting me. I was shocked. I had never experienced this kind of violence in my life before. Immediately afterwards, he became very apologetic and told me that I had pushed him too far. He said he had lost control, but that he would never do that to me again.

I don't know if it was my naivety that made me believe him, or if it was the sheer shock of the moment. It may seem strange when you hear a battered woman say that she actually believes the man didn't mean to hurt her, but I was once one of those women. At only twenty years of age, I was dealing with a level of shame I had never imagined possible. I was ashamed of myself for ending up in that horrific situation. I was ashamed of what people would say because I was living a very public life. I was ashamed that I had not seen the signs that I was getting involved with an abusive man. I don't know what it is about shame that makes people choose to keep things like this a secret, but that is exactly what I did. I made the choice to shut my mouth about the assault and just carry on with the relationship.

It didn't take long for Dingaan to go back on his promise to never lay a hand on me again. One day, while I was visiting him, another woman showed up at the gate, demanding to see him. I went out to see what the commotion was about and there she was, claiming to also be his girlfriend. You can imagine how painful that was for me, especially as he physically assaulted me for a second time for 'believing some crazy woman'. Yet still, I stayed.

In April 1995, I attended the Rand Easter Show with my little brother, Tshehla, and Dingaan. It was always fun going to that annual consumer exhibition. There were stalls selling all kinds of goods, as well as live performances. I bumped into some old friends from the University of Venda. Some had been colleagues in student politics and others were just glad to see me because I had not returned to campus since being crowned Miss South Africa the previous year.

It was so good to see them all again and to catch up, but while I was chatting with my old school buddies, little did I know that my boyfriend was becoming more and more agitated. We eventually left and, as we got into the car, Dingaan made it known that he was very angry. I remember him saying that he thought I was more famous than him. I didn't know where that comment had come from, but the next thing I knew he'd hit me twice with a back-fisted hand that had a big ring on it. My head hit the headrest so hard, I was bleeding and hysterical, and I had to be hospitalised.

Again, the shame of it all came crashing down on me. The media had caught wind of my injuries, and I really didn't want to deal with news coverage of poor, abused Basetsana. So I lied. I told everyone that I had been mugged and that the assailants had injured me in the process. Unbelievably, I went back to him yet again.

The final straw came a few weeks later, when I had finally made up my mind to end the relationship. When I told him it was over, he pulled out a gun and aimed it at my head, and said that there was no way I was going to leave him. He said that if I ever tried, he would kill me. I was absolutely sure he would. Later, when he went out, I took my little weekend bag from his house and ran for my life. And I finally found the courage to tell my family.

He didn't go quietly. He called incessantly, wanting us to get back together, apologising and then saying 'you made me do it'. It was the typical abuser mentality. It went on for months. He was relentless. I was scared of him, but thankful that the Rosebank apartment they had put me in as Miss South Africa had security, who were told not to give him access. I also got a full-time bodyguard.

We live in a country where the abuse of women is rife. Statistics show that South Africa's femicide rate in 2017 was five times the global average. 'In South Africa, every eight hours a woman is killed and at least half of these women die at the hands of their intimate partners,' one government minister said. My silence had a lot to do with the shame of being abused and always thinking about what other people would say. Here I am, loved by a nation, yet the person who professes to love me is the one hurting me and breaking me down. Eventually, though, I thought of my father, who totally adored me and had never hurt me.

He had never so much as given me a hiding! I figured that love should not hurt. Love should love. And so I finally left. I am blessed that I had a strong male figure in my dad, who showed me love in its truest form. I am a firm advocate for women leaving abusive relationships. Walk away with your life!

So it was an extraordinary year, but it wasn't all easy. What I found most difficult, being an introvert, was to be in a big crowd of people and to be the centre of attention. I often felt anxious and awkward going out in public and having to mingle and make conversation. It took great effort for me to do that.

Even though I was often surrounded by people, I felt quite isolated at times. It was therefore such a blessing to have Johanna around that year. She had finished her degree at Rhodes University and was back in Johannesburg doing her articles at KPMG. We spent a lot of time together, and she was a great companion and support.

When I think back on that year and all that happened, it seems like I grew up overnight. I became an adult, a serious, mature individual with big responsibilities. It changed me fundamentally. It changed my outlook on life, and it completely changed my vision for my future. I thought I would be content living a quiet life, going to school, teaching, coming back home at the end of the day. But all that went out the window, and I am not complaining! My year as Miss South Africa showed me possibilities that I didn't know existed for somebody like me. In my 'hood, there was a limited range of options for what you could do with your life. You had teachers, nurses, social workers and police officers. That was my frame of reference, and a great one too, and it was all I knew. Miss South Africa opened up a whole new dimension for me and allowed me to be bold and have audacious dreams.

As I said earlier, gradually things started to crystallise in my head and I got a glimpse of what I truly wanted to do with my life. I knew then that I wanted to chart my own future in my own way. At the time I didn't know exactly what that would entail, or in what field, but I knew I wanted to be 'the master of my fate' and 'the captain of my soul'. I absolutely love that line from the poem 'Invictus' by William Ernest Henley. I wanted to create jobs and to bring others along with me on that journey.

I knew that I needed to continue my studies. I had left university in my third year, when I made the finals of Miss South Africa, and I wanted to finish my degree. During my reign, Nelson Mandela spoke to me about my studies. He took education very seriously, as do I. He asked me what my passion was, and I told him I was passionate about politics and helping to bring about change in society. He said he thought that Georgetown University in Washington, D.C., would be a good place for me, and he offered to help me obain a scholarship to go and study there when my reign was over.

It was a very generous gesture and a great honour, but I was reluctant. It would have meant four years of study in America. I was cognisant of the change that was happening in South Africa. There was a palpable new energy in our country. It was an exciting and inspiring time, and I wanted to be a part of it. Leaving the country at this time wasn't an option for me.

I thanked him, but said, 'Tata, I'm not going to be able to leave now.' I explained to him my reason, and I gave him my word that I would go back and complete my degree one day, and he accepted my decision graciously. I learnt a lot from Madiba, including the discipline to always finish what you start. A few years later I enrolled at the University of South Africa (UNISA) and finished what I had started, just as I'd promised. In the meantime, I was on a one-year crash course, learning so much every day, with Doreen as my 'teacher', helping me navigate this new world.

Another thing I learnt about Madiba was that he was a stickler for time. Once Johanna and I were invited to his Houghton home for lunch. Just after we arrived, his motorcade swept down the drive towards the house, and there was a real sense of urgency. I thought maybe he was rushing to meet someone important, a head of state or some such. When he got to the house, I said, 'You know, Tata, I see you are in a rush. We understand if something has come up. We can just come back another time.' And he said, 'No, no, darlings, I said we'd have lunch at one o'clock. I was rushing for you.'

That was Madiba, though. Time is important, but more than that, *you* are important. This was very apparent in how he treated people. I often had the privilege of introducing him at an event, and I noticed how he would stop and greet everyone with such kindness and humility, from the waiters and waitresses to the VIPs. I was in awe of him in so many ways, and when people ask me about that year, and what the highlight was, I can honestly say that it was the time I spent with Nelson Mandela.

In November 1994, the Miss World pageant came to Sun City. And what a spectacular extravaganza of a show it was! Watched by millions of people across the globe, it's a really big production. The winner of each country's title competes, and in that particular year, ninety-four countries were represented. In the lead-up to the finals, all ninety-four girls stayed together for a whole month and did all sorts of activities in preparation for the big night. We were together the whole time and the schedule was absolutely gruelling.

As the month goes by, you start to get a sense of who is looking strong. I knew Aishwarya Rai, Miss India, was a contender. And Irene Ferreira, Miss Venezuela, of course – there is always a Venezuelan girl in the top five; they are just amazing, those Venezuelan girls. There was a frenzy before the pageant. People were very vocal in the media, placing bets on me or Aishwarya to win. At this point, I remember telling Doreen, 'I don't want to win this thing!' Soon it was down to the top ten, and I was among them, and I realised that I was looking pretty strong. I started to panic!

You see, winning meant leaving the country to live in London for a year. As I said, I was so aware of what was happening in South Africa, and I did not want to miss seeing the change and new dawn first-hand. When my name was called for second place, I was so relieved. Miss India won – a huge Bollywood star today, she is honestly one of the most beautiful women I've ever seen – even Julia Roberts is quoted as saying 'Aishwarya Rai is the most beautiful woman in the world' – and the lovely Miss Venezuela was second princess. I was so pleased to go home!

There was another significant highlight before I handed over my crown. South Africa had the honour of hosting the 1995 Rugby World Cup. Now I can't say I was a huge rugby fan or even understood the rules of the game. In those days, it was very much a white people's sport. Black South Africans were more likely to watch and play soccer.

But the vibe around the Rugby World Cup was so incredible that you couldn't help but be drawn into the spirit of the spectacle. Nelson Mandela was very strategic, and used the opportunity to create a sense of unity in the country, to bring the citizens of all races together in support of our national team.

South Africa not only hosted the 1995 Rugby World Cup, but we won it too! I joined Francois Pienaar and the winning team on an open-top bus in a Victory Parade Tour around Johannesburg. It was amazing. Amazing! The whole city – it felt like the whole country – turned out to congratulate them. People lined the pavements of the CBD, stood on top of office buildings and leant out of windows. It was an actual ticker-tape parade, just like in the movies.

In case you were wondering, I didn't have to wear a green Springbok rugby jersey. But I did wear a green Julian jacket with major shoulder pads and a black skirt. And the sash, of course. When you're Miss South Africa, you don't go anywhere without that sash!

It was incredible to see how people received the team and rooted for them, and how proud we, as a nation, were of our collective achievement of creating a new, democratic and inclusive South Africa. I got a warm welcome too, which was lovely. The whole experience was just beautiful and truly memorable. And I have to say that the rugby squad were very warm towards me. It felt strange for me, as a young black girl, to be on a bus with all these big, strong, rugby-playing men. They really were huge! But I found them amenable and friendly.

Not long after that, my time as Miss South Africa came to an end. It had been the most incredible year, and when it came to passing on the title, I was awash with mixed emotions. '(I've Had) The Time of My Life' by Bill Medley and Jennifer Warnes kept playing in my head – you might remember the song from the movie *Dirty Dancing* with Patrick Swayze. It's still one of my favourite songs. Yes, I'd had the time of my life, and what a time it was!

I remember sitting down to write my farewell speech, which would be pre-recorded and played, along with visuals of the highlights of my reign, as I took my final bow, before the new Miss South Africa was announced. The memories just came flooding back: the faces of the people I had met and with whom I'd interacted, from all walks of life;

the places I had visited in South Africa and abroad; and the things I'd done, from cover shoots to visits to schools, hospitals, old-age homes and children's shelters.

I recalled the visit my parents and I had made to my alma mater, the University of Venda. The entire student body and faculty had welcomed me on campus in the convocation hall. Wow, I had left university a simple girl with big dreams and come back a true reflection of and a face for hope of what is possible if you dare to dream. The unending applause reduced me to tears.

When it came time to hand over the crown and close that chapter of my life, I was overwhelmed and emotional, but most of all I felt a deep and profound sense of gratitude for an experience that had changed my life irrevocably, and for the better. For that journey, for 1994, I remain grateful.

PART III

FINDING LOVE

TEN

I'll get to it later, but when I started working on *Top Billing* in the year of my reign as Miss South Africa, and then at my production company, Tswelopele Productions, with Patience Stevens, I spent a fair amount of time at the South African Broadcasting Corporation (SABC). Believe it or not, in the pre-digital era, when a show was finished and ready to be aired, we would take the tape – the actual physical Betacam tape – to the SABC and hand it over to be loaded and flighted. Patience and I were running a tight ship with a very small team, so it was often left to us to deliver the tapes personally. We had to make sure that the tape was ingested on time, otherwise there would literally be nothing on air. When I was wandering around the corridors of the SABC, I would regularly bump into this guy called Romeo Kumalo, whom I'd previously seen singing a song by Lionel Richie on a television show called *Shell Road to Fame*. *Shell Road to Fame* was a talent competition that flighted on the SABC. Each week, contestants would perform on stage in front of a live studio audience, and these performances would be broadcast. I'd also seen Romeo presenting a music show called *Ezimtoti* with Caroline Fassie on CCTV, before it became SABC1. And occasionally I'd run into him when I was out with Bra Si. Bra Si knew just about e'r'body, and I mean e'r'body, *ekasi* (in the township).

Romeo was heading up sales and marketing at CCTV at the time. That was his eight-to-five, Monday-to-Friday job, but his first love was music, and he DJ'd on the weekends as a side gig. He had

71

this slot on Sundays on Metro FM, the famous 'Romeo's Romantic Repertoire'.

Whenever I went to deliver the tapes, lo and behold, who would I see but Romeo Kumalo. For someone so busy, he certainly seemed to have a lot of time to spend in the corridors of the SABC, where I would generally find him. I later discovered that he knew my schedule, and when I was supposed to deliver the tapes he would be there, waiting to see me. When we 'bumped into' each other, he would always accost me and try to charm me and ask me out on a date, but I thought, oh no, not this guy, not interested. I figured he was too good-looking, and I would be looking for trouble if I dated him. Romeo was clearly very nervous every time he asked me out. I could tell it was not an easy thing for him to do, and I even noticed that he stumbled over his words. He later confessed that he had stuttered in his youth, and that I made him so nervous, he couldn't get the words out. The problem was that I had just come out of a very traumatic relationship and had made the decision to give myself a break from dating. But he was very persistent!

So at one point I thought, you know what, I need to get this guy off my back. I'll just go for a coffee with him so that at least I don't have to feel awkward when I see him back at the SABC. At the time I was living in Hyde Park in an apartment I had bought after my Miss South Africa reign, right near the shopping centre, and I said I'd meet him there, in the mall. It was very public, and on my territory – no 'intimate private dinner for two'-type vibes ... *nton nton*! We would just have a quick tea or coffee, and when it was over I could say, okay, we've had our coffee, that's it. This was in 1996.

Romeo was already sitting at the table when I arrived at the restaurant. Of course, I had made sure to arrive fashionably late, so I didn't look too eager. I distinctly remember that when I got to the table, he stood up to greet me. I was quite impressed by this gesture and thought to myself, 'This guy has good manners.'

Like any other first date, there was some awkwardness at the beginning while we exchanged pleasantries. But as the afternoon wore on, we found ourselves relaxing into an easy, natural sort of conversation about our respective interests and careers. I told him that I knew about his radio show, and we realised we had very similar tastes in music. Well, the 'quick coffee' became a six-hour date, and we ended up ordering dinner. He seriously made me laugh that night, and I haven't stopped laughing since that day in April 1996. I remember thinking, is this guy for real? On the one hand he's goofy and tells the most hilarious jokes, but on the other hand he's one of the smartest guys I've ever met and also quite serious. And I later came to know him as one of the most decent, kind, authentic and present beings who loves deeply. I'm so glad we decided to multiply his genes and his goodness with our tribe.

From the first date, I fell head over heels in love with this guy. I was literally giddy when I left the restaurant. From that day, he was very clear. He said, 'You're going to be my wife.' I thought, yeah right, we'll see about that.

During our long courtship, we had the best time together. I was travelling all over the world for *Top Billing* and sometimes Romeo would come with me, or meet me at my destination. Or we would go away together for a holiday. We also just loved being together either at his place or mine, just hanging out.

There was one thing he was very sneaky about, though. In the early days of us dating, he invited me to his place in Sandton, and he had prepared this meal. Wow, I thought, this guy has got potential! He's so good in the kitchen – what a catch! Let me tell you, that was the one and only meal I ever got. After I agreed to marry him, never again. Here we are, married for twenty years and the guy hasn't yet met the stove. When I tease him about it, he is unrepentant. He just says, 'My baby, I had to work every move, every move. You were my dream girl ...'

He was so romantic, and still is. When he was at Metro FM he would play this song, 'April Showers' by Dru Hill, and dedicate it to me, because it was in April when we sat down and decided that we really did like each other.

Television kept me busy, but that wasn't all I was doing. Over and above my television work, I was being asked to MC events. I began to hone my public-speaking skills, and I soon had a busy schedule of events, some of them very big, such as the prestigious Loerie Awards (which I did for three years in a row), the launch of the newly rebranded South African Airways and the relaunch of the SABC. I basically MC'd every big gig in town. Corporates also started to invite me as a motivational speaker for their staff, to tell my story, from Soweto to Miss South Africa, *Top Billing* and the world stage.

In 1997, my sister Johanna started a travel management company, Travel With Flair, together with partners Robert Wilke and Tibor Zsadanyi. I joined the company two years later. Collectively, we wanted to build a brand that had substance, relevance and visibility. We wanted to be a brand with aesthetic appeal, style and timelessness, and to build a business that people could touch, feel and experience. We never intended to become a corporate travel agency; we thought we'd be a leisure travel agency selling packages and holidays. But we saw a gap in the market and redirected our strategy towards the corporate sphere, and the company has grown significantly, employing 800 people to date.

It was a busy, busy time. I was a girl on the move! In an average month, I might have ten or fifteen speaking engagements – that was over and above my television production company and broadcaster work on SABC. I made a decision to show up and be present. I took all the gigs. I realised that there was huge leverage in being such a recognisable face, and that at this time in my life I had a unique opportunity to earn well and build some assets.

Of course, you can't keep going at that pace forever. There's a limit. I pushed myself to the point where I was totally burnt out. I was doing too much. In addition, I was constantly travelling and my body just couldn't cope with the time changes and the jet lag. Everything caught up with me. I wasn't sleeping. I was exhausted. I started to get easily emotional, crying all the time. I was in a deep hole, to the point where I didn't want to do this any more.

Johanna was the one who said to me, 'This is not normal, you need to see a doctor.' I did, and of course the doctor told me I'd reached burnout and actually had to take time out or else I was going to really, really crash. So I took about three months off for a sabbatical. I didn't travel. I didn't do any gigs. I didn't see people; I didn't allow myself to be seen. I didn't take calls or allow any visits. I had to look after myself, restore myself and make myself well again. The world was not going to do that for me. It was time to just regroup and recover.

Experiencing that burnout changed a lot of things for me. By this time, I had already met Romeo. We were in a relationship, but frankly

I hadn't been giving it much attention because I was so focused on building my career. I loved the guy, but I also loved my work. I wanted to do something and become something, and I knew that this opportunity might not be around forever. I prioritised that over my person and my relationship.

Thank God Romeo was patient and stuck around. Bless his heart. When I took time out, he was always there, very present. I started to think a bit more clearly about the relationship. At this time, when I was getting better, I was fully engaged and present.

We got married in December 2000. Romeo proposed twice. I remember that the first proposal was at his place. We were sitting watching TV, and very casually he says, 'You know, I would like to send my uncles to come and see your uncles.' There was no ring and no bended knee, but when an African man refers to a meeting between his uncles and yours, you know things are getting very serious. I got the shock of my life. In my head we were just hanging out, and now he wanted to marry me! I was so not ready for those uncles. I took my bag and left. I didn't take his calls for a week or two because I felt so overwhelmed; the idea of getting married just seemed so daunting.

Romeo realised that marriage was not something that I wanted to entertain at that moment, so when we finally started talking again, we just went back to dating. Then, a year or so later, he proposed again, and I was like, 'Uh uh, you and I are good like this. We don't need these uncles ...' But then I began processing the idea of a life with him, and it felt comfortable, safe and right. There was something beautiful and peaceful about 'us'. So one day, we were just sitting together at his place and I said, very casually, 'So when do you think your uncles want to come and see my uncles?' His face lit up. He was quick on the uptake after that. He didn't waste time, don't you worry! Two weeks later those uncles were there, the deal was done and dusted, and I was spoken for. No dude could even say HELLO to my fine young self!

My parents got my uncle from Botswana to negotiate *lobola* on behalf of our family. *Lobola* or 'bride price' was originally paid in cows by the groom's family to the bride's family in order to secure her hand in marriage. In urban areas, people don't have cows any more, but the principle remains the same. Older male members of the family, usually referred to as 'the uncles', are invited to a meeting where the potential groom's family indicates the young man's intention to marry the other family's daughter. The bride's uncles start by saying how many cows they require in order to give their blessing to the union. This is usually the beginning of a long negotiation in which the groom's family tries to reduce the figure by as much as possible. Eventually the two families come to an agreement, money changes hands and an informal contract is signed by all parties to confirm that *lobola* has now been paid.

Uncle Dan Kwelagobe had served in the Botswana government for a very long time, in many different ministerial positions. 'Good shot,' I said when I heard he was to represent us, 'that's the guy we need! We need a tough negotiator.' When my soon-to-be husband heard that, he said to me, 'Baby, your people must not kill me ...', of course all in jest.

Besides Rra Itseng Kwelagobe, there were other relatives from my dad's and mom's sides of the family: my mom's brother, Uncle Seiiso, was there, as well as Rakgadi Mandu Makgalemele and Rakgadi Prella Maseko from my dad's side. Romeo is from the East Rand, where his parents live, but his roots are in KwaZulu-Natal, and his uncles on his father's side came from Winterveld and on his mother's side from Rustenburg. It was quite a crowd.

Romeo wasn't present for the meeting, of course, as culture dictates. I was there, but I was not part of the negotiations. As the potential bride, you are not allowed to be on your feet from the time the delegation arrives. My mom told me that when the negotiations are happening, you have to stay off your feet so that you do not suppress the deliberations. I'm not sure exactly how that works, but I obeyed Moeder in these matters. It sounds crazy, right, but I was told what to do and I did exactly as I was told, so the whole day I was not allowed to stand. I used the opportunity very propitiously, though, sitting there saying, 'May I have tea, please?' or 'I need some water, please' or 'I'm hungry', while my cousins who were in the bedroom with me ran around. They vowed to get payback.

The negotiations started with the uncles asking all the young maidens of the house to come to the lounge. So my girl cousins and

I all went through with our headwraps on and looking down, not making eye contact.

Then Uncle Kwelagobe asked Romeo's uncles, 'Do you know who you are here for?'

And Uncle Don Kumalo replied, 'Yes, we are here for Makgalemele's daughter, her name is Basetsana, for her hand in marriage,' but the way we say it in Setswana is really beautiful. It's something like, 'We are here to ask for a calabash of water.' *Re tlo kopa sego sa metsi.*

Then my uncle said, 'But who are you here for of these young maidens in this home?'

And, indicating me, his uncle said, 'We are here for this one here.'

Then we girls were summarily dismissed. We returned to the bedroom and waited while the negotiations for *lobola* took place, back and forth, back and forth between the two parties. It went on for hours and I was getting anxious calls from Romeo.

'What's going on? Is it not finished? Your uncles mustn't give my uncles a hard time.'

And then, an hour later, 'Are they still at it? Babes, do you think it will go well? Why are they still at it?' That man was in a state! I tried to calm him down. And still we waited.

Eventually, the uncles found a happy medium, whatever that was. An agreement was reached and a little invoice drawn up to say, 'We have received these cows from the Kumalos' – although they were not actual cows in this case, of course.

Once *lobola* had been negotiated, there was a big lunch. Romeo didn't attend; the groom is not included or allowed to be there. Later on, when my uncles and his uncles had left, and it was just me and my family at home, and Romeo called to ask if he could pick me up. I asked my parents if that was okay. My dad said, 'He has done the right thing and he's most welcome, officially, in this home.'

So Romeo came to pick me up, and I remember my dad saying to him, 'You look after my baby girl,' and Romeo saying, 'Yes, sir, I will look after your baby girl,' and he's lived up to that. He's more than lived up to that.

That evening, we went out for dinner at the Russian Tea Room, which was near my place in Hyde Park. We loved that restaurant with its plush furnishings and ambience, and we went there often. It was a special place for us. Sitting there, we were both like, 'Wow, we're getting married.'

That was in April 2000. Once the *lobola* was paid, we had the traditional welcoming of the groom to the Makgalemele family and of *umakoti* (the bride) to the Kumalo family, where I was given my married name of Sibongile. It is customary that after the bride is welcomed into the groom's family, she receives a new name as a sign that she is now one of them. My name, Sibongile, means 'we are grateful' in isiZulu. Afterwards, in December, I married the love of my life, my smile-keeper and my true friend at the wedding of my dreams.

ELEVEN

April 2000 was such an exciting time in our lives as Romeo and I planned our wedding. As was customary among black people, we would have a traditional ceremony, followed by what we call a 'white wedding'. I imagine it's called that because, much like a Western-style wedding, the bride wears a white dress and the ceremony takes place in a church.

I wasn't the first girl in my family to be married. In fact, we got married in order: first, the oldest, Lerato, then the second-born, Johanna, and then me. Number three. It's interesting, almost like my mom scripted it, you know – no one is going to have a child out of wedlock, you are going to get married, one, two, three. As you know, we girls did as we were told. We followed the rules of the house, which is to say Moeder's rules!

I have to tell you, my traditional wedding was spectacular. It took place at home in Protea North, Soweto, and the whole neighbourhood came. In our tradition, you don't send out invitations. The minute they see a marquee being erected, the neighbourhood knows: it's going down! Everyone is invited and everyone comes. When I say everyone came to our traditional wedding, I mean 1500 people (if not more) came to celebrate with us. It was a merrymaking festivity second to none. People had so much to eat and drink. To this day, people still talk about it and say that the Makgalemeles throw the best *mncimbis* (parties)!

When I think about it now, probably the best part was when Romeo and his people arrived. I should mention that when I married him, I became part of his lovely family: his mom, Jennifer; his dad, Mpho; his younger brother, Jabu; and his younger sister, Refilwe. We all got along well – my family and his family – and they were very involved in the wedding planning.

A big crowd of Romeo's friends and family arrived at our traditional wedding, some in minibus taxis. As they made their way down the street from the taxis to our house, they were singing – we could hear them approaching from a block away. And my people went out to meet them halfway to bring them to the marquee, and we were singing too, and it was this competition, singing our hearts out, trying to drown each other out. There were men and women, so many of us on both sides. We came closer, they approached . . . and the singing . . . our voices ringing through the streets of Protea North in Mark's Square. It was incredible. For me, it was overwhelming to see Romeo there with his people and to realise that this is it, we are really doing this, it's happening.

The traditional wedding was beautiful and colourful. Guests were dressed in their traditional attire. My parents said, this is the process we follow, the *lobola* and *umembeso* (the giving of gifts by the groom's family). When it comes to *umembeso*, each family hopes it's not a shopping list of relatives who have to be dressed. However, the Makgalemele clan is huge, so the Kumalos must have bought thirty blankets and headwraps. My father received a coat, an axe, a walking stick and a hat. I was given a three-legged cast-iron pot, an *ucansi* mat made of reeds, a *seanamarena* (a Basotho traditional blanket), and a wedding song that says '*Ntate nthekele seanamarena*', which is a very symbolic gift that is bestowed on a bride. To me, it's all part of my culture and part of who I am, the essence of my roots. I wore a Zulu-inspired outfit with an *isiqolo* (traditional Zulu hat), *nebheshu* (skirt), white vest and beads. An ox was slaughtered. The ceremony was held in the traditional manner that represented both of our cultures, customs, heritages and lineages.

When I think of my life, I am aware that I have always straddled both the modern world and the traditional one. In many ways, I've lived as a modern woman. I've travelled, I've made my own way in business, I love the work that I do. But I am also very comfortable with the traditional aspects of who I am, and with my roots. I inhabit both those worlds harmoniously and comfortably. I am modern and I am African!

When we got married, I took Romeo's surname. People said, 'Why would you change your surname? That's how you're known, it's your brand. Why not at least do a double-barrel?' I said no, I'm a traditionalist in that way, and I will take my husband's surname and people will just have to get used to calling me by my new name.

So yes, I'm a modern woman, but I have never felt the need to rewrite the script and break the mould just to say, 'Hey, I'm this modern twenty-first-century woman.' I've found a balance that works for me, and I've managed to live easily in these two worlds.

Which brings me to wedding number two. I *loved* my wedding, like *totally*. Oh my goodness, everything that I ever envisioned and dreamt about as a little girl – the big wedding with the big dress and a hundred other details – came true that day, thanks, in part, to an intervention from Nelson Mandela.

Madiba was something of a father figure to me. When I saw that my relationship with Romeo was about to get serious, I told Madiba about him. Tata would teasingly enquire, 'Do you have a boyfriend?' So I thought I'd better tell him that Romeo had become a permanent fixture. Later on, when I told Madiba that I planned to marry this man, he said, 'Well, he'd better come and ask me for your hand in marriage.' So Romeo and I arranged to go to Madiba's home in Houghton. My dear fiancé was so nervous, shame, having to ask Madiba for my hand in marriage. His wife, Mum Graça Machel, was there. It was so lovely. I have a picture of the occasion, and, in fact, that picture appeared on the front page of the *Star* at the time, the two of us sandwiched between Tata and Mum Graça.

Madiba gave us his blessing, of course, and then he asked about our wedding. We were just in the planning stages, but I mentioned that I had always thought I would love to get married by a river. 'Oh, my friend Douw Steyn has got a house at the Vaal,' Madiba said. 'Zelda, please call Douw ...' Douw let us use his home, and I had my dream wedding by the river. Romeo and I worked very hard that year to save up for it. Everything else we did for the wedding was paid for out of our own savings. And it was just as I had envisioned it since I was a little girl.

One thing I did not want was a white dress. When I said I was going to wear an ice-blue dress, my mom was horrified. But *I* was getting married and I was going to do what I wanted to do. It was one occasion where I went against my mother. Designed by Gert van de Merwe, my dress was ice-blue from top to toe! Gert also dressed my gorgeous bridesmaids – my friends Peggy-Sue Khumalo and Kerishnie Naiker, and three of my cousins, Lindiwe Mdhuli, Zamo Sabela and Amanda Tjale.

Edith Venter was my wedding planner, and I must commend her; anything that I dreamt up, Edith made happen. As a child I had this dream of arriving at my wedding by boat, and it happened. Douw had a boat and we bedecked it with hundreds of cream roses from Mauritius. Hundreds. Mama, Papa, Johanna and I got into the boat at the hotel where we were staying and set off down the river for the wedding. It was calm and quiet, just the four of us, and we stood and held hands and prayed. My mom started the prayers, blessing this journey of marriage, this chapter of my life and this day. I was very emotional and started tearing up, but then I remembered my make-up! When I think back on that day, which was just gorgeous in so many ways, I think that is one of the most beautiful memories – me, my parents and my sister on the boat, praying.

The boat drew up at the pier, and I couldn't believe what I saw: a sea of white parasols, which we'd had made for all the ladies. In my childhood fantasy wedding, I walked through a guard of honour with crossed swords (I think I saw that in the film *An Officer and a Gentleman*). Edith made it happen. She even had the swords inscribed with our names and surname, and we still have them in our cellar. I stepped off the boat and walked through the guard of honour, and then I saw the crowd, all the people we loved, gathered together. White doves were released. Women ululated! It was a dream come true.

Janine Price, a pianist from church, was playing 'Amazing Grace' when I arrived at the chapel that had been erected by the river. Pastor Ray McCauley married us in a beautiful service. I literally cried throughout the entire thing, and Romeo just kept squeezing my hand and giving me reassuring glances.

And then the party, which was in a massive marquee, draped ceiling to floor with flowers, crystals and chandeliers. The legendary Stephen

Falcke was responsible for the Delft-blue décor and setting. The marquee had to be huge, because the guest list just kept getting longer, what with my list and Romeo's list, and then my mom's list and his mom's list. You know how tricky it is with wedding guest lists! We ended up with about 500 people.

Romeo had a big surprise for me at the wedding. He made his speech, thanked the guests for coming, and then he started singing George Benson's 'Nothing's Gonna Change My Love for You'. OMG! I couldn't believe it! I knew he had a good singing voice, but he has to be in a comfortable space in order to sing. He's actually shy and reserved, and for him to sing for me in front of 500 guests ... I was blown away, totally blown away. I discovered later that he had been practising in secret for weeks.

That was the highlight of my wedding. I was so surprised and moved, and in awe of this guy who had just become my husband. This beautiful gesture totally blew me away and sealed the deal ... like, the guy sang at our wedding! He sure is a keeper. I wept buckets. I had been weeping for most of the day, I was just so emotional. Even through the vows, I just couldn't stop crying. The man I loved was singing a love song to me in front of 500 people – well, that *really* set me off.

We opened the dance floor to our favourite song, 'I Finally Found Someone' by Barbra Streisand and Bryan Adams. In fact, music was a key element to our day. The theme of our wedding was the coming together of R&B, and each invitation to our guests was accompanied by a CD of the top ten songs that we loved, wrapped in a blue box. We played those songs at the reception as well.

The wedding felt truly blessed. Even the weather played along. That year, 2000, it hadn't rained in a long time. But the weekend of the wedding it rained heavily, and the night before, it really poured. It also showed no signs of letting up, which would have totally messed with our plans. On the day of our wedding, however, the rain stopped, the sun came out, the parasols went up and we released the doves. Everything went exactly as planned, in this fresh, newly washed world. That evening, at seven o'clock, the heavens opened again.

It really felt like a blessing. The strange part is that one of my names is Motlalepule, which means 'the one who brings rain', and whenever there is a significant event in my life, it always rains. The same thing happened before our traditional wedding – there'd been no rain, and then the night before the festivities it had rained, and then again after everyone had left. My mom used to say that rain is a sign of blessing, and she was right, I really believe that.

Looking back, I have so much to be grateful for, not least the fact that my father was able to walk me down the aisle. Two years later, he passed away. But I can still see him there, beaming from ear to ear, with so much pride in his eyes, and I feel so blessed to have had him there.

It was the most beautiful, memorable day. I loved, loved, *loved* it.

And then it was over. I remember, finally, when we went back to the hotel: the world was gone and it was just the two of us. It was calm, peaceful and beautiful. It felt so right. I looked at Romeo and I knew for sure, without a shadow of a doubt, that I had married an incredible human being. After three years of dating and twenty years of marriage, I still look at him and think I married an incredible man. Through all the ups and downs of life, he's been the good guy, he's been my guy. He *is* my guy.

TWELVE

Our honeymoon was a cruise on board a luxury liner called *Voyager of the Seas*. We started in Miami and cruised around the Caribbean islands – Jamaica, Tahiti, Cozumel and so on. Maybe not our best idea, as it turned out. It was my first time at sea and I discovered that I get horribly seasick. That's a honeymoon passion-killer of note! We spent another week in the Bahamas to make up for it.

We started our married life together living in my two-bedroomed townhouse in Hyde Park. We had sold Romeo's place in Sandton and were building our first home in Northcliff – on a plot on the ridge with stunning views.

Through *Top Billing* I had met many interesting people, including a number of architects. I particularly liked the work of Suzette Hammer. We had featured quite a few of her homes on the programme and I really liked her style. And the fact that she was a woman made a difference, I think. She built for a family, not just for purpose or aesthetics. She created spaces and structures in the house based on how families can and should live, and we were building our life and our home with a family in mind. It was very exciting, designing and building our dream house.

During the early part of our marriage, our Sunday routine was usually the same: we would wake up and go to church, then I would cook Sunday lunch and we would sit and read the newspapers. Lovely. Until I picked up the *Sunday World* one day and saw a picture of our almost-completed house splashed on the front page: 'The palace Romeo is building for Bassie!' It was incredibly invasive, sort of a 'check out that lifestyle' article, and no one had approached us for comment. We were very upset. The worst part was that they had printed the address, which we thought was extremely irresponsible. We were a young couple with a public profile trying to build a life, and really, we did not want the whole world knowing where we lived. It's not good for security, for a start. And when we did move in, we had people coming to take a look and stopping to take pictures.

In the end, the house was everything we dreamt of – the views were spectacular – but it never felt right. We had security on the property, but we were burgled. After two years, we decided to sell up and move.

I must say that those early years of our married life were carefree and great fun. We had married young – I was twenty-six and Romeo was twenty-eight – and it almost felt like we were playing house. We were figuring life out together. We were also working hard. I was now a business owner working full time in the television industry, both in front of the camera and behind it. *Top Billing* was still very successful, and we had started producing other shows such as *Pasella*, *Top Travel* and *Top Dogs*. Romeo was an executive at the SABC and subsequently joined Vodacom South Africa.

We were never big club people, preferring to host house parties, like dinner for twelve at our place. I'd cook and lay the table, and we'd get dressed up and Romeo would play the music. At that time we did it regularly – later, we had less energy for that sort of thing, but I still remember those occasions fondly.

We were working hard, but we also had so much freedom. No kids, no responsibilities. We could just pack up our bags and go. We used to do crazy things. Once we decided, out of the blue, that we would go skiing. We booked a package in Bulgaria – what did we know about skiing holidays? – and off we went. Oh my word. The first sign that it wasn't going to be quite what we'd expected was the shuttle from the airport – more like a beaten-up old car with actual holes in it. It took us to the most rundown, shabby hotel. The room was dusty, with cobwebs and poor television reception. We'd been schnaaied!

Although the package had been bought and paid for, we were out of there so fast. Straight back to the airport. We got there and said, 'Where is the next flight going? We'll take it.' It happened to be a

British Airways flight to London, and we didn't even stay over one night, we just came straight back to South Africa. It was so awful and we were *gatvol*. Then, because we had both taken the week off from work, we ended up going to a bush lodge. The two of us are such city slickers, we really don't do the bush all that well. We can do two days, three max. Anything more than that is just too much. So we had our three days in the bush, which was a lot better than a dusty hotel room in Bulgaria, and went back to work.

PART IV

LIGHTS, CAMERA, ACTION!

THIRTEEN

A major part of being Miss South Africa was doing media interviews. My very first radio interview was on Talk Radio 702 with a presenter by the name of Noeleen Maholwana-Sangqu. I was so nervous, but she was patient and kind, and it went off without a hitch. Little did I know then that we would end up being good friends for twenty-five years and counting. One of the interviews I did that year would change my life forever, although I didn't know it at the time. I was interviewed for the pilot of a new fitness programme that television producer Patience Stevens was shooting. After the interview, she asked if I would do the promo, and I did it in one take. 'Would you be interested in presenting for *Top Billing*?' she then asked.

At the time I didn't even know what *Top Billing* was; I had never watched it. I discovered that it was the pre-eminent lifestyle show on South African television, covering travel, entertainment, décor, architecture and fashion. What made it unusual was that it wasn't broadcast from the studios, but from exotic locations or inside people's beautiful homes. One of my goals was to travel the world, and this seemed like a golden opportunity.

In a moment of Divine Synchronicity, Doreen and Patience literally met on the street outside Ellis Park Stadium after the biggest rock concert ever staged in South Africa at that time. The cultural boycott had just been lifted and The Rolling Stones set the country ablaze with their Voodoo Lounge show on 25 February 1995. With the strains of 'Brown Sugar' and their encore performance of 'Jumpin' Jack Flash' still ringing in their ears, Patience asked Doreen whether she would like me to join the *Top Billing* team, and Doreen said yes immediately. My life-changing journey began almost at once.

Now there had never been a case of a Miss South Africa being a regular presenter of a TV programme during her reign, but Doreen, a broadcaster herself, as well as the owner and manager of the pageant, allowed me to take the gig. I started presenting *Top Billing* towards the end of 1994, and it was through the show that I got to see the world, interview amazing people and, eventually, reach my goal of being self-employed. At the time, Doreen received a lot of criticism for the fact that I was allowed to have a full-time job as a presenter on *Top Billing* during my reign as Miss South Africa. People were really unkind to her.

It was a steep learning curve. You have to research your stories, write your questions, script your own links – it really stretches you. From the very beginning, I was intrigued by television. You come up with an idea, conceptualise it, curate a story from start to finish, and see the end product on TV! Producing really appealed to me.

One of my very first interviews was with Jon Bon Jovi. Patience and I flew to Brazil, where he was in concert. We arrived to do the interview and he had his shades on. Now, rule 101 of television is: no dark shades for one-on-ones! The audience must connect with the interviewee's eyes. Patience asked Jon to remove them, but he refused, saying it was his look. What could we do? The interview kicked off and it was going beautifully, and before he knew it, the shades were off. Jon really gave me one of my best interviews. 'Your warmth completely disarmed him,' Patience said to me afterwards. Over the years I interviewed the likes of Madiba, Michael Jackson, Samuel L. Jackson, Sol Kerzner, Will Smith, President Thabo Mbeki, Winnie Madikizela-Mandela, Graça Machel, Hugh Masekela, Wesley Snipes, Blair Underwood, Al Jarreau, the Bee Gees, Quincy Jones, Luther Vandross, Sade, Gloria Estefan, Kenny Lattimore, Mariah Carey and Oprah.

I quickly realised that what really interested me about television was not being the pretty face in front of the camera, but rather what goes on behind the scenes. I asked Patience to mentor me and school me in what it takes to be a producer, and she very graciously shared her knowledge.

A bit of background about how television shows were produced in those days: if you had an idea for a show and you pitched it to the SABC – or any broadcaster, for that matter – and they liked it, they would pay you for your idea and they would own the intellectual property. You would be paid a fee, but they would own it and generate revenue through advertising and sponsorship. So *Top Billing* was being produced by Henley Studios, the SABC's in-house production company, even though it was Patience's brainchild.

I said to Patience, 'Let's start a company together, and I will help negotiate with the SABC to give us the *Top Billing* contract as independent producers.' And that's how our company, Tswelopele Productions, was born. The name is a Setswana word meaning 'progress', in honour of my father's lineage. I made the call to set up a meeting with the CEO of the SABC, Mr Zwelakhe Sisulu. One thing I was able to recognise was the gravitas of my title, and that if Miss South Africa leaves a message, it's very likely that the call will be returned. And so it was.

Mr Sisulu was the third son of struggle stalwarts Walter and Albertina Sisulu. Walter Sisulu had served as the Secretary General of the ANC and been jailed on Robben Island for twenty-six years. His son had taken up the post of SABC CEO in 1994. Mr Sisulu granted me an audience, and off I went to the intimidating twenty-seventh floor of the SABC building to deliver my big idea. I didn't have a fancy PowerPoint presentation or anything – I was just a twenty-year-old youngster with a crazy, wild idea. I tell you, my nerves were completely shot. I was a wreck! I was saying to myself, 'Don't stutter, don't pass out, keep calm. You can do this.'

I told him that we were a fifty-fifty women-owned business, an empowered company (empowerment was the buzzword at the time, and I threw that one in for good measure), and we wanted the SABC to give us an opportunity to be independent producers, to generate decent revenue streams for ourselves and to create jobs. Mr Sisulu kept quiet for a while. When he finally opened his mouth, he said, 'My child, the future of this country looks bright if young people can do what you have just done.'

It took eight months for them to make the decision to give us the contract as independent producers, but another challenge awaited us after the initial excitement. We had to raise capital to buy the equipment we would need to actually make the show. I had no way of raising that kind of money, so I made the difficult decision to sell my Miss South Africa car. I had grown very fond of that car, and I really loved the fact that I didn't have to use public transport any more. However, like everyone else, I had to make sacrifices in order to achieve my goals.

That was the start of the story of Tswelopele Productions as an independent production company, and we have gone on to produce shows such as *Pasella*, *Top Travel*, *Top Dogs*, *Expresso*, *No Reservations*, *Afternoon Express* and *Win a Home*. Twenty-five years later, Patience and I are still partners, and still producing *Top Billing*. We have been well supported for many years in the industry by so many people, and we have an amazing team of creatives who work really hard to keep the shows fresh every single week – not an easy thing to do for a quarter of a century.

FOURTEEN

When I started work on *Top Billing*, I was the first black presenter the show had ever had. Now you must know that I was not some model-C kid with a model-C accent. I went through the Bantu Education system, for school and university, basically. The so-called former model-C schools are government schools that are administrated and largely funded by a governing body of parents and alumni. In the early 1990s, when it became legal for black children to attend schools with their white counterparts, many of them ended up attending former model-C schools because they were more affordable than private schools. These children were taught in English from an early age and became far more comfortable speaking it, to the extent that they sounded more like white people compared to the average township schoolkid, who pronounced his or her words with a heavy African accent.

Not only did I not have the model-C accent, but I was also generally a very fast-paced speaker. My mom often said, when she and my dad had been watching the show, 'What train are you trying to catch, child? Because I heard nothing of what you said.' The mother was still a teacher at home, clearly.

There was a lady called Lizzie Staughton who worked at Tswelopele Productions and who was originally from England. She was an English teacher by profession, as well as a director for links shoots, and she became my elocution instructor. Dear Lizzie, she was on set with me all the time in the beginning, working with me. She taught me so much. I remember getting terribly frustrated at times, because I would mispronounce a word or not project my voice well, and we would have to do a retake, and then another take. I remember her distinct voice: 'Quiet on set, please.'

I began by doing links. These are the short pieces that are delivered directly to camera, and that join the various inserts – the travel pieces, the interviews, the fashion inserts and so on – of a show together. The links for *Top Billing* were produced and shot on location from someone's house.

To this day, I remember the first shoot I did for *Top Billing*. I don't know how many takes I had to do. We worked probably ten hours just for a one-hour show. I can still see the red-and-black chequered pantsuit I was wearing as host Neil McCarthy and I walked down the staircase and delivered our first link. Well, Neil walked down the staircase – I tripped down it! You basically had to glide down and simultaneously deliver your lines and make it look effortless. I couldn't even get my words right. It was a complete mess.

But I stuck with it and learnt as I went along. It took me a long time to really perfect my craft and to feel comfortable in front of the camera. The tough thing about television for me was that I had to learn on the job, live, in front of a television audience. I didn't go to film school or do a presenters' course. In the beginning, it felt like a 'fake it till you make it' kind of situation. I didn't necessarily feel comfortable or confident, more like I was winging it, but I absolutely knew that I wanted to do it. I understood what a great opportunity it presented.

It was a steep learning curve. Within a very short time I graduated from just doing links to doing inserts. That meant travel! When the opportunity to travel overseas came along, I jumped at it without skipping a beat. That was what I really wanted to do – travel and see the world. I loved it. But let me tell you, it was not as easy or glamorous as you might think. In those days, when you went on an assignment, you were not the big star just because you were in front of the camera. You were part of the team, and it was a small team, so everyone had to double up and do whatever needed to be done. You carried lights, you carried gear, you helped out, you hustled, you did everything. Meanwhile, you're still doing your research, you're working on your questions, you're doing your own make-up, you're trying to pin a microphone onto your outfit. In that business in those days, you really had to become an all-rounder. None of this travelling with a whole glam squad and a ten-man crew to carry your bags!

Patience Stevens was a mentor to me from the very beginning of my career, and she soon became a solid partner and a good, dear friend. We have each other's backs. We are able to agree to disagree as partners, but the loyalty and the love we have for each other is solid. We have great mutual respect and it's been the cornerstone of the success of our partnership.

When we first started working and travelling together, we would share a room. People want suites and first-class tickets now, but we flew economy and shared a room. The only problem was that Patience always wanted to sleep with the windows open, and I just can't do open windows at night. We decided, okay, take turns, one night windows open, one night windows closed.

One night we were staying somewhere, I forget where, and it was time for bed. She was in bed on her side of the room. I was on my side. I took out my Bible and started to read. I turned to look back at her, and she was doing the exact same thing. We had never talked about our faith, so this was a defining moment for us – I knew then that we were kindred spirits.

At *Top Billing*, we always did things differently. As I've said, we didn't shoot in a studio; we were always on location. Another thing that made the show interesting and different was that a lot of the inserts were very experiential. It was a far cry from my sheltered life in my mother's house in Soweto. The things I did, oh my word!

I flew on a fighter jet. I went to Scotland to go and find the Loch Ness monster (*ja* right, no sign of *that*, of course!). I went to Australia and played with kangaroos. I rode a camel in Egypt and an elephant in India. In Miami, I was picked up by a limo and taken to interview Gloria Estefan. I sang with the Bee Gees, sat in the front row at New York Fashion Week, and wore a kimono in Japan and ate frog soup. I went to Pakistan for the Cricket World Cup. It was a wild adventure. I did everything! Well, not exactly everything. I was the stereotypical black person who didn't swim. Shark diving? No, thank you. Luckily

Michael Mol joined the team – he did all the water sports and also took on the job of flying on the wing of a plane.

So I started with links, then travel pieces, and finally I got to interview entertainment stars and other high-profile people. That was the most challenging part of the job. On *Top Billing*, we don't do 'talking heads' interviews with stars. As the presenter or interviewer, you go and have an experience with them. You take them to Soweto, or you go wine tasting together, or you do something fun and interesting out and about in the world.

Interviewing someone is daunting, particularly if that someone is very famous and they know it. The reality is, even to this day I find it unnerving to be in front of the camera. I still get butterflies. I suppose through the years I've managed to make them fly in unison, but they're still there. I always say to myself, 'Basetsana, if you ever wake up and those butterflies are not there, you should call it quits.'

So yes, a bit of nerves is a good thing, but in my early days, I would be in a flat panic. My palms would sweat. Fortunately for me, I was surrounded by a team of people who made me believe I have what it takes. Patience was one such individual. She would compliment and commend me when I did it right, when I gave a particularly good performance or did a brilliant interview. There was also this fantastic director of photography, Lourens Human, who was a laugh a minute. He called me *'skattie'* and would crack jokes just before I delivered a link. He was such a sweetheart, always rooting for me. I would see him nod behind the lens as I was delivering my lines, signalling that I was doing okay or was on point. I loved him to bits. He was a brilliant cameraman.

One of my early interviews was with Samuel L. Jackson. Being part of the *Top Billing* team, you have to get out of your comfort zone, and Patience, who is a scratch golfer, had encouraged me to take up golf. I was actually not doing too badly at it, and so we set up the interview with Samuel L. Jackson on the golf course. So the two of us played golf. Man, oh man, that man is as hot as they come. My knees were wobbling! It's amazing that I managed to hit the ball at all.

I interviewed Will Smith also quite early on in my career. Will, *neh*, I mean, *Will*! I had watched him on *The Fresh Prince of Bel-Air*. I knew his music, as a rapper. And now I was going to sit down with him for a one-on-one. I actually couldn't sleep for days before the interview, I was so nervous and excited.

It was the press junket for his movie *Ali*, in 2001. I remember walking into the interview, and there he was. I said, 'Hello, my name is Basetsana, but you can call me Bassie,' and he was very friendly, really a very friendly guy, very affable. He could see I had a case of nerves, and he calmed me down. 'Hey, how you doing? How is South Africa? You look nervous, calm down, we're just chatting …' Long story short, he gave me the most beautiful interview and we took a picture together.

And then there was Michael Jackson. I was a huge fan, of course. He was staying at Sun City. He was launching a new CD, so the idea for the insert was that he would leave the Palace, I would walk with him to the record store in the entertainment area and we'd conduct the interview right there in the store. The trouble was that he spoke so softly, I couldn't hear a word he was saying. It was a very awkward interview, me leaning in and trying to hear him. I actually don't know what to make of that interview; it wasn't my best. All I can say is that I met Michael Jackson and shook his hand, y'all!

The other thing, when I look back on that interview, was that I was wearing the most ridiculous outfit! I had this oversized gold-and-black Versace shirt, and I wore it with an Escada jacket and my hair was all over the place. At that time, Escada and Versace were quite the thing, but the combo was totally wrong. What was I thinking? Blame it on the nerves!

In those days, we did our own styling and wardrobe for the inserts. We had a stylist, Robert Bell, who sourced clothes for the links and those links were properly styled, really slick and set in a beautiful location. But for the inserts you just had to put yourself together with whatever you had, working with your own wardrobe, and you had to do your own make-up. I had to figure it out by myself, and some of the time I got it wrong.

Those interviews are all coming back to me now. Oh, and Luther Vandross! Oh my goodness. Luther Vandross is one of my all-time favourite musicians. Let me tell you how this all went down.

It must have been 1997 or '98 when Luther Vandross came to South

Africa. The interview was scheduled at the Westcliff Hotel, on a Saturday. Now on that day a friend of ours from the beauty-pageant world, Augustine Masilela, was getting married, with my sister Johanna as matron of honour. The church service was in the morning, and I was going to slip out in the early afternoon to do the interview, then join the reception.

I'm not the only Luther fan in the family – Johanna is crazy about him too. She was determined to come along and was ready to leave the bride and skip out with me to see Luther, and then return for the reception! Fan number three: Romeo. He also loved Luther Vandross, and played a lot of his music on the radio. So Romeo was desperate to meet him. We were dating by this time, and Romeo said to me, 'Listen nicely, my babe, I am coming with you to that interview.'

'Babe, it doesn't work that way,' I said. 'This is my job. I'm going to work!'

Stars' managers are very strict at these junkets. They allocate you a specific amount of time for your interview, they count you down, and they tell you what you can and can't ask about. It can be intense, quite nerve-racking and even annoying, and you've got to be on the ball. You can't pitch up at an interview with another person, let alone two! But Romeo asked so very nicely …

I decided that Johanna would just have to forgive me for this one. I was taking my boyfriend! So, after the wedding ceremony, off we went, Romeo and I, to the Westcliff Hotel. I have to say, that day I got the outfit spot on. I had these sort of leopard-print culottes, what we called 'knickerbockers', and a matching off-the-shoulder top. I was going to a wedding and to meet Luther Vandross, and I was looking *fine*, honey.

As I arrived, Dali Tambo was coming out. 'I had the worst interview, Bassie,' he said. 'He wouldn't give me anything.' Dali was producing and presenting *People of the South* at the time. Now my nerves were completely shot. This was not good at all. If Dali, a seasoned broadcaster, couldn't get anything, how was I going to manage?

Anyway, I walked in and there was Luther Vandross in all his greatness. He got up to greet me and said, 'Hello, darling, you look so good, you are giving some supermodel a run for her money.' Luther just broke the ice. He said, 'Come on, sit down, let's chat.' We chatted, and when his people began counting him down to finish up the interview, he waved them away and said, 'Let the girl chat, leave her alone.' He gave me a stunning interview that extended way beyond the allocated time.

When it was over, I said, 'Mr Vandross, can I introduce you to my boyfriend?' He agreed, and Romeo came over and we took pictures with him, which I've still got. Romeo, Luther in the middle, and me.

That was a special interview. I was such a big fan of his. He invited us to his concert, too. His people gave us backstage passes, and when we saw him again, he greeted us warmly. Romeo and I took more pictures with him backstage. We were both just beaming from ear to ear.

Oh man, Luther. On that day I considered myself supremely blessed to do what I do. It was a privilege to interview people whom I had only ever listened to or seen on a screen or read about, and whom I never ever thought I might one day meet.

I should mention that Johanna still hasn't totally forgiven me for that one. To this day, she'll sometimes say, 'Girl, do you remember that time you dumped me for your boyfriend – okay, yes, he's now your husband – and I didn't get to meet Luther Vandross?'

To which I say, 'These things happen; a girl has to make choices.'

I think Romeo still owes me, come to think of it. Although he was very appreciative at the time, and also very proud of me and of the interview. He kept saying, 'Babes, you did great. You did great.'

All in all, that was a wonderful experience and it stands out in my memory. When Luther Vandross died some years later, I wept. I was inconsolable. I wanted to go to the funeral. Growing up listening to his music, he had a special place in my heart. Some of my favourite songs are 'Power of Love', 'I Know', 'Killing Me Softly', 'Endless Love' and, of course, 'Dance with My Father'. Ah, I love that song. It reminds me so much of my own father, and oftentimes when I miss my dad, I play it and think of him.

Never in my wildest dreams did I imagine I would meet all these amazingly talented performers and celebrities. Not only was I able to be in their presence, I was also given a platform to interview them on national television. Whenever I think back to those days, I feel truly blessed. Sometimes the dreams we have for ourselves are able to gain their own momentum and carry us further than even we thought possible.

FIFTEEN

In 2002, I had an incredible, life-changing opportunity to spend a day with Oprah Winfrey and Madiba in Qunu, the village where he lived, and to interview them both. Madiba, of course, was a great hero of mine, and Oprah had been an inspiration ever since I first came across her and her work. So as you can imagine, I was delighted to receive this extraordinary invitation.

At the time, Oprah had an initiative called Christmas Kindness. She would travel all over the world giving gifts and meeting children during the festive season. Madiba hosted an annual Christmas party in Qunu. He would give gifts to the children and cows would be slaughtered. It was a huge celebration for everyone in the village and beyond. The queues went on and on, people coming from all over the area to see Tata.

That year, Oprah came to South Africa to do her Christmas Kindness in collaboration with Tata. I travelled to Qunu and was able to spend a day with two of the most extraordinary human beings. It was an honour to glean from them their energy, their spirit and their magnanimity.

It was remarkable to see how Oprah interacted with the children. She gave each child a gift pack, which consisted of a backpack with books, a uniform, school shoes and so on – Oprah was very passionate about education, as was Madiba. Some were given bicycles, as many of them travelled long distances from home to school. When she presented each child with their gift, she looked them full in the face. Every single child.

She also put a mirror in each of those gift packs. Most of the children in the village had never had one. 'I put a mirror in each of those packs because I wanted each child to look into their own eyes and see who they are and the potential of what they can become,' Oprah told me. I thought that was such an interesting and thoughtful gift to give young kids, to help them to appreciate who they really are and to see their value and worth.

One of the questions I asked Oprah was why she felt it was important to give back. She answered with a quote from Martin Luther King, Jr: 'Not everybody can be famous but everybody can be great, because greatness is determined by service ... You only need a heart full of grace and a soul generated by love.' Those words have stayed with me and I still find them powerful and true.

It's difficult to describe the feeling of being in Qunu with Oprah and Madiba. It wasn't that I was in awe – it was almost like I had transcended into another realm of existence. All in all, I would say that that day in 2002 probably rates as the highlight of my television career.

I have interviewed Oprah subsequently. She's come to South Africa many, many times. Close to thirty, I think. Her love for this country is just incredible. She built a school in Gauteng, the Oprah Winfrey Leadership Academy for Girls, and she has a real commitment to sustaining Madiba's legacy into the future.

The next time I saw her was in 2004, when I interviewed her at the InterContinental Hotel in Sandton. I was pregnant with my son Nathi, and as I walked into the room where she was sitting, she got up to greet me and said, 'Can I put my hands on your stomach?' I agreed, and she put her hands on my tummy and spoke a blessing over my baby. It's all captured on camera. Unfortunately, my outfit was a disaster. Clearly porridge brain had already set in, because over this big tummy I'm wearing multicoloured stripes – everyone knows that you never wear stripes for television – in this bad, stretchy material. Oprah was wearing the most beautiful, elegant cream suit. Anyway, it was a wonderful moment and we went on to have a good interview. You cannot be in the presence of Oprah and leave the same as when you entered her space.

Oprah has played a significant role in my life and in my growth as an individual, a broadcaster and a producer. She has not mentored me in person, but I've drawn so much inspiration from her as a successful businesswoman and media mogul, and, more importantly, as an individual. I watched her talk show, I am a fan of *Greenleaf* (the drama series she produces), I have seen *The Color Purple*, I listen to *Oprah's Master Class* and her *SuperSoul Conversations* podcast, and I read her books. I find her wisdom almost unparalleled. She is someone whom I greatly admire and look up to.

Look at Oprah's background. She was born in poverty in rural Mississippi. She was sexually molested as a child and suffered so much heartache in her life, but she hasn't allowed the circumstances of her past to define who she has become, and that is exactly the ethos that I live by. I will not allow the circumstances of my past to define my destiny. If Oprah can overcome her circumstances to become who she is, it's almost as if the rest of us have no reason to fail.

As a black woman, I feel that in her I have a role model, a blueprint of what a black girl-child can be and achieve. Yes, we all live in different universes and we have our own struggles. But in a way, many of our stories are not so different from hers. Everyone has their struggle, which you can overcome if you set your mind to it, work hard, are determined and bring others along on the journey.

I've also seen how Oprah has used the powerful medium of television to shape minds, to educate, to inspire, to be a change agent and also to challenge the status quo. This has influenced how I understand my own responsibility with the content I produce, whether reality shows, lifestyle magazine programmes, documentaries or drama (a genre in which we have recently broken ground). I see myself as someone who can have an impact on people's lives, even if on a smaller scale.

I believe that there are people on earth who are here to serve a higher purpose. Oprah is one of them. Madiba was another. How can you not want to strive to be a better person when you have received the counsel of a Madiba or spoken to an Oprah? It is even more incumbent on you to do better and to make this world a better place. Whether it's through philanthropic work, through creating jobs, through educating children – we've all got to do what we can within our own ambit.

SIXTEEN

All in all, I was in front of the camera for ten years, from the time I was crowned Miss South Africa until just before the birth of our first child. Between 1994 and 2004, I was on television every week. I was in people's living rooms and became a public figure.

It is one thing to be in a pageant – when your reign is over, you carry on with your life. But *Top Billing* gave me national prominence. It made me a recognisable face. Whether I was buying groceries or catching a flight at the airport, people wanted to take pictures or get an autograph. South Africans are usually quite gracious – they don't mob you, they are polite – but I had lost my anonymity.

I had to grow comfortable with the fact that my life would never be normal. I would be recognised. Everything I did would be scrutinised, and I would be criticised, if people were inclined that way. Everything in my life was magnified by virtue of being a host of an iconic TV show.

I must say, I sometimes battled with living in a fish bowl. I realised I couldn't just schlump around in a tracksuit when I felt like it. It took a lot of effort to keep up appearances day after day, and there were days when I didn't have the energy. I just wanted to go to my mother's house and eat her *pap*, *vleis* and atchar, or her *magwinya* (deep-fried fat cakes) and white liver, and not have to be out there in the world. I am grateful to have had that space to go to, to sit on the floor and just be.

First in front of the camera, and then increasingly behind the camera, that decade at *Top Billing* taught me so much. I had to come out of my shell and interact with people, even though I am naturally quite introverted. Early on, I learnt that being shy doesn't pay the bills. If I wanted this life, I had better step out of that shell and own the stage.

Through *Top Billing*, I not only learnt to present, I also learnt to become a researcher, a producer, a director, a businessperson and an entrepreneur. It armed me with so many skills. To this day, I will use one of those tools and remember, *Top Billing* taught me that. Really, it was my university and a formidable grounding.

It taught me discipline and hard work. And patience! Television is a hurry-up-and-wait business. You arrive on set and you're ready to go and things go wrong. You have to wait your turn. Talent can make you sit the whole day just waiting for them to show up.

During that time, I learnt to cultivate my own strength. I knew I had to be brave, because I was pushing boundaries. For one thing, I was the first black female host of a show that was being watched predominantly by white viewers. White South Africans were the core audience when I joined *Top Billing*, but that soon began to change as black people, who aspired to that lifestyle, started to watch the show. It was inspirational and aspirational at the same time; it allowed people to live and travel vicariously in the comfort of their armchairs at home. Here was this black girl – and not a private-school girl, a local girl from Soweto – and she was presenting and interviewing and travelling the world. Black people took this to mean that here was a show also for them. And, moreover, that this lifestyle was now also attainable.

I was the first Miss South Africa to become a television host (thanks to Doreen Morris), and many others subsequently followed that path. A lot of them, in fact. Some joined *Top Billing* and *Pasella*, which Tswelopele Productions has produced for the last seventeen years. Dr Michael Mol, who was Mr South Africa, and I worked and travelled together for a long time, and we were a formidable duo. He has a beautiful, generous heart and was the MC at my wedding, and he's still my friend. It's one of the many lifelong friendships I made through my time at *Top Billing*. Friendships that I hold dear to this day.

So, the *Top Billing* journey changed the trajectory of my life in unimaginable ways. Would I do anything differently? No. I wouldn't change a thing.

While I was still on air, in front of the camera, I gradually came to realise that I was really more comfortable behind it. Being a public figure was always a bit of a conflict for me, and I came to increasingly love and thrive on the other side of the business. With Patience as my mentor, I was learning the craft and the business of television, which was so exciting and fulfilling. Remember, we started small, just the two of us, and we had to do everything, from answering the phone and sending faxes to clients to booking crew and scripting, the whole gamut. And Patience still had to sit and edit the shows. It was great for all-round experience.

By this time, we had employed more people, including a bigger team of presenters, so that our tiny crew didn't have to fly around the world so much and do absolutely everything. We could at least take a break every now and then, and weren't constantly on the edge of burnout. When I wasn't under so much pressure travelling and being on camera, I gravitated towards being on the other side of the lens. I was directing, researching, looking for locations, and coming up with ideas for inserts and guests. With more people on board, I was able to focus more on the bigger picture and on stakeholders rather than the nuts and bolts of production. Part of my responsibility was to market the business, so I was meeting with clients and working hard to bring in advertisers and sponsors. I was in constant negotiations with the SABC to renew our contracts. More and more, I focused my energy on those aspects of the business. And it was business as usual.

My journey with *Top Billing* consistently took me out of my comfort zone, forcing me to trust my own abilities. At every turn I made the decision to believe in myself, even when I was completely out of my depth. In the beginning it was very scary to do this, but through the years I have realised the power of my mind to influence my reality. This doesn't make me special or different from anyone else. I have come this far by believing and having hope.

PART V

FAITH

SEVENTEEN

Romeo and I had planned a special Cape Town holiday for December 2002. A couple of days after Christmas, my parents came to see us off and we flew down for a week or so of sun, sea and sightseeing.

A day or two after we left, my beloved papa had a stroke. He was at home with Moeder when it happened, getting ready for their daily ritual of tea in front of their favourite soapies, *Days of Our Lives* and *The Bold and the Beautiful*.

A week earlier, my dad had had what they described as a 'small accident'. He and my mother had gone to a relative's funeral, and he had been crossing the street and a taxi had knocked him. He wasn't badly injured; the doctor had just bandaged up his leg and sent him home.

A week later, when they were getting ready for the tea-and-TV ritual, Moeder took off his bandage so she could soak and massage his feet. That's when he had the stroke – it is presumed there was a blood clot, an embolism, and the removal of the bandage made the clot that had formed in his leg break loose and travel to his brain via the bloodstream. My brother was at home at the time. He put Papa in the car and rushed him to the Lenmed clinic in Lenasia, which was about ten minutes away.

Papa was admitted to the ICU. He was in a coma and unresponsive. The family decided not to tell me; they would monitor him. Moeder apparently thought it best not to worry us, to let us have our holiday. They knew how close I was to Papa, and, of course, they hoped for the best outcome. Papa was going to be fine, Moeder believed, and we were coming home in a few days anyway.

Completely unaware of what was happening back home, Romeo and I went to a New Year's Eve *jol* with friends. Our cellphones had been off, out of battery probably, and it wasn't until New Year's morning that I looked at my phone. Romeo was driving, the roof was down of the convertible we had hired as a treat, the sea breeze was blowing – we were ready to enjoy the first day of a bright new year. I switched on my phone, and here was Johanna, saying, 'Girl, you've got to come home.' Now I knew my family wouldn't call me home if it wasn't serious. And then she said it was Papa.

I started screaming.

Romeo took the phone and Johanna explained that Papa'd had a stroke, he was in hospital, and it wasn't looking good. She thought we should come home.

Growing up, I had always had a terrible fear of what would happen to us if Papa and Mama passed away. What would we do? What would happen to me? What would happen to us? They were not only my moral compass, they were my world, my cornerstone, my safety, my place of belonging.

'Romeo, we're going to the airport,' I said. 'Whatever is at the hotel, I don't care, it will get sorted out.' We drove straight to the airport, got on a flight and, when it landed, we went to the hospital to see Papa.

He wasn't moving. There were tubes everywhere. My hero, my giant... He had never been sick a day in his life, never been hospitalised. I never imagined that I would see him so vulnerable. It was unbearable to see him in that state.

At least I got some time with him. 'Hello, Vader,' I said. I spoke to him and read his favourite scriptures to him, Psalm 23 and Psalm 91, every day.

Psalm 23: 'The Lord is my shepherd, I shall not want ...'

And Psalm 91: 'Whoever dwells in the shelter of the Most High will rest in the shadow of the Almighty ...'

Every day, like he had taught me.

We brought him earphones and played music to him – his favourite jazz tracks and gospel music. I really thought he was going to make it.

© Simon Manana

The first pic of the lovebirds ever taken, at a dinner at the Carlton Centre

Romeo's teenage swag years, in yellow!

Romantic Repertoire — I am in love with a DJ

'I will have your back and walk with you' — our traditional wedding in 2000

My father receives gifts from the Kumalo family from Malome Doctor Khunou

Makoti — with my aunt Prella Maseko as the elders advise me on marriage

'I will honour you and respect you'

My father walking me down the aisle

Just married!

Mr and Mrs Kumalo

The love of my life

Dancing with my mother and Koko Peggy Mogale

Honeymooning in Jamaica

Wanderlust — on holiday in Capri

One of my favourite photos of me and my man

My best friend and protector of nineteen years!

Meeting the legendary Hugh Masekela

With Africa's incomparable songbird, Mama Miriam Makeba

A conversation and timeless moment wih the king of pop, Michael Jackson

A *Top Billing* interview with Mariah Carey

The legend behind the legends, Mr Quincy Jones

Romeo and I with Luther Vandross, a highlight that never gets old!

Jamming with the Bee Gees, Barry, Maurice and Robin Gibb

Gloria Estefan, quintessential songstress

Chilling with Wesley Snipes

Award-winning actor Alfre Woodard

Isn't she lovely? Miss World 1994, Ashwarya Rai

With hotel magnate Sol Kerzner in the Bahamas

Celebrating South Africa's 1995 Rugby World Cup victory at a ticker-tape parade with captain Francois Pienaar

The day before he passed away, he started to respond – or at least to move his right hand ever so slightly – but he stayed in a coma for two weeks, and my beautiful father, my great dad, passed away on 19 January 2003, at age seventy. I was shattered. I was broken. My siblings and I had lost a protector and a patriarch who was always ready to give of himself in service. My poor mother had lost her soul mate and partner, the father of her children. She was never the same afterwards. That fearsome fire in her eyes had been diminished.

But Vader watches over us. He's our special angel. I feel so blessed that he was there to walk me down the aisle, but I must say that it is a great sadness to me that he never got to meet my kids. They would have absolutely adored him. He was that kind of man.

EIGHTEEN

From the time I was a little girl, I wanted five children. That was my dream. A husband, a big house and five children running around. Romeo and I started trying for a family as soon as we got married in December 2000. I was twenty-six, so it seemed like time.

A year went by, no pregnancy. In the black culture, nine months after the wedding, people want to see a bundle of joy. Whenever I went to a wedding or a funeral, anywhere where the community gathered, the aunties would say, 'So where's the baby?' Even complete strangers would have the audacity to come up and ask, 'So when are you going to have a child?' It was quite disconcerting, invasive and rather rude, I thought. As I used to say to my friends, it's not as if you can pick up a baby from the supermarket. If I felt up to being nice, I would say, 'When God wills.' Other times, when I wasn't up to entertaining unwarranted questions, I would just shrug my shoulders and walk away. But the fact of the matter is that these questions hurt me deeply and made the struggle even more difficult and painful. At one family gathering a few years into our marriage, when I'd been trying for a while to conceive, one of my aunts said something to the effect of 'You should really be getting on with having a child.' I told my mom, and don't you worry, Moeder went to see that auntie. 'What right have you got to talk to my child like that?' my mom demanded. 'What right have you got to put pressure on her? You don't know her struggles and it's not your place.' There was a major falling out with that aunt and my family. Some time later, bless her heart, she came to apologise. 'I was wrong,' she said. 'I know I hurt you, and it was not intentional, but I apologise.'

The second year of trying without success, my gynaecologist prescribed a tablet to stimulate ovulation. Still no conception. It was now 2003, and we were really starting to worry when, lo and behold, we discovered we were pregnant! When the doctor confirmed that I was carrying new life ... that was the best news I had ever received. I was just over thirteen weeks and we could see the baby on the scan. We were over the moon, delighted.

Our happiness was short-lived. At sixteen weeks, I started to bleed. I went to the hospital, but my baby didn't make it. I had to have a D&C. I was devastated. Romeo and I both were. It was gut-wrenching. I couldn't leave the house; I just cried for days.

It was deeply painful, but the interesting thing is that I never lost hope. I had faith that we serve a good God and that His timing is always perfect. His ways are not our ways, and so it was not for me to try to control the situation. I just knew in my heart of hearts that one day He would make good on all His promises to me, including giving me and my husband a baby to complete our little family. There was one thing I'd always known for sure, just like I knew Thursday followed Wednesday, and that was that I was going to have children. Romeo did too. My husband pulled me out of that hole. He said, 'Baby, don't worry, we are going to have babies, and we are going to have lots of them.'

I would go on to have a total of seven miscarriages in all. The worst part was having to be admitted to hospital for the dilation and curettage procedure. Basically, the doctor would dilate my cervix and clean out the contents of my womb. Any woman who has been through one of these will tell you that there is nothing quite as painful. It's not the physical pain as much as the fact that the life you were carrying is just gone when you wake up. I went to the hospital so many times that one day an admissions clerk looked me dead in the eye and said, 'Maybe you should consider a timeshare, because you're always here.' I could not believe she had uttered those words. Romeo and my sister Johanna were furious. There was really nothing any of us could say to this woman, but her words were like a knife through my heart.

Romeo was amazingly loving and understanding through all our fertility challenges. He told me that he hadn't married me to bear him children; he'd married me for me. He loved me. Whether I was fertile or not, it didn't matter to him. But it mattered to me. I knew what Basetsana truly wanted. She wanted a family.

In 2004, we got pregnant again. There's a saying in our culture that a pregnancy isn't told, it's seen. It means don't go around telling people about your pregnancy too early. Keep your business private, in case people wish you ill. For my first pregnancy, the news appeared in the papers, and I think I was even on the cover of a magazine. When she found out, my mother scolded me. She told me I should never have done that, that it's not what we do. For this second pregnancy, I did things differently, but news of the pregnancy still got out and appeared in the papers, but now at least I knew better.

The baby was due in April 2005. I gave a lot of thought to what that meant in terms of my public life. Towards the end of 2004, Robert was styling me very strategically. I was wearing a lot of black, and they were mostly shooting my head and shoulders, not showing my tummy. I had already stopped doing inserts and travelling and was only doing links.

On *Top Billing*'s Christmas 2004 show, I announced that I was having a baby and that I would not be back the following year. I bid the audience farewell, and thanked them for loving me and believing in me, for embracing me and welcoming me into their lives and their homes every single week for ten years.

When I stepped off-camera, it was like this mini-sabbatical. I didn't go to the office every day. I took time to rest and to read and to nest … I enjoyed the pregnancy so much. Despite the struggle to conceive and the grief around the miscarriage, I had an unwavering faith that this time it was all going to be fine. There was peace in my heart that all would be well and that we would come home safely with our baby.

I did notice at some point close to the end of the pregnancy that Romeo was behaving somewhat oddly. He was not his usual self. He seemed anxious, as if something was bothering him. Eventually, he came out with it. He had been offered a big promotion. Vodacom wanted him to take up the position of managing director of their Tanzania operation. The contract would start in May, a month after the baby was due.

I took a deep breath and calmly said that of course he should go. It was a great opportunity, and it wouldn't be fair of me to hold him back. He was completely taken aback. He kept saying, 'Are you sure?' We agreed he would take the job, but that the baby and I wouldn't join him in Dar es Salaam. We had tried so hard and waited so long for this baby, and I wanted to be within close proximity of the doctors we knew, like his paediatrician and my gynaecologist, and my mother. We agreed that the baby and I would stay in Johannesburg. So it was decided. Romeo accepted the job.

On 18 April 2005, our baby boy was born. I held him in my arms, and we named him Nkosinathi Gabriel Kumalo. Nkosinathi, 'God is with us', and Gabriel, 'the strength of God is mine'. It was interesting looking at names. While God is *my* strength, I love the fact that Nathi will forever know that the strength of God is his as well. Nathi was perfect. Just perfect. Beautiful and peaceful. I don't think I've ever been so happy in my life as I was at the birth of my first-born child. My son. Bone of my bones. Fruit of my loins. Being mother to this boy was the highest privilege that God could have bestowed on me.

To hold Nathi, to breastfeed him, to smell him – it was extraordinary. I never expected to love another human being like that, so selflessly that I would give up my life for him in an instant. As I write this, he is fourteen and has just started high school. He is just a beautiful son. He's kind, considerate, compassionate and respectful, and has impeccable manners. I was truly favoured. My son is a good kid, even if I say so myself. You know that saying, 'When they are good, they are Mommy's, when they are bad, they are Daddy's' ... but on a serious note, he is a remarkable young man, and I am daily just in awe of the man he is becoming.

We took Nathi home to our Northcliff house, and a week later, Romeo left for Tanzania. It was one thing being calm about our decision before the baby was born, but now that I was a breastfeeding mom with a newborn and a body full of hormones, the reality of Romeo's departure hit me hard. When I watched him actually get on the plane, I fell apart. I just cried and cried.

The saving grace was that Romeo's mom, Jennifer, came to help me with the baby. My mother-in-law is an amazing woman. She is very present, and she really loves Nathi and loved looking after him. Let me tell you, she will take a bullet for me. And Rakgadi was there, of course, and she was wonderful. My mother also came to 'oversee us' every day, though she didn't stay with us. Even so, I started to question the decision Romeo and I had made. When Mama Jenny left after a month or so, I was saying to myself, 'What was I thinking? This isn't part of the script, bringing up a baby alone with Romeo coming home every four or six weeks for a weekend.'

I even started to feel resentful. Romeo was miles away, his career was flourishing. I was fat and on maternity leave, stuck at home all day with a tiny baby. As much as I wanted this baby, as much as I loved him, the wheels were coming off. Only later, when I thought back on it, did I realise that I was probably suffering from postnatal depression. And I really, really just wanted my husband home. There were days when I felt, well, what is the point of being married? I might as well just be doing this by myself, seeing as I was, in essence, a single mother.

It was hard for Romeo too, because he was missing out on seeing his son grow. We spoke every day, and he would say, 'You know how I want to be there to see him, to play with him, to put him to bed and to be with you.'

Our relationship took a lot of strain. Every time Romeo came home, it was almost like we had to get to know each other all over again, restart the engine, relearn how to communicate. I believe that this period was defining for our relationship; it was either going to make or break us. And, thank God, it made us stronger, more solid, a team. To me, the fact that our marriage survived that period means we can take on any of life's challenges.

As difficult as it was, it was the right decision. My husband is a selfless guy. He has always been clear that he is the wind beneath my wings, and he wants me to fly and fulfil my divine destiny, what God has called me to do. Romeo had been so supportive of me and my career, and now it was my turn to support him in what he really, really wanted to do and achieve. I would hate to have refused him this great opportunity and then have him resent me for a lifetime. It was a turning point in our relationship, and in his career. It set him on the trajectory that has brought him to where he is today, in his life and in his business.

After Nathi's birth, I took time out from Tswelopele Productions and curtailed my travels dramatically. I always knew I wanted to be a mom, and I wanted to really focus on being with this little boy whom we had tried for and longed for and waited for.

I made a decision to breastfeed all my children for a year – everyone got a full year – so I really had to keep them close by. I took six months' maternity leave, and when I went back to work, I took Nathi with me. The joys of being your own boss! He came everywhere with me – you know, they are very portable when they are little, so it's actually very easy. I even took him overseas with me. Whether he was in the pram or in those baby-carrier things you wear on your front, he was always with me. Rakgadi too, of course – what would I have done without her? Rakgadi, with her warmth and familiarity, had the ability to make any place feel like home. Her presence kept me grounded and reminded me of my roots. But above all, I knew I could trust her to take good care of my baby, and that was very important to me as a working mother.

NINETEEN

Nkosinathi was a three-year-old toddler in 2006. Romeo was still working in Tanzania, and Rakgadi and I had settled into our own daily routine.

My mother had a lifelong dream to attend the opening of Parliament in Cape Town. She often told us that she wanted to pose for a photograph on the steps of the parliamentary building in her traditional Xhosa garb. She wanted to be part of the celebrations that she had seen so many times on television, and who could blame her? There are very few experiences like it. The red carpet, where glamorous politicians and celebrities are photographed in their evening wear and traditional regalia; the fabulous snacks and drinks that are served as guests wait for the president to arrive and deliver the State of the Nation Address. The whole thing is broadcast live to millions of viewers all over the country, and the following day the newspapers carry wall-to-wall coverage of every detail.

Well, in 2006, Johanna and I were able to fulfil our mother's dream. It was such a proud day for her, to be there with her daughters and all the VIPs and the who's who of South Africa. We introduced her to everyone, from ministers to businesspeople, and they all welcomed her. Some said, 'Happy to meet you, ma'am,' while others referred to her by her clan name, Dlamini, and even Moeder. We took a picture of her, just as she'd planned, on the steps of Parliament in her orange-and-black Xhosa outfit. It was a great experience for her and we were so glad that we were able to make that dream come true. To top things off, we were going to stay on in Cape Town for an extra day or two. Nathi was with me. We would have a little holiday.

During that trip, Moeder had a heart attack. My whole life, I had known that, despite her formidable, stoic nature, my mother's health was fragile. The way she told the story, when she was a young girl of about nine, she went on a bus trip to the Eastern Cape, and it was freezing cold on that bus. She contracted an illness that left her with a rheumatic heart condition, and she also suffered from asthma. Moeder was on a daily regimen of pills and medications, and had been in and out of hospital over the years, but there was nothing to indicate that she was terribly ill until she collapsed.

She was rushed to hospital, where the medical specialists managed to resuscitate her, but she had to undergo a triple valve-replacement operation. The cardiologist who operated on her at the Panorama Mediclinic was none other than Dr Wouter Basson, a talented cardiologist with a very dark past. He had previously served as head of the apartheid government's biological and chemical weapons programme, codenamed 'Project Coast'. He was initially responsible for gathering information on experiments in foreign countries, but in 1981 he was appointed head of the whole operation. Project Coast was allegedly involved in attacks and assassination attempts on members of the anti-apartheid movement in the eighties and nineties, and this had earned Basson the nickname 'Dr Death'. Despite his past, he was one of the best heart doctors in the country, and he took good care of my mother. The surgeon who assisted him was Dr De Wet Lubbe, who was lauded as one of the best heart surgeons in the southern hemisphere. My mom received superb care from an excellent medical team and the surgery was a success.

About a month after the operation, she was discharged. The doctors advised us that it was best for her to recuperate in Cape Town, rather than fly back to the Highveld. The sea air and the oxygen would do her good, and she could return to Johannesburg in the spring, when the cold, dry winter was over.

Nathi, Rakgadi and I moved to Cape Town, and I worked from Tswelopele Productions' Cape Town office, so that we could be with my mom. Once she had healed from the operation, Moeder was in quite good health and fine spirits. There was a lovely young guy called Paul Potgieter in our Cape Town office – in fact, he still works for me – and he would drive my mother around if she needed to go anywhere. He's a jovial, jocular sort of chap, with a great outlook on life and a nice manner. My mother absolutely adored him. The two of them got on well and would even go out for lunch together and have a fine time.

One day during this period, Moeder, Rakgadi and I were sitting watching TV. I recall that Nathi was learning to walk – you know how they cruise around the coffee table and you're always worrying that the child will fall and bang his head. I can't remember what prompted it, but Moeder turned to me and said, 'Setse, the little things you do for me please my soul.' My mom was a woman of few words, but when she spoke, you knew you had better pay attention, because it's likely something profound or important. When she said that, it was her way of saying, 'Thank you, my child, thank you.'

While my mother was in Cape Town recuperating, Johanna and I took shifts, alternating weekends. One weekend I would be in Cape Town and she would be in Johannesburg. The next Johanna would be there to look after our mother and I would return home. One weekend in August, it happened that neither of us was in Cape Town. Romeo was going to be in Johannesburg, and Moeder insisted I go home and spend time with my husband.

She was in fine health and recuperating really well, and the plan was that we were all going to return home to Johannesburg in three weeks. Because Moeder was asthmatic, her chest sometimes gave her problems, though, and one day she called Paul and asked him to take her to the Constantiaberg Mediclinic. It was nothing serious; she just wanted to be put on a nebuliser to open up her chest. I used to say that my mother was practically a doctor, as she had been ill most of her adult life, always knew what was wrong with her, and knew all there was to know about medicines, down to the last milligram of what medication she should take for what ailment.

Moeder went to the emergency room, explained her condition and told the staff that she needed a nebuliser. Now, my mom, she didn't care much for worldly things. She was a very simple woman, in her shweshwe overalls and slippers. If you saw her, you'd think she was just a *magogo* (granny), totally unassuming and gracious. Such a lady she was! There was a young locum at the mediclinic who insisted that he was the doctor and knew what needed to be done. They put her in a bed and he gave her an injection.

At this point, Moeder phoned Johanna and told her what had happened. She was battling to breathe and was in agony. She started to bequeath her possessions. She was telling my sister that the papers for this car are there, the key for the safe is there … Johanna was confused. 'Moeder, what are you talking about?' My mom said she didn't think she was going to make it. She was very incisive and gave a clear description of the locum, who was of slight frame and wore specs. She said she needed to get back to the hospital where they did her heart operation to see her doctor, Dr Basson.

Johanna and I were in Johannesburg, trying to make our way to the airport, but Moeder kept saying, 'You won't make it in time. They did something to me. I am not going to make it.' I phoned Patience and asked her to please go to the hospital. She rushed there. My mother was not speaking much by then. Over the phone we had asked that she be transferred to Panorama Mediclinic, but the staff at Constantiaberg wouldn't listen. Patience now put up such a fight, threatening that if the ambulance parked outside didn't move Mrs Makgalemele immediately, there would be big trouble. They finally agreed to put my mom in the ambulance and send her to Panorama, where Dr Basson and his team were waiting.

Patience stayed with her and was constantly on the phone, keeping me updated. I could hear the commotion on the other side of the line: doors opening and closing, people shouting 'move, move, move'. I was hysterical. 'Put her on the phone,' I said to Patience. I could hear Patience saying, 'Bassie, talk to her, she can hear you.' She had put her phone to my mom's ear.

'I love you,' I said to Moeder.

'She heard you, Bassie. She heard you,' Patience said. Moeder had nodded.

Patience and my mom had a special bond, and I am so grateful that she was there for Moeder and for our family. When they arrived at Panorama, they rushed my mother in and tried to save her, but they couldn't. By the time she got there, she had already had three heart attacks.

Moeder passed away on 11 August 2006 in the evening. She had been recovering so well that we were just three weeks away from taking her home. People in her community of Protea North had been very concerned – we were meant to be away for two or three days, and instead had been gone for months. We told them that Mama would be coming back in September and were planning a little get-together so that everyone could come and greet her and welcome her home. It felt as if we had been robbed. We *were* robbed.

Moeder was a simple woman, so we buried her simply, as per her wishes. Sometimes, when we sat together as a family, talk would take a morbid turn and she would say, 'When I die, please make sure that you wrap me in a white cloth and bury me in a tomato box,' meaning just a simple coffin.

In this, she was the complete antithesis of my dad. Vader would say, 'You, my dear, you go with your tomato box. I want a casket. I want to wear my three-piece Versace suit, and I want to lie in state. And don't you forget my Nunn Bush shoes and my Rolex.' Because he was a server in the Anglican Church in his younger days, he did get to lie at the altar at St Augustine's church overnight. We had to get guards to guard him. My mother got her simple pine coffin. They both were laid to rest in peace, exactly as they had wanted.

The shining light in my life at that painful time was my Nathi. He was the sweetest little boy. He didn't cry much and he slept well. But one night, not long after Moeder passed, Nathi started to cry, and he just wouldn't stop. Rakgadi had gone to bed and Romeo was in Tanzania. It was just the two of us, and the boy just wasn't going to let up. Well, if he was going to cry, I was going to cry too. 'Okay, dude, let's cry,' I said. 'I want my mama too.' He was howling, I was howling. I think I felt better after that, though.

My siblings and I considered taking legal action against Constantia-berg. But it was all just too much. We sat down as a family and decided that suing the hospital was not going to bring her back. She wouldn't want us to relive the horror of how we had lost her and be tied up in the courts for years. She would want us to let go and live in peace, and that's what we did. We let her rest in peace.

TWENTY

In around 2007, we built our dream house in the country. We had moved out of the Northcliff house, where we'd had a couple of worrying security incidents and some unwelcome visitors stopping by to take pictures. While the new house was under construction, Romeo put us up in a secure townhouse in Bryanston.

We had decided to go and live out in the sticks in order to be out of the public eye and off the beaten track. We chose a beautiful, secure equestrian estate surrounded by fields and horses, bought a plot and set about building our family home. Building this home was such a special experience for us. Suzette Hammer, whom I had met through *Top Billing* and who did our Northcliff house, also worked on this house with us. It's a real privilege to create a space that is your haven, your sanctuary, where your peace lies. And to put a plug where you want it!

We had some more happy news in 2007: I was pregnant. Better yet, this time it was twins, a boy and a girl. It seemed like I was going to have my childhood dream of a big house full of children after all.

Romeo was still working in Tanzania at the time and spent a weekend at home every four weeks. In December, he came home for an extended period over the Christmas holidays. I woke up one morning not feeling great. I was halfway through the pregnancy. Romeo took me to the doctor, who said there was nothing to worry about. I should take it easy, put my feet up, and not worry. The following day, I woke up soaking wet. Romeo took me back to the doctor, who immediately admitted me to hospital. It turned out my amniotic sac had ruptured.

Now it was just mayhem. Drips, injections – it was absolute chaos in that ward. They tried everything, but I went into labour. The babies were just twenty weeks old. I could feel their every move, their gentle flutters and the Braxton Hicks contractions. They were such an intimate part of me for twenty weeks, but they didn't survive. The doctors put me in a labour ward. At one point I started to lose consciousness, and they told Romeo that we had to make a decision. The doctors gave me the option of a general anaesthetic and a Caesarean, but I said no, I wasn't going home with a scar and no babies. I chose to go into labour and give birth to them, even though I knew I was not going to be able to take them home with me.

My sister Lerato had gone to our home to fetch my Bible and my father's crucifix, which was the one thing I asked to keep when his belongings were being distributed after his passing. When she came back, I told her to read me my father's psalms. They put his cross around my neck and they read me Psalm 23 and Psalm 91. With the curtains closed, I delivered my babies, a boy and a girl. The nurse quietly came and asked if I wanted to see them. I said no; let them go in peace. Romeo was there every step of the way, holding my hand. I cried, he cried, we both cried. It was painful.

I went into a severe depression when I lost my babies and didn't get out of bed for weeks. I just didn't have it in me. I started to question myself. All the 'what-ifs'. I went through a phase of thinking that maybe I should have seen them. If I'd seen them, maybe I would have had closure, maybe I would have dealt with the loss better.

My siblings were so present. With my mom and dad gone, we had no parents, only one another. Lerato is such an extraordinary human being, an angel on two feet. She carried me through that time. She'd arrive and order me out of bed and run me a shower. 'Come, into the shower; I'll get into the shower with you if I have to.' She'd put me in a robe and comb my hair. My brother Tshehla would sit with me and say, 'Tell me what to do, please tell me what to do.' I'd say, 'There's nothing you can do. Just be here.'

My husband, bless him, just wanted to make my pain go away, but he didn't know what to do. He had lost his kids too, and he was deeply sad and grieving as well. He would try to be brave in front of me, but I knew that he was broken inside. He would hold me at night and say, 'It's going to be okay, honey, it's going to be okay.' The reality is that when you are in that place, actually, what do you know? What do you do? You are trying to process it, but you can't think straight.

I tried therapy, and the therapist wanted to put me on antidepressants, but I had a strong feeling that I had to work through this pain so that I could get to the other side. I didn't want to numb what I was feeling. I felt that, if I did, it would somehow manifest in some other way at some other time. In that terrible situation, you don't know if you're making the right or wrong decision. Actually, there *is* no right or wrong. But my spirit just told me, 'Basetsana, walk through this and work through this and you're going to be okay.'

One thing that tortured me was that there would be no burial, no funeral, for my children. If a child is born too early, without signs of life, it is termed a stillbirth and they don't issue a birth certificate, which means you can't bury them. I just felt that when someone passes away, you should bury them. They did not just come into the world and then disappear into thin air. It made no sense to me. I couldn't process it at all. To me, they were my babies: they were human, I had felt them move, and I had a deep bond with them.

Furthermore, in African cultures, when a loved one passes, it is customary for the whole community to gather and break bread together. Our funerals, like our weddings, are open to everyone, and so it's not unusual for a few hundred people to attend. Even in the week leading up to the funeral, people come in numbers to pay their respects and support the family. On the day of the funeral, there is usually a service, followed by a procession to the gravesite where, after a final blessing, all the men take it in turns to fill in the grave, using shovels. We then return to the home of the deceased to wash our hands and share a meal. It is a tradition that brings healing and closure.

While it was true that my twins had not yet come into this world, they were still very much a part of our family. I needed to say goodbye. Seeing my struggle, Uncle Seiiso came to me and said, 'My child, I think what you need to do for them is to have a ceremony to honour them and respect them. Plant something in their remembrance so that you can have the closure and finally find peace.'

So the family gathered at our new home and we prayed and sang and had tea. We made a little garden outside the kitchen window and planted two fig trees. I'm glad I did this. When I wake up in the morning, I go into the kitchen and I open that window and I see these fully grown fig trees in our courtyard. We put a little bench out there, and often I sit there and have my tea, and it is well with me.

When I lost my twins, I came to realise that I hadn't really processed either my father or my mother's passing. I had refused to go there fully, because it was just too painful. I wasn't ready for my father's death; it wasn't time. And my mother, she had been through the worst and was healing. It shouldn't have happened the way it did. I was grieving, I was in denial, I was angry and I hadn't worked through it. I was dealing with so much loss. I had been unhinged. Somehow I think that, through grieving for my twins, I got to deal with the loss of my parents, too.

Some days were better than others. What they say about grief is true. It gets better with time. I don't think you ever completely heal. I think what time does is make the pain and void more bearable. Gradually, I picked up the pieces of my life and myself. After all, I still had a two-year-old who needed me.

PART VI

BRAND BASSIE

TWENTY-ONE

I f you drove into Soweto from Potchefstroom Road, entering at the Chris Hani Baragwanath Hospital side in the late 1990s, you would have seen a massive billboard featuring me in a flowing red dress, a scarf and a big smile, advertising the Revlon Realistic range of hair relaxers. The tagline: 'I wanted to dazzle the world and my hairdresser said relax.' The product was being rebranded and relaunched with a bang, and I was the face of it. To be asked to do a Revlon endorsement was a real honour – I mean, Halle Berry was the face of Revlon! The most beautiful women in the world were connected to the brand.

It's quite an experience seeing your own face plastered all around the township and across the city. That image was in all the women's magazines of the day too: *Bona*, *Pace*, *Thandi*, *True Love*. Some of them no longer exist, but at the time they were a big deal, those magazines.

It's funny to think back on that time, because things have come full circle for me in terms of hair. Four or five years ago I decided to 'own my roots', quite literally. I stopped relaxing my hair, cut off the relaxed part and grew out my natural Afro. Black women's hair is a political issue, and when you wear dreads, or an Afro, for that matter, it is seen as a sign of rebellion for some reason. But I decided that it was time to join the changing the narrative around black beauty and to set an example for young women so that they could be part of it too. The year 2016 saw a major student protest when staff at the Pretoria High School for Girls in South Africa's administrative capital began telling black students to 'fix' their hair. Some had even been told to use chemical straighteners. I was rather proud to see fifteen-year-old schoolkids standing up for themselves and owning their roots. Thirteen-year-old Zulaikha Patel led the charge. Those are the daughters we want to raise, young women who stand up for themselves and others. Schools should not be used as platforms to discourage students from embracing their African identity.

When I was young and getting started in the beauty-pageant world, the beauty industry espoused slick and smooth hair. The standard for beautiful hair was long, silky, Caucasian-looking hair, and the absolute ideal was to be able to flick your hair. You could wear it pulled up in a bun or in a ponytail, but there was no way you could enter a beauty pageant with an Afro in those days. You would stand zero chance of winning the title. So black women relaxed their hair to get it as smooth as possible.

Thus, in my beauty-pageant days, and for most of my life, I relaxed my hair. But the process was far from relaxing! Those relaxers would burn your scalp. The fact is that they work by permanently breaking down the protein bonds within the hair to loosen its curl. The chemical process was torturous, to say the least. You would sit in the stylist's chair while your hair was being treated, and your scalp would be on fire! If they left the relaxer on for too long, you would actually have scabs on your scalp from the chemical burns. And for what?

Some people actually believe that 'beauty is pain', but that doesn't have to be the only narrative for African hair. It is one part of our identity that we have to reclaim and reframe. Before the advent of colonialism, Africans embraced their looks because there was no external force demanding that they alter themselves in order to be beautiful. Village women would spend hours grooming one another's hair, and this kind of communal self-care was passed on from mother to daughter for generations.

Our hair remains important as an expression of individual identity. Everywhere you go in Africa, you will find a hair salon. It might be located in a dilapidated shack or on a street corner, or – like you find in the township – in your neighbour's garage. There will be a lady there who knows how to do the best cornrows and a guy who is an artist when it comes to men's haircuts. These spaces are a part of who we are.

Recently, the conversation about hair has moved onto the big screens of Hollywood, where a new crop of black actors and actresses have made the decision to commit to their natural hair. Women like Lupita Nyong'o, Danai Gurira, Letitia Wright and the amazing Viola Davis are using their platforms to tell the world that we are beautiful just the way we are. While the politics of hair remains contentious, at least our kids can now see people who look like them in the media.

Since having Bontle, I have realised that raising a daughter who embraces her true self is a deliberate act of acceptance of who you are as her mother. It is important to encourage her to see herself as the ideal standard of beauty just the way she is, not as someone who needs to be 'corrected' or changed in order to be acceptable.

Today, when I plait my little girl's hair and see how beautifully her Afro is growing, it makes me so proud. It's good to know that she will grow up and look at herself in the mirror and see that she's completely perfect the way she is. Later, if she decides to grow her hair into dreads, or wants to relax her hair, that's her decision. There is nothing wrong with how a woman chooses to wear her hair. But for now, while Bontle is under my roof, we've decided to go back to our roots, to own them and to fix each other's beautiful crowns!

So, thankfully, attitudes are changing around hair, and I am pleased to be a part of that change. But at the time, endorsing such a big brand was a turning point in my career. I still remember the actual shoot. My word, there must have been twenty people running around on set. I knew that something had happened in my life. I was not only a former Miss South Africa any more – I had grown into a national brand. I began to see that I had potential longevity in this space as a public figure, well beyond the twelve months of my reign.

Because my full name, Basetsana Makgalemele, was a bit of a mouthful for some, a lot of people had taken to calling me Bassie for short. I didn't mind it. I was increasingly using this shorter version of my name. It had a good ring to it and worked well as a 'brand name'. Being asked to endorse Revlon was amazing, and I think that also got me thinking about how I could expand the Bassie brand into other areas.

The early 2000s were significant in terms of building my brand. They were pioneering years for me as an entrepreneur. My own cosmetics range was an obvious next step. Patience and I partnered with three gentlemen, Sam Alexander, Barry Chrystal and Ian Stern, to create a cosmetics line called Bassie Cosmetics. It was a beautiful range, with good-quality coloured palettes, and beautifully packaged. We had everything, from foundations, eyeshadow and blush to volumax mascara, lipstick, eyeliner, lipliner and moisturising lipgloss. The range was extensive and came with a training manual, which was used by make-up artists and consumers alike. We distributed through the big retailers: Pick n Pay, Checkers, Clicks, and so on. The range did well and I saw that the Bassie brand had potential for growth. I started to think about other areas I could expand into.

So, next I partnered with Torga Optical and we created a whole range of eyewear as well as an optical range, which was distributed through their outlets around the country. Torga had a big national footprint, and our range was advertised via TV commercials, a print marketing campaign and on radio. It did very well and was successful for about ten years. Later on I partnered with Spec-Savers to create the Bassie Sunglass Collection, which also enjoyed a good run.

I have always loved fashion and I have an eye for it. I was keen to develop a range of women's wear under my brand. I wanted it to be accessible to the mass market, so I partnered with Ackermans in a range called Stature by Bassie, which was available in 230 of their stores in South Africa, Namibia, Botswana, Lesotho, Mozambique and Swaziland. It was quite an extensive collection with a wide range of fine garments, from suits to fashionable dresses and stylish leisurewear. It was great working with a big brand like Ackermans, because they had a whole team of merchandisers, buyers and so on to support the range. I'm not a fashion designer, but I was deeply involved in the design, choosing the look, feel and fabric. The range did exceptionally well.

It was at this time that *Femina* nominated me as one of the top ten most glamorous women in South Africa, the *Sunday Times* and *Elle* magazine voted me as the most stylish female entertainment host, *Style* magazine nominated me as one of South Africa's best-dressed women, and I was listed as one of the top personal brands in the *Sunday Times* Top Brands Survey. I was also named one of the 100 Most Influential South Africans and was a brand ambassador for LG Electronics. I also had the pleasure of cruising in the Cadillac SRX as the face of the brand when it launched in South Africa.

I wanted to be sure that the people who bought into the Bassie name and brand received a quality product. When I was involved with a product, I was always very hands-on. For my cosmetics range, for example, I went to Italy to trade exhibitions and scoped out the current trends. I travelled with the Ackermans buyers to build our new season range and went to China to source the eyewear range. It really was quite a commitment developing a range that I was prepared to attach my name to. Critical, though, for me, was to create brands that were accessible to a larger market, not niche products that cost a fortune so that people had to save for months to purchase them. It was also about being in the right place at the right time, with the right concept. My products and my brand had to espouse three aspects: integrity, credibility and innovation.

So, the late 1990s and early 2000s were intense in terms of building the Bassie brand. I was really breaking new ground in the way I leveraged my public personality and built a business out of the brand. Of course, it helped that I was on television in people's living rooms every week. One of the interesting things – and something that really benefited me – was that I had crossover appeal. People of all races embraced the Bassie brand, so there was a broad market for the cosmetics, eyewear and clothing I was offering. It pleased me that the products that carried my name were accessible and accepted by so many South African women.

But my brand was not only making an impact within the borders of South Africa. People from all over the continent responded to my story and identified with my life. My products, whether clothing or make-up, carried the name of a black woman, and that resonated with fellow Africans. Furthermore, the quality and standard I demanded were attractive to consumers, even if they didn't know me personally.

TWENTY-TWO

As satisfying and exciting as building a brand like Bassie is, you're constantly walking a tightrope. When you are a public figure and you go into a partnership, or you decide to create or endorse a product or brand, it's not something to undertake lightly. You can't just put your name to something and collect the cheque at the end of the month. Your own personal brand is at stake. Which is why what happened next with Cycle Lab was most upsetting.

One thing that really bothered me after Nathi's birth was that I was carrying way too much weight. During my pregnancy, I had put on a good thirty kilograms, and despite breastfeeding, the pounds just wouldn't budge. Months went by and I wasn't winning the battle of the bulge. I wanted to fall pregnant again, and that was my main priority, so I didn't want to go on some crazy diet or start running marathons while I was trying to conceive.

Now, of course, in the beauty-pageant world you have to be a particular size and shape, but that had never been a problem for me before. I was a skinny kid, and even as a young woman I'd never had any issues with my weight or my body. And then I wake up one day and I weigh ninety kilos! Like really, knocking on 100 kilos! Horror of horrors.

I was extremely conscious of my weight, and I didn't like what I saw in the mirror. I had very low self-esteem and felt awkward, to the extent that I did not want to be seen in public. I didn't fit into my clothes, so I got to the stage of thinking, well, let me just stay at home. And then I would open some newspaper or magazine and read some nasty story about how big I'd got.

It was an odd time. I was a happy mom with a beautiful baby, but I was also this fat girl with chubby cheeks (okay, my cheeks did look cute) whom I just couldn't relate to.

I was desperate, and desperate to do something about it. Eventually, I decided that I was going to tackle this weight problem once and for all. I said, 'Basetsana, you have got to do something. This is just ridiculous.' But nothing seemed to work. A whole year went by and, despite breast-feeding solidly – which uses up millions of calories and really should help with weight loss – I still wasn't able to get rid of all the weight. Oh, and by the way, I wasn't eating seconds or thirds either, just in case you were wondering!

My husband was very, very sweet. He didn't put pressure on me. He just kept telling me I was beautiful and shouldn't put so much pressure on myself. But he could see how it was affecting me. He saw my poor self-esteem, how self-conscious I got, and his position was, well, if you don't like it, do something about it and I will support you.

Romeo is a health fanatic, like seriously health-conscious, and he wanted me to be healthy and happy. He is also very fit. He runs the Comrades Marathon (known as the ultimate human race) and the Two Oceans, he's in the gym, he cycles. But his approach was to encourage me rather than pressurise or criticise me. I have to say, that would *not* have worked with me. I would have throttled him.

Romeo was cycling like crazy at the time (he had done the 94.7 Cycle Challenge twice by then), so he said, 'Babes, maybe you should try cycling. Let's go buy you a bike.' I wasn't winning with this weight thing, so I was prepared to give this riding business a go. So, in February 2007, off we went to Cycle Lab in Fourways to purchase a bike, helmet and gear. I was trying on the helmets when one of the staff came over and took a picture without asking me. It's one of the tricky things about being a public figure. You don't want to be photographed without being asked, but you also don't want to be rude. So I was caught in that slightly awkward situation, but I thought nothing of it. If anything, it might be used in some staff communication or put up on a notice board, or so I thought.

Not long after that I got a call from my good friend Peggy-Sue Khumalo. She had picked up an in-flight magazine on 1time Airline titled *abouTime*. 'Sisi,' she says – we call each other sister – 'I see you're endorsing bicycles now and I don't think you are aware of it, judging by the picture.'

According to Peggy-Sue, there I was in the in-flight magazine, in an ad 'endorsing' Cycle Lab. I soon discovered that the photo taken that day in the store was being used not only in *abouTime* but also in *Cycling News*. As it happened, Romeo was riding the Argus that particular year, and who should he see on the Cycle Lab flyers being distributed to participants? Me! My initial reaction was one of total incredulity. How was it possible for someone to take my image and use it in this way without having at least engaged with me first? I initially wondered whether there had been some kind of error or mix-up. Had some kind of communication been sent to me about publishing the photograph, something I had missed? Uh, no.

You must understand that at the time I was doing a lot of endorsements: Cadillac, Queenspark, LG, Lux. These were all carefully chosen, because there was a synergy between my profile and their brand image and messaging. I was making top dollar with these endorsements. I also had my own personal brands: Bassie Cosmetics, Bassie Clothing and Bassie Eyewear. And along comes Cycle Lab, just climbing on the bandwagon. I was outraged by their absolute audacity, thinking that they could just use my image without asking my permission, without having a contract in place and, of course, without paying for its use.

It was clear to me that I could not continue to live my life assuming that everyone I encountered had only good intentions towards me. Don't get me wrong: I will always believe in the human spirit and its capacity for good. These were the values instilled in me by my mother and father, as well as my community at large. Where I come from, everyone's fate is inextricably bound together. We all need each other in order to survive. Family members have to find ways to contribute, because poverty and marginalisation demand that we club together like a tribe. The only problem with being raised by such a close-knit community is that a strange kind of naivety settles in. Where I was raised, there's a good chance the person you meet on the street knows you and wants you to thrive. Unfortunately, that's not always the case in the bigger, wider world.

I had long known the importance of my image and likeness as a business tool and a brand. I was now coming to see that its value in the public domain would need to be protected from those who would seek to subvert it for their own gain, be it financial or otherwise.

As has happened so many times in my life, the rules of engagement had changed right before my eyes. I was now faced with a choice. Was I going to allow these people to misuse the good name I had worked so hard to build, or was I going to stand up for myself and anyone else who might be going through something similar?

In this world, there is a lot of pressure to be liked. In fact, an idea exists that being liked is more important than being true to oneself. I decided to be true to myself. I chose to push back. My decision was not an easy one to make, but it was certainly the more courageous one. Yes, I thought, it might make me less palatable to a segment of my audience, who preferred a more submissive sort of beauty queen. Yes, the media might portray me as 'litigious'. But it was not the first time I had made the decision to go against the grain, and it will certainly not be the last.

So I brought a lawsuit against Cycle Lab. As you can probably guess, this was the beginning of a complex and lengthy legal battle that turned into a precedent-setting court case. It both greatly challenged and changed me as a person.

In the late 1990s, Adams & Adams had registered my name as a trademark in different classes. I consulted attorney Bally Chuene, and he advised me to pursue a case of *iniuria* (a Latin term meaning 'outrage' that I only came to know and understand during the trial). Basically, we were going to sue Cycle Lab for wrongfully and intentionally infringing my interests. This turned out to be a greatly simplified version of what would ultimately unfold. What I quickly realised between writing affidavits and meeting with my lawyers was that the law is never simple.

Even knowing for sure that I had been wronged, and that I wanted and deserved justice, did not make the inevitable public scrutiny any easier to endure. I knew I had made a decision that would change the way the media reported on me, and maybe even the way the general public would feel about me. I was no longer merely a 'celebrity', the former Miss South Africa who attracted mostly positive attention. I was now the kind of person who should not be provoked unless you were willing to defend yourself against a solid legal team.

It took four years for me to get my day in court. The wheels of justice turn slowly, but they do turn. I think Cycle Lab thought they would frustrate me, that I'd lose stamina. A lawsuit is costly and they may have thought that I would give up. But that's not me. When I was eventually given my court date and the trial started, it was complete media mayhem. I had to go to court every day for a full week. I had to unpack in detail what had happened on the day the photo was taken, as well as when exactly I had become aware of its use. This was the question of fact: What were the actual events that had precipitated the complaint that I had brought to court for adjudication? The legal question would be answered by the interpretation and application of the law by the attorneys and the judge. I also had to disclose all of the endorsement contracts I had in place and how much I was being paid for each one. I felt that this was a total violation of my privacy.

Since it was common cause that Cycle Lab had, in fact, incorporated my photo in their advertising, there was no dispute in this regard. What *was* in question was whether I had consented to my image being captured in the shop that day. This would later go to the question of wrongfulness, because if I had agreed to being photographed, could I really claim that I had been unaware of the possibility that my image would end up being used in that way?

I remember very clearly that when the member of staff, a Mr de Villiers, approached me in the shop, I was trying on a bike helmet. As I looked up, there he was, having already pressed his camera's shutter button to capture the moment. The question of whether I had actively consented could be answered with a resounding no, even from the point of view of the defendant. Mr de Villiers had not walked up to me and asked if I had any objection to being photographed. I had not reverted to him by actively saying yes or no. The moment had already happened, so there was no need for my permission, whether active or tacit. The point was moot.

Mr de Villiers testified that he thought I had granted consent, but he couldn't remember whether I had signalled so expressly or tacitly, by nodding my head. Both Mr de Villiers and Andrew McLean, a board director at Cycle Lab who was actually present in the shop that day, conceded that they had never sought my permission to use the photo in magazines or brochures for advertising purposes. They also conceded that, because I had not objected to the photograph being taken or engaged them about its use, they had decided they could go ahead without my input. During the trial, I was flummoxed when McLean said, 'I just saw a black woman and didn't know who she was.' Now I am not even going to give credence to the racial tone of that comment.

My position was very clear. I did not agree to the taking of the photograph or to its use. And just because I am the kind of person who is loath to make a scene does not mean I consented to be photographed that day. All it means is that I have operated in the public space for so long that I know when not to create unnecessary waves. I cannot shout from the rooftops every time someone takes an ill-timed photo of me; that is part of the life of a public figure.

There would not have been an issue if the photo had been published with my knowledge. But it hadn't. I was perturbed, shocked even, that these two men ostensibly intended to exploit me for commercial gain without my knowledge or consent. My image had been abused and my privacy invaded.

What further incensed me was the terrible quality of the photo, which was unflattering, to say the least. In the public space where I have been for over twenty-five years, there is no getting around the fact that looks *do* matter. We are judged for our weight, our hair, our skin, every single possible aspect of our physique. This is why anyone in the public eye is careful to put the proverbial best foot forward. It does not mean that I subscribe to these impossible standards of beauty every day of my life. Of course I don't always wear make-up when going to the mall or doing the school run. I do, however, want to have control when my face is going to be used for a marketing campaign. It is the difference between me having a day out with the family, and me using my brand for a very specific business purpose.

My claim against Cycle Lab was threefold. The first was for damages based on the common law *iniuria*. The second was for constitutional damages arising from the violation of my rights to dignity and privacy.

The third was an alternative claim in case the first did not succeed. This was a claim for special damages sustained as a result of the unauthorised publication of the photograph.

The court found that my image had, in fact, been used in a misleading way, because of the false impression (which it created) that I myself personally endorsed the products sold by Cycle Lab and its campaign to promote cycling among women. This was found to be a wrongful violation of my right to identity, and was therefore considered *iniuria*, which was deserving of legal protection.

Ultimately the court found in my favour, setting a legal precedent and sending a clear message about the right to privacy and the protection of personality rights. The case was widely publicised, and it has subsequently been included in the law syllabus of most of South Africa's universities and higher-education institutions. It was even covered in the *Harvard Law Review*.

This legal battle was not at all easy. In fact, it was extremely stressful. But I'm glad that I was bold enough to stand up for myself and for any other public figures who may have been exploited in this way in the past or potentially in the future. It reminded me of those days selling hard-boiled eggs after school, and how Ma-Rooi had leveraged her age and my politeness to bully me into letting her take eggs on credit. And I remembered Moeder setting off down Msitshana Street full of purpose and coming back with what was owed to her. Bullies exist in every sphere of life, whether on the streets of my childhood Soweto, in business or, increasingly now, on social media. Bullies must be dealt with decisively. This was the message I received loud and clear from my parents. You stand up for yourself! So I thought of the court case and I thought of Moeder and the eggs and I thought, yes, I am my mother's daughter and I will stand up for myself.

This was the first time I would go to court to defend my name and my brand, but it would not be the last. One thing I have learnt through the years is that life comes in waves. One minute all is calm, and the next you are hit by a big surprise that knocks your feet right out from under you.

TWENTY-THREE

From the day I was crowned Miss South Africa, I was a public figure who attracted the attention of my fellow South Africans. I never think of them as fans and I am not a celebrity; I am just someone who happens to have a more prominent public platform. I am very clear about this. There's something about the word 'fan' that does not sit well with me, and that does not befit the sisters, brothers, husbands, wives, mothers, fathers, boys and girls who just want to write me a note or have a chat with me, or get a photograph or autograph to mark the moment, or who decide to follow me on my social media platforms. It is not asking too much.

Starting out, I had no idea of the kind of attention my presence would attract in a shopping mall or restaurant, for example. And I guess I should be used to it by now, but I still find it surprising when someone recognises me and comes over to talk to me. My introverted nature requires that I do some mental readjustment in these kinds of situations, but I have learnt to deal with them as best I can and, hopefully, as graciously as possible.

Over the years, I've received letters from South Africans from all walks of life. It always touches my heart to know that someone has taken time out of their day to write me a personal note to wish me well or to give me a shout out on social media, to express their love and support. And I've experienced so much love when I've been among people that I hardly give a thought to my safety at public engagements. Unfortunately, when you are a public figure, not everyone you come across is harmless or wishes you well.

In the *Top Billing* years, there was a sharp increase in the volume and frequency of letters and faxes (this was before email, remember), so there came a point where it was just not feasible for me to read them all personally. The task fell to my then personal assistant, Leanne Smit, who swiftly took charge of what was fast becoming a mammoth undertaking.

At some point, Leanne discovered a worrying chain of communication from a man referring to himself as Freddy Bokaba. He had been sending me letters, faxes and, eventually, emails for years. He claimed to have met me in 1989, when he was a high-school student. In his correspondence, he spun an elaborate tale, a fantasy with me as the subject. It was an extremely convoluted fiction with multiple plot lines, twists and turns, taking place over many years and settings. There were various other characters in the story, including friends – real or imagined, I don't know – who he claimed had introduced us when we were children. He made deranged and completely false claims, including that he had visited my father to arrange *lobola* negotiations.

What started as something strange and unsettling soon became quite shocking and scary. The letters became more frequent, more urgent, more unhinged, until I became genuinely fearful for my safety. In April 2003, a five-page fax arrived at the offices of Tswelopele Productions describing in great detail an incident in 1989 when he and some of his friends had taken a trip to a certain flea market and seen me there, dressed in camouflage pants and accompanied by someone he referred to as Augustine. Apparently this was the moment he knew I would become his wife.

The fax was written in erratic and illegible handwriting, and attached to it were documents about the author's academic aspirations and track record. These were apparently relevant because he intended to complete his degree in accounting so that he could take up a high-flying marketing job and have the financial means to 'finally meet' me. Apparently he dreamt about me every night and intended to buy me various pieces of jewellery on credit he would secure using his disability grant. Most disturbingly, the writer ended his letter by saying that I would soon receive a 'surprise present' from him.

This potential surprise gift really scared me. It told me that he either had my home address or planned to obtain it. It was clear that he was not like the other stalker-types I had previously encountered, who were basically harmless admirers who would eventually go away if I ignored them or reported them to the police. This man was determined to achieve his sinister agenda, and he was not going to stop unless I took decisive action.

I decided it was prudent to go to the police. On 29 September 2003, I laid an official complaint at the Parkview police station. In my affidavit I explained that Freddy's correspondence had become increasingly disturbing and urgent, to the point where it was clear that he was becoming a danger to my colleagues, my family and me. He had also taken to incessantly phoning me on my work number, which was affecting productivity.

In response to the subsequent police investigation, Freddy – whose real name, we discovered, was Rakawu Joseph Bokaba – penned an even more disturbing affidavit that confirmed we were dealing with a very sick man. What I found most chilling was the fact that he actually believed I had been returning his phone calls and his barrage of letters because, in his own words, 'we were going to get married' one day. He also believed we'd had many encounters over the years, whereas the truth was that I had never met him.

Freddy proved to be a single-minded, persistent person who went to great lengths to find me. We received information that he was sleeping at the petrol station down the road from my home in Northcliff. He had been there for a few days, presumably hoping to catch a glimpse of me while I was getting petrol, or to get information about my address from the petrol attendants.

Despite this information, the police case of intimidation went nowhere.

On 24 February 2005, two months before Nathi was due, I arrived home from work and Rakgadi informed me that a parcel containing baby toiletries, socks, bibs, bottles, nappies and school stationery had been delivered. I cannot even summon the feelings that went through me in that moment when I realised who it was from. He had managed to breach security at our home, which included a full-time guard. We used a weekly garden and maintenance service, and when Henry

Rashaka (who still works for me at Tswelopele Productions) opened the gate to let them out, Freddy just walked in and said he had come to drop off some presents. Thinking nothing of it, Henry accepted them and gave them to Rakgadi, who put them in our bedroom. After all, the whole country knew we were expecting, and gift deliveries were not unusual.

Romeo had been incensed from the moment he learnt about this stalker. The gift incident just ratcheted up his concern for my safety and for that of his soon-to-be-born son. To be honest, for the longest time he wanted to deal with the matter 'kasi-style'. I told him that I would not have a husband in jail and a stalker on the streets. We had to follow the rule of law. We decided that I would have a permanent security detail and that we would retain a lawyer to approach the courts in an attempt to keep this man, who clearly had mental issues and an unhealthy obsession, away from my family and from me. We decided that a restraining order was the best way to proceed.

In my founding affidavit, I requested that the case be dealt with as a matter of urgency, because it had been interfering with my life for a very long time. By this time I was a new mother with a husband who worked outside of the country, so I needed it to be resolved as quickly as possible. The court had to stop this man from entering my home or my place of work.

While I was visiting Romeo in Tanzania later that year, my personal assistant discovered that Freddy had somehow got hold of my old mobile number and had started calling and sending strange text messages. He had also sent more faxes to the office, attaching forms from the Department of Home Affairs, which he had completed on my behalf. There was an application to change my surname from Kumalo to Bokaba. He was trying to do the same for my baby too, by applying for a 'late registration of birth'. There was also an application for authority in terms of Section 26 of the Births and Deaths Registration Act, which would give him the legal standing to make these amendments to my and Nathi's government records. All the forms were signed 'Freddy'.

There is something very sinister about someone who feels they have the right to amend another's name. To add insult to injury, when I got married I chose to take my husband's surname. It was my personal choice. I didn't feel a double-barrelled surname was for me. Besides my beliefs, can you imagine writing 'Basetsana Julia Makgalemele Kumalo'? Yhoo, that's a whole sentence; it would take all day to fill in forms! So to have my name usurped by someone I had never met was a grotesque violation of my rights. It just seemed unreal. I had a hard time accepting that this craziness was, in fact, happening.

In May 2005, the notice of motion for an urgent High Court application was to be served on Freddy in preparation for a hearing. As part of the civil procedure, my lawyers applied for a preliminary protection order, called a *rule nisi*. This would serve to temporarily restrain Freddy from coming to my work or my home, or within 100 metres of my person, until the conclusion of the court case.

Before we could proceed, however, we had to locate an address for Freddy, because legal documents have to be hand-delivered by the sheriff of the court. The police found him in Mamelodi, living with his mother. Freddy's entire room was covered wall to wall with every single picture and article that had ever been published of me. The investigating officer said he'd never seen anything like it before in all his years on the job. Freddy's mother had apparently been telling her son to stop his 'craziness', as it would land him in trouble.

According to the court process, Freddy was to appear that same month to give reasons why the preliminary protection order should not be granted and to respond to my claims. After various postponements, where he claimed either that the process had not been explained to him or that he had no legal representation, the responding affidavit he eventually prepared confirmed our suspicions about his mental health. According to Freddy, he'd been involved in a major car accident in 1991, which left him with amnesia and epilepsy. He had also been admitted to the Dr George Mukhari Hospital in March/April 2005. I do not know if the part about the accident is true, but it might explain his delusions. Perhaps he had been trying to access his memories and piece his life back together, and what he thought had happened in the years before the accident was a string of false memories, mixed up with the reality.

When I read about his history and difficulties, I could not help but sympathise with what Freddy had been through. I am not a medical professional, or a psychologist or psychiatrist, but it seemed that maybe he was just a man with severe mental issues who simply wanted to be loved and accepted.

The court granted my restraining order on 9 June 2005, but the relief was short-lived. It did not stop Freddy from harassing me. Nor did it stop the media from making a meal of the story. While I lived in fear, articles were published that made light of the matter, suggesting that I had been heavy-handed in approaching the courts. I had to remind myself that I was doing what was best for my own and my family's safety, which was of paramount importance. I had to shrug off the destructive commentary and stay focused.

Although Freddy faced imprisonment if he continued to write to me, he did not stop. In April 2007, he started sending emails and making calls to a mobile number that had previously been mine but which I was no longer using. If I had ever been disturbed by this man before, I was now terrified. He was arrested for being in contempt of the restraining order and was sentenced to two years in prison, of which one was suspended, but he only served a few months. On his release, I received another string of faxes from him. This time the tone was overtly sexual. The details of his sick fantasies are too terrible to repeat.

I continue to be the victim of a sick stalker. It has been almost twenty years since Freddy Bokaba entered my life, and he has not stopped writing to me and looking for me. At this point, I cannot say I fear him. I don't! I have dealt with every possible emotion, from the anxiety of being powerless to the pity I felt when I read about the car accident that may have resulted in his mental illness. I have cried about the situation and I have laughed. I have now come to accept the fact that the type of life I have chosen lends itself to these kinds of experiences. I realise that Freddy might never stop, but I cannot afford to let his behaviour consume and change my life. I go to public events and speaking engagements, I buy groceries at the store and take my kids to school, I go out with my friends. I know he is out there, but his reality is not my reality. His is a very sad tale. You pray for such people and leave them in God's hands. I live, I love, I laugh, I am fully present in every moment, and I don't live in fear.

TWENTY-FOUR

On the afternoon of Tuesday 5 June 2018, I was at Ade Hair in Sunninghill undoing my braids when my friend Nyeleti Makhubele phoned me.

'Hi, friend, how are you?' she asked.

'I'm great, friend.'

We chatted for a while. I asked after her twins, and it was just a normal conversation between two people who have known each other for a long time. But as we spoke, I began to realise that she knew something I didn't. Eventually, she decided to just come out with it. 'You're trending on Twitter, you and Romeo.'

Totally oblivious to the drama that was about to unfold, I asked her what she was talking about. She said that it would be best if she sent me the screengrabs, which is what she did.

This is what I saw:

Just over heard a painful conversation, a Female TV mogul ...
Pleading with one of my girls not to share videos of her drunk
and her husband rimming a celebrity boy!!!!! What the hell!!!
Kanti what kind of marriages do we have now!!!

I was still confused. The tweet came from someone called Jackie Phamotse, who seemed to be a self-published author. I'd never even heard of her. What did this have to do with Romeo and me?

A few more screengrabs made it clear. People had started commenting that the couple in question was Romeo and Bassie.

It suddenly dawned on me that earlier in the day I'd received quite a few messages from people I hadn't spoken to in a while, saying how much they loved me and sending me good wishes. One sweet message was from Thembisa Mdoda. 'We love you and appreciate you,' she wrote. I had responded by saying: 'Thank you honey, gotta lotta love for you.' I realised that while I was unaware that we were 'breaking the internet', my friends had seen what was going on. These weren't just the usual loving messages – they were messages of support from friends who knew I was being targeted on social media. Apparently, it had been trending since one o'clock that afternoon. I was the last to know.

I called Romeo and sent him the screengrabs. He was as oblivious as I was. 'What the f*ck is this about?' he demanded.

I was still in the hairdresser, my hair half-done, while all this was happening. Next, a WhatsApp message popped up from Ronnie McKenzie, asking if I was available to talk. I took the call. Ronnie told me that he had in his possession a video of my husband performing sexual acts with another man, and that he would send it to me.

I had met Ronnie McKenzie years ago at an ANC ward meeting in Midrand. I had always suspected that he held a grudge against me for refusing his unwelcome and persistent advances, but this was confirmed when on one occasion he promised that he would 'get me' for rebuffing him.

At the time of Jackie Phamotse's tweet, Ronnie was the administrator of a WhatsApp group called Open Politics, to which Romeo and I belonged. The group included 196 influential people, from government ministers, deputy ministers and directors-general to journalists, CEOs and captains of industry. The purpose of the group was to discuss current issues and politics, but in hindsight I think it was set up by Ronnie to give him relevance and provide a platform for his own vitriol. The Open Politics group has been at the centre of a couple of defamation lawsuits in recent years.

Ronnie didn't immediately send me the video, but he did put a series of screengrabs of tweets that were doing the rounds on the Open Politics WhatsApp group. People were talking about me and Romeo.

At around seven o'clock that night, while I was still sitting in the salon, Ronnie finally sent me a video – of two Caucasian men having sex. At this point my shock made way for incredulity and confusion. Here I was, sitting in a very public place, watching pornographic material. Of course, neither of the participants was my husband. What was going on? It was the stuff of nightmares, or perhaps a B-grade TV drama or a sick joke.

Next, Ronnie put a screengrab of a tweet from the Twitter handle @AdvBarryRoux on the Open Politics group. The tweet stated that Romeo was gay and that we had 'an arranged marriage'. The next screengrab was of a tweet from Penuel Mlotshwa that featured a Photoshopped picture of the rapper Nasty C and my husband. I have to admit that I'm not very up to date on rappers, and so I had never even heard of Nasty C before.

My hair finally finished, I drove home in tears. I could not even see the road. I was a wreck when I opened the door and saw Romeo. 'Do people hate us so much?' I remember asking him. Romeo is not easily fazed; he knows who he is and he knows what's important. He opened his arms and held me, and after I calmed down, he took my face in his hands and said, 'Look at me, we know who we are, what we are about and what we stand for. It's going to be okay.'

Later that night, someone sent a message to the Open Politics WhatsApp group reminding participants that Romeo and I were on the chat, presumably to warn everyone to be cautious about what they were saying. Someone else pleaded with the others to end the conversation, but his request fell on deaf ears. The messages went on for most of the night and into the next day. Every time I heard the ping of a WhatsApp, my heart sank. I felt completely violated and powerless as my husband and I continued to be baselessly attacked.

The following day, Ronnie posted another Photoshopped picture, this time of the 'pregnant' rapper Nasty C, who had supposedly slept with my husband. It was the most diabolical thing I had ever seen. I am sure it seemed very funny to the people scrolling through their messages, but it made me sick to my core.

I still had no idea who was behind it, or why anyone would want to hurt and humiliate us in this cruel way. Then I started receiving telephone calls from concerned friends, asking if I knew Jackie Phamotse.

She was the one who had sent that first tweet, which was now getting hundreds of likes, shares and retweets. Although she had not mentioned either my or Romeo's name, she had used phrases such as 'female TV mogul' and, in another tweet, 'former Miss South Africa'. I do not know of any other former Miss South Africa who went on to become a TV executive, and it was clear from the comments that the general public assumed it was me, and that Jackie Phamotse did not attempt to correct them.

In subsequent tweets, she claimed the 'TV mogul' had been calling her and 'pleading with her' not to release the video. And she made further spurious allegations, including that this person was an alcoholic. Most disturbing, however, was the allegation of the 'TV mogul's' presence in the room when the sex video was made, and that it had been 'secretly' recorded by a friend in the mogul's home. This allegedly would be the same home in which Romeo and I raise our children. It was just beyond preposterous.

What Jackie Phamotse did not do was post the video she said she had. Now, as we all know, if there's a salacious video doing the rounds, it'll be all over the internet in a matter of hours. People on Twitter started saying as much – 'If you've got the video, why don't you post it?'

The reason, of course, is that there was no video. The story was completely fabricated, a figment of her imagination. I had never even heard of this woman, let alone met her. I struggle to make sense of why anyone would launch an attack on a total stranger in such a blatant way. The only explanation that held any water was that she invented the story and orchestrated a targeted character assassination to boost her social media profile and her book sales. What was even more hurtful and inexplicable was that so many people – some of whom we actually knew – saw fit to share her lies.

The matter did not end with Twitter; some newspapers and online publications picked up the story and put their own spin on things. We decided not to respond until we had consulted our attorneys and explored all courses of action available to us. We also felt we needed time to process the assault. We would respond in due course, after thorough investigation and reporting the matter to the police. Our first step was to lay a charge of *crimen injuria* and apply for a protection order against Jackie Phamotse and Ronnie McKenzie (by this stage, we were convinced Ronnie was somehow involved). We engaged the services of Ian Levitt Attorneys.

A really low moment was having to sit at the breakfast table the next morning with our thirteen-year-old son, Nkosinathi, and having to tell him a story that I still struggle to believe to this day. Romeo and I had decided that it would be best if it were us informing him about the social media lies that were doing the rounds before he saw the tweets for himself or was told by his friends at school. Nathi was at an age where this kind of thing would surely find its way to him.

I think all mothers reading this will understand the horrible discomfort of that moment. I don't wish it on anyone. But his response warmed my heart and brought me to tears. My beautiful, clever boy said, 'I know who is raising me, I know my parents, so nothing the world says is going to change that.'

I realised in that moment that I had a responsibility to our children to take back my story and to tell it for myself. I decided I was going to have my say. I did not get to choose what happened to me and my family that day, but I *was* in full control of how I responded. There would be no knee-jerk reaction or brash response. I was going to use this painful experience to grow my resolve. I knew that I had to take control of the narrative, and that is exactly what I am doing by writing this book.

I know that these malicious and indecent rumours could hang over us for a lifetime. One day, our children might find a headline on the internet that will shock them to their very core. Will they think we have been lying to them their whole lives? What kind of person and mother would I have had to be to live a lie in a debauched sham of a marriage, saying one thing to them, yet doing another? I owe my children my truth – they deserve that.

Romeo and I decided to approach the courts in order to address the victimisation and cyberbullying. Before we had children, I would have just thought, let them talk. But this was a different time. Our family was under threat. The rules of engagement had changed.

Once the case had been filed, we were ready to break our silence. We released a joint statement on 16 June 2018:

We were so deeply shocked and hurt by the salacious content and manner in which it has been recklessly shared and spread. We feel it is our duty to take a stand – both against the specific individuals involved in spreading these baseless allegations about us and, more broadly, against all those keyboard warriors who so swiftly jump on the bandwagon to share harmful content about others – without considering the long-term harm that this can cause.

It is our hope that, in taking a public stand against this type of malicious and reckless behaviour, we will send a strong message to all those who regularly and carelessly share false and harmful information about others without fact-checking or considering the tremendous harm to be caused on a personal, professional and reputational level.

In the days that followed, I had to endure headlines such as 'Bassie's claws out' and 'Bassie vs Jackie'. It seemed so unfair – I didn't start this fight. I had been forced into it, in order to protect my reputation and my family.

On 26 July 2018, the Randburg magistrates' court granted us a protection order against Jackie Phamotse, preventing her from engaging or even attempting to engage with us, from enlisting the help of another person to harass us, and from making any malicious allegations on any social media platform with regards to us. The court also ordered her to remove all malicious allegations against us from all of her media platforms, and confirmed that should she violate the order, a warrant of arrest would be issued, resulting in a five-year jail sentence. (The case against her co-accused, Ronnie McKenzie, was set aside, but that is a fight for another day.)

Overall it was a victory, not just for my family, but also for the many other victims of cyberbullying who have endured these kinds of public attacks in silence. As much as it was a painful experience, I consider myself lucky, because I had the resources and the support system to be able to stand up for myself. This is not the case for many others, especially young people, who are often unable to cope with the shame and are on occasion even driven to suicide. I took this on for everyone who's worked hard, built a career, raised children and lived a decent life, and seen it destroyed by a malicious bully. And I took this on for all the young people I mentor to show them that it's okay to stand up for yourself and fight back when you've been wronged.

According to an Ipsos Global Advisor study completed in 2018, South Africa has the highest prevalence of cyberbullying of the twenty-eight countries surveyed. Twenty-five per cent of South African parents who took part in the research reported that their child had been cyberbullied. The report showed that more than 80 per cent of South Africans said they were aware of cyberbullying and almost three-quarters believed that the anti-bullying measures we have in place are insufficient.

I believe that by acting the way she did, especially on a public platform, Jackie Phamotse and her accomplices have caused serious harm to my and Romeo's reputations, and violated our children and their innocence. This matter has hurt us in many ways, and we are still dealing with the consequences of their actions.

It has been a year since that first tweet and I believe I am stronger for having had the experience. Surprisingly, we have grown closer as a family too. We went through the lowest of lows, but we did it together.

Despite the protection order, Jackie Phamotse continued her campaign against us on social media. On 24 May 2019, she was charged with two counts of *crimen injuria* and issued with a summons. At the time of publication of this book, the courts were dealing with the matter and the trial had begun.

TWENTY-FIVE

I n 2007, I got involved with the Businesswomen's Association of
South Africa (BWA). The BWA was a thirty-year-old organisation,
the largest businesswomen's network in the country. It played a very
important role in the development of South African businesswomen,
including me, as it turned out.

The president of the BWA was Dr Namane Magau, a brilliant
change agent with a doctorate in education from Harvard University.
She was one of my mentors, and to this day she is someone I look up
to. When she asked me to consider taking over from her as president –
with board approval, of course – I was very daunted. As I've said before,
as a former beauty queen I was pigeonholed. You know, the usual
comments: Is she really the sharpest knife in the drawer? What's she
got between her ears, except her pretty face? At the time I hadn't finished my degree, so that was another point against me. But Dr Magau
believed that with my public profile, I could help reposition the BWA
brand strategically, as well as with stakeholders, and also make it more
appealing to younger women professionals and entrepreneurs.

I decided to take on the challenge. There was a lot of scepticism when
I took over as president, and at times I was undermined. But I knew I
could make an impact, and believe me, I worked ten times harder because
of that scepticism. One thing about me: if you say to me I can't do something, that's when I go out and do it! I call myself a rebel with a purpose.

By this time, South Africa was thirteen years into democracy. We
had one of the most progressive constitutions in the world. The country

had a stated agenda of transformation and equality. And yet, women were underrepresented in the workforce and disturbingly rare in the boardroom.

The BWA was determined to change that. Our mandate was to give women a voice, promote their interests in the workplace and take on a corporate South Africa that was reluctant to bring women into the economic mainstream, particularly in management and on boards.

If you want to change the status quo, if you want to change legislation, you need information and statistics. Every year, the BWA undertook an important annual census that tracked how women were doing in the various spheres of business, whether in the corporate world, as entrepreneurs or in government. The census tracked how many women were in lower and middle management, how many were in senior management, how many sat on boards of JSE-listed companies, and so on. And let me tell you, the stats were alarming. Transformation was moving at a snail's pace; the needle had hardly moved since 1994. Because the census was public, the results were all over the media. We would name and shame those companies that were not transforming – 'call them out', as we might say today.

There was one big supermarket retailer that did not have one single woman on its board. Not one! Think about that. Who takes that trolley and walks those aisles and picks what the family is going to eat? The woman in the family, that's who. And yet there were no women in the boardroom. When I looked at the lack of transformation – and let me tell you, it is not a whole lot better today – I saw companies that were missing out on an incredible pool of talent, and of insight. Women should have been in those boardrooms, not because of tokenism, but because they worked hard, they were educated and they had a lot to bring to the table. Yet they sat in organisations where they were disregarded, even undermined. As president of the BWA, I was committed to changing this – I regarded it as my national duty. I always said to myself, 'Basetsana, all of us have to serve, and you have been given this platform, so make the best of it and make a difference.'

There were various aspects to the BWA's work. Bringing women together and developing networks was a big part of our focus. Empowering women through development and training was also key. We would give women tools to navigate negotiations in the boardroom, for example, or pitch ideas, write business plans or raise capital for a start-up. It was about building skills, but also about building confidence and a generation of world-shakers and history-makers. We wanted to teach women that speaking up for yourself and being bold and courageous are not signs of arrogance. It's not brash and harsh; it's your right and it's what you need to do to change the status quo, not only for yourself but also for future generations.

One of our high-profile activities was the BWA Businesswoman of the Year Award. Every year we hosted a big gala dinner and gave out awards in various categories: professionals, start-ups, entrepreneurs. When I took over as president, we included a category for women in government and the public sector. The inclusion of different categories was important. We knew that we had to inspire women across the board, whether it was a florist trying to open her own flower shop, a doctor or a lawyer who was a pioneer in her field, or an entrepreneur who had started a business with zilch and was now listed on the JSE.

Those awards were really inspiring. The winners were incredible women, like Marina Maponya. Growing up in Soweto, everyone looked up to the Maponyas. That family was the epitome of black excellence and achievement. They owned a BMW dealership in the township and developed the Maponya Mall. When the late Mama Marina won the award in 1982, I was only eight years old. She was a beacon of hope and inspiration for so many of us. It was her generation of women, the Marina Maponyas, the Pam Goldings and the Jane Raphaelys, who moved the needle for women. Other formidable leaders who won the coveted BWA award include Dr Thandi Ndlovu, Futhi Mtoba, Maria Ramos and Nolitha Fakude.

The BWA was a national organisation headquartered in Johannesburg, with regional offices so that we could reach women everywhere. We held Regional Business Achievers Awards around the country, and the winners would have the opportunity to compete for the national award. I remember in late 2009 going to the regional awards in North West province. We were not a flashy organisation; we were a non-profit and we had to mind the pennies. So we set off in a kombi over these gravel roads. I was pregnant with the twins at the time, and my instinct told me not to go on those roads, but I guess I was committed to the job. In December, I lost the twins, and I have always wondered if those trips around the country had something to do with it, although I don't advocate living a life of regret.

As I said previously, that time with the BWA was important to my development as a businesswoman. It taught me so much: how to be a sharp business mind, how to hold my own in a boardroom, how to pitch ideas, how to work for a common cause and, more importantly, how to tangibly and meaningfully impact the lives of women. Thanks to the BWA, this shy person was able to sit in boardrooms, hone her leadership skills, sharpen her strategic thinking and own her voice. Later, in my mining businesses, I benefited greatly from these skills.

One thing I was very clear about was that I was not going to try to be a man just because I was a leader. I led with femininity. I wasn't going to go around in a grey pinstripe suit. I could wear my floral blouse and my fishnet stockings and my high heels, because what was important was not what I looked like but what was in my head, what came out of my mouth, and my heart's intentions.

The term of office for the president of the BWA is three years. I served from 2007 to 2009, and for those three years I did everything I could to grow the organisation and contribute to the true empower-ment of women. When I was asked to consider another term, I said no. I remembered Madiba's example. He taught us a lot about so many things, and one thing he was very clear about was not hogging power. African leaders are inclined to want to be president for life, but he was happy to serve only one term. Leadership is also about giving other people the opportunity, and allowing a new leadership to emerge, build, grow and contribute.

I believed that I had given everything I had to the BWA, that I had done what I could. I had focused on raising the profile of the organisation nationally, putting systems in place and driving the women empowerment agenda with everything I had. I'd renegotiated the Nedbank sponsorship deal, which ensured the BWA's sustainability beyond my tenure. It was now someone else's turn. I also knew that the time and energy I had put into the BWA had taken its toll on my businesses. I could see the effect on the bottom line. I needed to refo-cus my attention. I had served. It was time to move on.

TWENTY-SIX

Following my term at the BWA, I was nominated to the Forum of Young Global Leaders, a non-profit organisation of the World Economic Forum, managed from Geneva, Switzerland, under the supervision of the Swiss government. Its mission is to create a dynamic global community of exceptional people with the vision, courage and influence to drive positive change in the world. It nominates leaders under the age of forty. The Young Global Leaders are change-makers and disruptors, young people who have the potential to improve the world. They are led by a board of world and industry leaders, who lend their ideas and passion to the community of young leaders' success and development. I made it through the selection process and was inducted into the 2011 class of Young Global Leaders.

During a transformational five-year experience, young global leaders are inspired to be bold in taking shared responsibility, to have an impact and to be ambitious. So, in that time I completed a Harvard Executive Education Program titled 'Global Leadership and Public Policy for the 21st Century' at the John F. Kennedy School of Government, and participated in the 'Leadership and Decision Making in the 21st Century' programme at Yale University. It was an extraordinary opportunity. I spent time at an Ivy League school in the States, where the education, information, networking and exposure I experienced were beyond my wildest expectations.

The people on these programmes were incredible and diverse. In a lecture hall at Yale you might be sitting next to the youngest billionaire on the African continent, the head of McKinsey, an Israeli government minister or a Mexican mayor. To be exposed to these extraordinary minds, these world-shakers, had a fundamental impact on my life. And then there was the network. The Young Global Leaders are a community; there's always a member you can look up when you are in a foreign country. On my subsequent overseas travels, I would often reach out to the alumni, and there would always be someone willing to meet up or introduce me to contacts in my areas of interest. The forum is a remarkable, powerful and influential body.

So the years between 2007 and 2012 represented a lot of personal growth for me. I was very focused on honing my business skills and learning from the best of the best. The BWA raised my profile as a businessperson and organisational leader, and the Young Global Leaders accelerated my growth trajectory and experience. Increasingly, I was invited to give keynote addresses at corporate functions and motivational talks, often to management and staff, or to do presentations on change management or how to turn an organisation around. The topics varied.

This was a time of political growth, too. Working in organisations like the BWA, I had become more politically conscious, and it was partly for this reason that I decided to go back to UNISA and start a new degree and major in politics.

I'd had the privilege of attending the inaugurations of presidents Mbeki and Zuma. It was an honour to sit in the amphitheatre at the Union Buildings, to see the torch of leadership change hands and to be part of that experience. I understood the importance of getting involved, of not just sitting on the sidelines, casting stones from glass houses. I began to ask what I was going to do with the platform I had been given. How was I going to add my voice and hopefully have an impact?

My own life experiences, my time in the BWA and my passion for the empowerment of women led me to speak out about women's rights. It was important that I used my voice to raise the voices of other women and to demand a fair playing field, to say that women should be given the same opportunities as men to be key players in the mainstream economy.

When women are economically emancipated and independent, when they have financial freedom, only then are they truly empowered. That's when we can make better choices for our bodies, our children and ourselves. When we have financial freedom, only then can we create a better society, a better country and a better people.

I was not asking for women to be given favours. No. If a woman has what it takes, if she has the qualifications and the know-how and the skill set, she must take her rightful place at the table. I think it was Mum Graça who said to me something like, 'If we are not going to be rightfully given a seat at the table, well, you find your place and you pull out a chair.'

Part of my narrative – and this is something I've spoken about in my speeches and talks – is about how women need to work and build together. As women, we cannot afford to have PhD syndrome – Pull Her Down syndrome. If you get in the boardroom, don't slam the door shut behind you. When you climb the corporate ladder, don't kick that ladder away so that no one else can ascend it. Rather offer a hand to the woman coming up behind you. We finish stronger when we finish together. I get so angry when I hear someone say proudly, 'Oh, I'm the only woman on the board of such and such.' That is such absolute nonsense! It's just not acceptable, not in this day and age.

This has been part of my messaging throughout the journey of my life, and I feel as strongly about it now as I did then. Honestly, when I look at the current census figures and the current composition of boardrooms and management, it's quite disheartening. Women's involvement as key players in our economy is simply not accelerating fast enough. I mean, look at the JSE companies. We are still falling short in terms of numbers and wage disparity. Government has historically been better than business in terms of the ratio of women in administration, but even there we have not made enough progress.

As a society, we do not take the advancement and safety of women seriously. We live in a country where gender-based violence is the norm. Women are being raped and murdered at an alarming rate. Dockets are being lost at police stations. I speak from a place of absolute pain and distress as a mother raising a daughter. We all want to be able to raise our children in a secure country, in a progressive country, in a country that values women, not in theory but in practice. It is an indictment that South Africa, with the most progressive constitution in the world, has fallen so short.

Nevertheless, as you know by now, I am an eternal optimist. We can only hope that these important conversations do eventually take place and, more importantly, that they manifest tangibly. I believe in this country. I believe that, collectively, the men and women of South Africa can effect meaningful change for the betterment of all. This is the South Africa in which I have hope.

TWENTY-SEVEN

When I won Miss South Africa, I was in the third year of a BA degree majoring in education at the University of Venda. I didn't finish the degree – life happened, as they say – but I made a commitment to myself that I would go back to school and finish my degree one day. To this end, in between working in my various businesses and being a mom, I studied through UNISA. On 3 May 2012, I was set to graduate with my BA degree, majoring in politics and communications.

But there was one small problem: I was in hospital.

Much to our delight, Romeo and I were expecting our second child. I had started getting contractions at thirty-two weeks and had been hospitalised and put on bed rest. When it came time for the graduation ceremony, I had been in hospital for two weeks. I was on a drip and the doctors were giving me medication to strengthen the baby's lungs in anticipation of an early delivery.

I was desperate to go to that graduation. I remember begging my gynaecologist, Dr Rene Janse van Rensburg, 'Please let me go and graduate. It will just be three hours – I promise I'll come straight back!' He thought about it and thought about it and then, rather reluctantly, said okay, I could go, but I was to walk as little as possible, and I was to come right back to the hospital and get back on the drip as soon as the ceremony was finished. Romeo was in the United States at the time doing the Advanced Management Program at Harvard Business School, so my friend Nomsa Ntshingila picked me up, took me home to change and fetch Nathi, then drove me to Pretoria and watched me graduate.

I was adamant that Nathi was going to witness his heavily pregnant mother receive her degree. It was important to me that this moment imprint on his little mind, and that he know that his mother took education so seriously that she made the decision to study and then graduate at the height of her pregnancy. I firmly believe that it's not what you say, it's what you do that really impacts on children and shapes their thinking, their value system and, indeed, their lives. Children learn by example and role-modelling. I wanted this son of mine to learn about the value of education and commitment at the tender age of seven.

So I dressed Nathi up in a little pinstripe suit, and myself in a black dress and pearls – I mean, I even made the effort to wear stockings! – took my robe, hood and cap, and off we went to Pretoria. It was a magnificent sight, that hall full of graduating students. President Mbeki gave the commencement address, and then they began to call the students' names. One by one, the graduates made their way up to the stage to be capped and receive their degree. When they called my name, I made my way very slowly to the front. The entire audience rose and started to clap as I took those steps across the stage to be capped. I was so heavily pregnant that I was walking like a duck. Slowly, slowly I walked over to be conferred and have my picture taken.

There was a wheelchair waiting in the entrance hall to take me back to Nomsa's car. She said she would have loved to take me out for a celebratory graduation dinner, but we had to get back to the hospital as per the doctor's orders. She did, however, grant my wish for a Streetwise 2 takeaway from KFC. When I got up to the ward, the black dress and pearls came off, the drip went in, and I tucked into my graduation dinner of chicken pieces, mash and gravy. It was delicious! Nomsa then took Nathi home.

Two days later, I started having contractions, and it was clear that our baby's birth was imminent. Romeo jumped on a plane in Boston and landed on the evening of 6 May. Kgosi was born the following morning, and Romeo left that night to go straight back to finish his course. It was crazy, coming all that way for a day and a half. I'd told him it was okay, he didn't have to come, but Romeo said, 'My child is going to be born – I'm going to be there.'

Our second son, Kgositsile, was born on 7 May 2012 at thirty-four weeks, weighing 2.2 kilograms. He was tiny. Such a tiny, beautiful boy. I was discharged and sent home after four days, but Kgosi had to stay in hospital. He was very small, so he needed to be in the neonatal ICU, and he also had jaundice. It was a tough time. It broke me to have to leave him. I was expressing milk every three hours and being driven to Sandton Mediclinic to deliver it. Kgosi was being fed via a feeding tube. I would arrive there at six in the morning and stay all day, and 'kangaroo'-carry him until they said, 'Mrs Kumalo, we really think you should go home now and rest.' That might be ten o'clock at night.

We called our new son uShaka Kgositsile Emmanuel. We named him Shaka, after the king of the Zulus, because of his bravery and courage in fighting to come into and stay in this world. His second name, Kgositsile, is Setswana for 'the king has arrived'. His Christian name, Emmanuel, means 'God is with us'.

He fought and fought – he was such a brave soul – and finally he was well enough to come home. Bringing Kgosi home was just the most wonderful experience. I was a mother of two! I felt completely fulfilled and whole.

About two weeks later, Romeo's programme finished, and he graduated and came home to us. We were a family again. A family of four. Somehow, Kgosi's presence changed the energy of our home. It was delightful to see how Nathi took to him. There is a big age gap, seven years between them, and Nathi was so protective of Kgosi and so loving. He wanted to hold him and to bathe him. It was a joyous period, a very sacred and special time for our family.

All was going well with the Kumalos. We had our two children safely home. I was focusing on being a mom and raising our boys. I had never been happier. I have done many things in my life and I've loved them all. I've succeeded in business, but I honestly do believe that being a mother has been my truest and highest calling. And I have been very lucky to have a partner to support and assist me on this journey of motherhood. Romeo had come back from Dar es Salaam and was now CEO of international business at Vodacom. He was working hard and doing very well in his career, but he always had time for his family.

My husband loves his children. He is a very present father and an exemplary dad. When he comes home after work, he hugs and kisses his children. The way he looks at them makes me fall in love with him all over again. He lives for them, and he works hard for them because he wants them to have the opportunities that he never had, like studying overseas. He encourages them to read and to educate themselves. He affirms our kids. He will say to Kgosi, for example, 'Who's the champ, who's the star, who's the brightest kid?' And of course Kgosi will say, 'Papa, I am.' He will say to Nathi, 'Who's the greatest, who's the smartest, who's the gifted boy?' And Nathi will confidently answer, 'I am, Papa.' I love watching him with his boys and seeing how he is raising them!

Romeo often says to me, 'I want them to be great and decent men.' And I say to him, 'They're going to turn out good, because look who's raising them. Who is their primary role model? YOU.'

When I see the impact that Romeo is having on his boys, I feel very sad and concerned about the absence of fathers or father figures in a lot of children's lives in our country. Boys and young men in particular are suffering because of this. They are not fulfilling their potential and using their God-given talent. They don't know who they can be, because they've never *seen* who they can be. They don't know their greatness, they don't recognise their gifts or the men that they are destined to be, men who can make this world a better place. Instead, our boys and young men are getting into drugs and joining gangs. One of the main contributing factors to so many of our societal woes, like crime and gender-based violence, is that so many dads have abandoned their role and their responsibility to raise good men. To my mind, this is one of the great challenges we face as a society.

It is in our interest as mothers and fathers, politicians, economists, social change-agents, activists, world-shakers and history-makers to own our collective responsibility, to create a new generation of legends and leaders and groundbreakers, to champion the Winnie Madikizela-Mandelas, the Maya Angelous, the Oprah Winfreys, the Malcolm Xs and the Martin Luther Kings.

TWENTY-EIGHT

Whoo-hooo, the girls were going to Vegas! Sister had lost all the baby weight and she was living in hot pants!

I was turning forty in 2014, and my good friend Shumi Dantile was turning fifty, and we had big plans for a combined celebration. A group of fifteen of our girlfriends was going to Las Vegas. We had arranged a special package, and it was all booked and paid for. We had even organised a combined black-tie birthday dinner with all of us dressed to the nines. Come March, we would be partying it up in Vegas and painting the boulevard red. Later in the year, I was going to have a party with forty men and women who had journeyed with me over the last four decades.

I wasn't sure about this forty thing. For a start, I was exhausted! We'd been on a family holiday to Dubai over December and I was just the sleepiest girl. I couldn't keep my eyes open. My family and I would lie on the beach and I would literally pass out into a deep sleep. Talk about a passion-killer! If this was a sign of what forty felt like, I wasn't keen.

Can you guess where this is going? Yes, I went to the doctor in late January and discovered I was pregnant.

I had experienced a world of pain and heartbreak, and had struggled to fall pregnant time and again. I'd had a total of seven miscarriages. I felt very blessed to have my two healthy sons and had given up any thought of having another baby. And now, a surprise. My long history of fertility problems meant that I wasn't particularly fussed about contraception. And besides, I was about to turn forty. A pregnancy was the last thing I expected. Needless to say, I was most delighted.

I called my friends together around mid-February and explained that there was to be no trip to Las Vegas. My girlfriends still hold it against me that I robbed them of that holiday – all in jest, of course. 'We want to go to Vegas,' they still protest. Who knows, maybe for my fiftieth ...

So I was pregnant at forty. Given my history, I knew I had to be very careful. But it was the easiest pregnancy imaginable. I wasn't sick, not a single day, and I went to full term. It couldn't have gone smoother.

Romeo and I had only ever found out the gender of Nathi before he was born. Having had two boys, we had it in mind that this one was probably going to be a boy too. It wasn't something we gave too much thought to, though. The fact that I was carrying life was blessing enough; it didn't matter whether the baby was a boy or a girl.

The Caesarean was booked for 23 July. I lay on the theatre bed, Romeo all suited up in hospital scrubs, holding my hand. My sister Johanna was my birth partner, as always. The baby was delivered safely, and only after a minute or two did Johanna say, 'Doc, what did we have?' And the doctor replied, 'Oh, it's a girl.'

Well, I had tears streaming down my face. Romeo was in tears, my sister was in tears. We named our little girl Bontle ba Morena, 'God's beauty'. Her second name is Jasmine. She is the sweetest girl, the sweet fragrance of our lives.

This girl changed my life and brought total completion to our family. There I was, the queen of my castle with these three men in my life, and now this gift, the joy of my heart, my best friend for life, my heartbeat. She restored my faith in so many ways. She taught me to continue to believe, to never lose hope, and reminds me of my mom in her strength. She is strong-willed and very determined. She's not afraid, and has a mind of her own. Cute as a button, she gives those sons of mine a run for their pocket money! Bontle is five now, and already she challenges the status quo and speaks her mind. She's also very affectionate and doting. My word, the things that come out of her mouth! She will tell me, bless her heart, 'I love you, you are my marshmallow, you're my cutie pie, you're my cupcake. You are so delicious, Mommy. I prayed for you to be my mommy. I hold you in my heart, Mama.' She bowls me over.

It's such a joy having a daughter. I am keeping some of my favourite shoes and gowns for her. I still have my wedding dress, although I somehow doubt that she will ever want to wear it. But the fact is that – God willing – I will be the mother of the bride in a big hat.

Bontle is my mini me, and we do sometimes dress in matching outfits that I have had designed. On vacation, we have matching swimming costumes.

As you can imagine, this girl has her father wrapped around her little finger.

When Lerato had her daughter Mantwa, after her son Mofuthi, Mama said to her, 'My child, to have a daughter is such a blessing, because she will be the one to close your eyes one day.' Johanna also had a boy first, Ndalo, and then, when her daughter Khethile arrived, Moeder told her the same thing.

When Bontle ba Morena was born, I remembered Moeder's words. God willing, I will live a long life, but my daughter will be there to close my eyes.

Celebrating twenty-five years of producing *Top Billing* with Patience Stevens. We call each other DFP — Dear Friend and Partner. A meeting of minds that's stood the test of time

Romeo and I with the one and only Oprah Winfrey

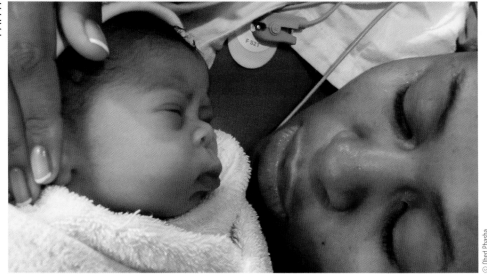

© Obed Phasha

© Obed Phasha

© Obed Phasha

Parenthood bliss with our first-born son, Nkosinathi

© Gordon Harris Photographic

© Johanna Mukoki

© Johanna Mukoki

Graduation Day, UNISA, 2012: 'Education is an important tool no one can take away from you'

The birth of our second-born son, uShaka

The birth of our daughter, Bontle ba Morena

'I am my brother's keeper'

BESTIES!

Cuteness overload

'Who's the king?'

Cupcakes with sprinkles and icing

Rakgadi Agnes Mofokeng — Godsent, my angel on earth!

© Obed Phasha

Family affair

© Sibusiso Sibanyoni

Do you know what today is? Our eighteenth anniversary!

© Obed Phasha

Nathi with Mama Graça Machel

BE BEAUTIFUL BY

BASSIE

The birth of Brand Bassie in the 1990s, which gave rise to many great ventures

Bassie Gold, one of my signature cosmetic ranges

Bassie eyewear, a bestseller!

One of my early campaigns and brand endorsements was for Revlon in 1995

The face of South Africa's first National Women's Day. What a great honour!

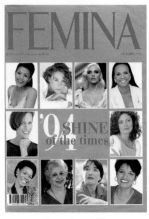

December 1994

March 1995

July 1995

November 1995

June 1996

October 1999

January 2001

June 2001

October 2001

June 2003

June 2003

June 2006

August 2008

September 2008

Face of Lux, 2008

March 2009

September 2009

Destiny, May 2017

© Linga Moonsamy

With Mama Graça Machel and Josina Machel

© Ramonda Jordan

With Dr Phumzile Mlambo-Ngcuka

With former Public Protector, Advocate Thuli Madonsela

PART VII

ON THE SHOULDERS OF GIANTS

TWENTY-NINE

I was always welcome at Madiba and his wife Mum Graça's homes, whether in Maputo or Houghton. Mum would say, 'Darling, come home, come and have lunch.' One of the things I absolutely loved was watching them together. It was so special to see this mature, beautiful kind of love. They were still giddy with love and just doted on each other. Her eyes would light up when she saw him, and he would look at her with such deep and profound love. I saw what true love looked like when I was with them.

We often went to lunch at Houghton. There would usually be oxtail and samp or tripe and *idombolo* (dumplings) on the menu. Or *umngqusho* – Tata enjoyed his samp and sugar beans – and other traditional foods like the humble chicken dish *umleqwa*. Their cook, Xoliswa Ndoyiya, would later release a book of all Tata's favourite recipes, titled *Ukutya Kwasekhaya*, which means 'food from home'. South Africans have many local delicacies and eating is a big part of our culture. Most families gather for Sunday lunch, where the 'seven colours' are served: beetroot for red, spinach for green, pumpkin for yellow, and so on, to create a plate that is bright with colour and packed with flavour.

It was a great privilege and joy to visit Tata and Mum Graça. He would sit at the head of the table and Mum would sit on his right, and they would often hold hands. Mum Graça was so attentive to Madiba. She called him Papa, as a term of endearment. 'Papa, can I do anything for you?' she would ask. 'Papa, would you like something else?' She would even tenderly cut his meat into perfect bite-sized chunks.

The conversation was always convivial. Tata was interested in people and their take on things. We'd traverse politics, children and business. But often he would just ask one simple question: 'Are you okay, darling?' He really did care.

They always kept the door open for me, and over time I became close to the Machel family too, particularly Mum's daughter Josina. I'll never forget the day I met her. Romeo and I had gone to formally inform Tata and Mum that we were getting married. Mid-conversation, this young woman comes running in, shrieking, hugging Madiba, hugging Mum, dancing and skipping around the room. It was Josina, who had come home for the holidays from the London School of Economics, where she was doing her master's degree in sociology. She had pulled up and found a Toyota RAV4 in the garage, wrapped in a ribbon. Security had opened the garage door by mistake and she'd seen her surprise present. That was the reason for the shouting, hugging and shrieks of delight.

When she calmed down, she noticed us and introduced herself and apologised most graciously for interrupting us. It was so sweet, though; she was so excited! So that is how I met Zina, as I came to call her. She calls me Mana, which means 'older sister' in Portuguese. We connected and have stayed close over the years. I was at her wedding when Madiba walked her down the aisle, and I love her children, Ziga and Fanon Mucave, like I birthed them. But I've never forgotten that first meeting.

I have another special memory of the family. This is a story I've never told in interviews. It just felt like it was something sacred and private, a precious and cherished memory for which I am grateful. One day in 2012, Mum phoned and said, 'Oh darling, do you think we could come for lunch if it's not too much trouble?' Too much trouble? Of course not! It would be an honour to have Madiba and Mum Graça in our home. Zina was to come with them, and I invited my in-laws, Jennifer and Mpho, and Romeo's and my siblings, so it was just a few of us.

Their security detail came the day before the lunch to scope the route from Houghton to our home and to determine how close we were to the nearest hospital, just in case of any problems. It was all rather difficult explaining to the guards at the estate that all these mysterious people would be coming the next day and that they didn't need to sign in. Of course, we didn't tell them that our guest was to be Nelson Mandela.

The next day, Tata and Mum Graça arrived. I had put two wingback chairs on the patio. Tata preferred to sit up straight in a wingback. If you visited his home in Houghton, he was always sitting in a wingback. So he and Mum sat in those chairs, overlooking the garden. I had set the table on the patio as well. After lunch, they sat on their wingbacks, and at one point Tata just closed his eyes and slept for a few minutes while the rest of us chatted away with Mum. It was all so peaceful, just a perfect, beautiful Sunday afternoon.

Funny, but I still remember what we had for lunch. Madiba was a man who was modest in his habits. I knew he didn't need fussy food. I love a good roast, so I made roast leg of lamb, a big, stuffed roast salmon, and chicken. I decided to cover all the bases with three proteins! I also knew Madiba liked a little glass of sweet Nederburg dessert wine from time to time. I wanted to make sure I had everything just right, so I ordered a case of that wine, but of course Papa only had one small glass.

Oh, it was magical, having those two beloved people in my home, with my family, breaking bread together. I tried to make sure everything was just right, you know … At some point, Mum said, 'Darling, relax, everything is fine.'

It was a privilege to have such extraordinary people in my life. With my dad passing in 2002 and Moeder in 2006, I am incredibly grateful to have had Mum and Madiba take me under their wing and raise me as their own.

I must also at this point pay tribute to Mama Winnie Madikizela-Mandela. I met her when I first met Madiba, when I was sixteen and took part in Miss Black South Africa. Mama Winnie was an extraordinary woman who'd had a very difficult life. She was treated appallingly by the apartheid state, yet she remained brave and resolute, and broke down barriers throughout her lifetime. She fought hard for our liberation and freedom and to keep Madiba's name alive when he was incarcerated. Mama Winnie represented a generation of women who were not afraid to die for their beliefs. The women of my generation stand on her great shoulders. I don't think she was properly honoured while she was alive for her immense contribution to the freedom we enjoy today.

My second-last interaction with Mama Winnie was when I was admitted to Milpark Hospital with a fractured ankle after a freak accident at my eldest son's piano recital. At around midday on 17 March 2016, I had left the office, saying to my colleagues that I would be back in an hour. Little did I know I wouldn't be back for three months!

It was a rainy day, and I slipped and fell in the school courtyard after the recital. I hit the back of my head and was concussed, and also suffered a complex fracture and dislocation of my right ankle. My injuries included a fracture of the fibula, a transverse fracture of the medial malleolus and an oblique fracture of the lateral malleolus. The fall itself was so bad that I lost consciousness, and on arrival at the hospital, it was determined that I needed emergency surgery to insert two long plates and a total of eleven screws.

I had never experienced such grotesque pain in my entire life. To hear your own bones break into multiple fragments is something else. It is difficult to describe the pain after that operation – it was so bad that I had to be placed on a morphine drip. I was wheelchair-bound in the weeks that followed, and went from a cast to a moonboot. After prolonged physiotherapy, I had to learn to walk again. All of that aside, it was so hard for me to lose my mobility and independence and be bedridden for weeks on end. It was just debilitating.

Mama Winnie was in Milpark at the same time for a back operation, and we were both in the executive wing. When she heard I was in the hospital, she extended an invitation for me to visit her. On that particular day, Penny Mkhize, one of the young ladies I was mentoring, and my friend Patience Mlengana were visiting me. (I was helped on my journey of recovery by my friends, who had a roster and would bring me my favourite food – I do love sushi, darling, and being in hospital for three weeks can drive a girl crazy.) I struggled into my wheelchair and Penny and Patience wheeled me next door to Mama's room.

When she saw me with my drips and cast, Mama exclaimed, 'Bassie, is that you? What happened to you?' She leant forward to embrace me – according to the nurse, it was the first time since her surgery that she'd done that. 'Look at you!' she kept saying, her eyes beaming as she held my hand. 'The last time I saw you was when Madiba had just passed and you were standing at the bottom of the stairs looking defeated and your eyes expressed so much pain,' she said. 'All I could do was hold you. You really stood in the gap for the family during that time, do you remember? You CANNOT be in this chair, Bassie, you need to get out of this chair.' I promised her I would. We talked for some time, and towards the end of our conversation, she charged me and all young women to take the baton from her generation, run the race and make a difference in the country. I took that to heart.

My final engagement with Mama Winnie was when I interviewed her for *Top Billing* on her eightieth birthday in September 2016. By then I was not doing on-camera work for *Top Billing*, but of course, when it's Mama Winnie, you dust off your microphone and you show up for the honour of conversing with her. My goodness, what a beauty she was, even at eighty, and always impeccably put together. She was still so full of vigour, with a sparkle in her eye, and she had great faith in our country and our people, even though we were not where we wanted to be. I hope everyone who watched that interview went away with a sense of responsibility to take the baton from the old guard, from the likes of Nomzamo Winnie Madikizela-Mandela, the one and only, and to do what they can to effect change in their own sphere of influence. I know that I feel her impact greatly in that regard every day.

THIRTY

In 2013, Madiba was in and out of hospital. We all knew that his health was precarious. Early that year I was called to a meeting at the SABC and asked whether Tswelopele Productions, and specifically *Top Billing*, could help them with Project 10, which was the codename for the programming they were preparing and that would run during the ten days of mourning when Madiba passed. They wanted us to interview people and have them talk about him in the past tense, even though he was still alive. They knew that I was close to him and his family.

I was horrified and absolutely livid when I heard this. I lambasted everyone in that boardroom. 'How can you even consider that it's acceptable to speak about somebody who's alive in the past tense?' I demanded. 'How dare you even approach me with this! This is an insult of the highest order...' The SABC was my biggest client at the time (I was producing *Top Billing*, *Pasella* and possibly *Top Dogs* and *Top Travel*, I can't recall exactly), but I told them they could keep their contracts, and stormed out. It was terribly upsetting, but the truth was that I knew he might pass at any time.

Towards the end of the year, as Madiba grew frailer, it was clear that the end was approaching. I remember the last time I saw Tata. I hadn't been to visit since he became so ill because I wanted to remember him as he was, but Zina and Mum Graça said to me, 'You had better come and see Papa. If you don't, you will always feel that you should have.'

So I went to Houghton and made my way through the media storm camped outside the house. Mum and Zina were there. They let me spend a few minutes with Tata. I told him I loved him and I thanked him for everything he'd done for this country and for humanity, and then I left. I left his bedside and I never saw him alive again.

A week or two later, Zina called. 'Mana, I'm going to call you from a different number later. When the phone rings, you must pick up, it's me.' She knows I don't answer calls from numbers I don't know. She also knew that her own phone wasn't secure. It was obvious that it was close to the end. The media interest in Madiba was at fever pitch. Everyone wanted to hear the news first from a reliable source, even if it meant tapping the family's phones.

The phone rang in the afternoon and it was Zina, saying it wasn't looking good. She asked if she could send her son Fanon over to my house. Of course she could. I kept saying, 'What do you mean, it's not looking good?' but she just said, 'I'll keep you posted.'

Later that afternoon, I got another call from Zina: Papa was gone. On 5 December 2013, we lost our beloved Madiba. The great son of the African soil had fought the good fight and finished his race. Now it was time for him to rest.

It was such a shock. It sounds crazy, because Tata was ninety-five and had been very sick, but I wasn't ready for him to go; people the world over were not ready. For many South Africans, it was as if we couldn't quite believe that Tata would ever leave us. He was not the dying type. It was almost as if we felt there would be some loophole for Nelson Mandela, as if we could negotiate with God to please let this extraordinary human live forever, because who would we be without him? What would become of humanity without his moral compass, his energy and goodness and magnanimity and leadership and being? He was, after all, our true north.

Tata's passing was such a great loss to the world. The death of Nelson Rolihlahla Mandela was the end of an era. But we are all better because he once lived. The world is a better place because of him.

So, after processing the news and curling up in a corner and having a good, ugly cry, I thought, well, what do I do next? So I went home; I went to Houghton. It was impossible to get near the house, of course, with the world's media outside and ordinary South Africans starting to arrive in droves to pay their respects. Zina arranged a pass for me and I managed to get through the crowd and into the gate.

Walking into Madiba's home, I automatically turned to the armchair where he used to sit. When you entered the Houghton house, the reception room with the piano was to the left, and to the right there was the reception lounge and that's where you would always find Tata. He would be sitting there in his armchair reading the papers with his feet elevated on an ottoman and this lovely cream mohair blanket covering his legs. Next to him would be a side table with all of the day's newspapers, even the Afrikaans ones, and he would read them all.

That December day, I walked into his peaceful home, the house in which I'd grown into an adult, and I turned to that chair and, of course, he wasn't there. Papa's remains had already been moved. The house never felt the same again.

There were so many people there. The family had gathered, and friends and dignitaries had come to pay their respects. I asked where Mum was, because I didn't want to be presumptuous and just go upstairs to her. I was raised properly. I was told to go to her upstairs, and there she was, sitting on a mattress on the floor, as is our custom when someone passes. Mum was broken. Not hysterical, but just hurting so deeply and intensely.

I stayed there with Mum and a few of her close friends. I remember Auntie Sheila Sisulu was sitting with her on the mattress, as well as Auntie Thandi Lujabe-Rankoe, an ANC struggle leader and later ambassador to Tanzania and Mozambique, and Auntie Tia Amelia Mingas, Mum's best friend since her university days in Portugal. Mum's daughter Zina and her son Malenga were there too. It was a sacred space, and we all just sat, mostly in silence. It is customary for people to come in to pay their respects, to offer a prayer or sing a hymn, but generally it's a place in which to be still and quiet, to be in the moment and to observe that moment and the sacredness of what the deceased represented.

Eventually, people started to leave. It was quite late, and I asked Mum what she would like me to do for her before I left, and she just said, 'Baby girl, do your best.' I've never forgotten that.

From that day until the funeral, I would leave my home at around five o'clock in the morning to go to Houghton to help Mum get ready and to make sure she had eaten and had her tea. All of Mum's mourning clothes were kept at my house, together with her headgears, shoes and bags – we had ten mourning outfits for the ten days of mourning. At seven o'clock, the world would descend on Papa's house, and she had to be up and dressed and in the lounge ready to receive the visitors who had come to pay their respects.

I remember arriving at dawn on one of the days. It was around five-thirty and the street was rather quiet. I stopped to look at all the tributes that had been left outside the house, and said a prayer. Every day, ordinary South Africans came to honour the memory of Madiba. They gathered in their hundreds. Many parents brought their children. People brought flowers and candles and pictures and thank-you letters. The corner of 4th Street and 12th Avenue was strewn with these deeply heartfelt gifts and messages; it was just an outpouring of love. It was beautiful to see the love his people and the world had for Tata.

On another day, I was upstairs with Mum when she asked me to go down and receive Oprah, Stedman Graham and Gayle King. They were accompanied by the actress Alfre Woodard and many of their friends. Oprah truly loved Madiba in every sense of the word and heeded his call to support education. She has done this so magnificently with her Oprah Winfrey Leadership Academy for Girls.

One night, I stayed until quite late, and when Mum was settled, I left the room where she was resting and went to turn off the lights around the house. I then made my way downstairs and curled up in a corner on the floor and just cried. Mandla Mandela found me. He is a gentle soul, and he said to me, '*Sisi*, don't cry. *Uwu gqibile umsebenzi wakhe* (Madiba has finished the great work). You should go home now, you need to get some rest.'

I was back the next day, and the next. There is a group of us – Rebs Mogoba, Malaika Motlekar, my sister Johanna, Dr Mashadi Motlana, and, of course, Zina – whom Mum Graça calls 'daughters of my heart'. We sat with her, made sure she ate and drank her water, reminded her to take her vitamins, and just made sure she knew that her 'daughters' were there to support her. It was my great privilege and honour to serve her and her every need in every way, at every moment. For Mum

Graça to trust me in her most vulnerable moment reminded me of her essence, her truth and her belief in humanity. She didn't *have* to love me or embrace me; she *chose* to raise me as a daughter. Mum: my *SHERO*, thank you. There is absolutely no need for me to say anything more, but *obrigado, ndo livhuwa, ngiyabonga, ndiyabulela, ke a leboga, dankie, ndza khensa, ngiyathokoza, enkosi, ke a leboha*. You, Mother, are an extraordinary leader, and it has been a privilege to sit at your feet.

Graça Machel is a truly phenomenal woman. Her life hasn't been easy, first losing her beloved husband, Samora Machel, in such a tragic way, and then, as a Mozambican, marrying a revered South African leader. The absolute grace with which Mum Graça carried herself – and continues to carry herself – is remarkable. This is one of the things I've learnt from her. Even in the midst of the storm, you don't lose your grace.

I also admire how Mum has kept the legacies of both her husbands alive. I visited her recently in Maputo for Josina's birthday and thanksgiving, and in the main reception room of her house, there are portraits of Papa Machel and Papa Mandela, the leaders and liberators of our people, side by side, taking pride of place.

THIRTY-ONE

The official memorial service took place on Tuesday 10 December 2013 at FNB Stadium in Johannesburg. Every South African will remember that day. It was raining as the public and dignitaries from all over the world came to say farewell. Mum Graça asked me to stay with her in the holding room, which I did. President Zuma and his wife Tobeka Madiba were also there, as was Ruth Mompati, a veteran and icon of the liberation struggle.

Mum Graça asked me to please make sure that Auntie Ruth got to her seat on the stage. Auntie Ruth was in her nineties and needed a stick to walk, so I took her bags and helped her from the holding room across the field, up the steps and onto the stage. Madiba's eldest daughter, Makaziwe, screamed at me as I climbed those stairs. 'You are not a Mandela,' she said. 'You are not welcome. There's no chair for you here.' She was quite right. I am not a Mandela. I am a proud Makgalemele. But I wasn't there for a chair; I was there to seat Auntie Ruth. In quiet composure, I held my tongue. I wasn't going to get into an argument. I was there to give Madiba a dignified send-off and do what Mum had asked me to do. I seated Auntie Ruth and made my way to the back of the marquee where I stood for the entire service, with the rain pouring onto my back. I stood there for a good three hours, unmoved, unshaken. I got pneumonia a few days later. I didn't know at the time that I was pregnant with Bontle, my gift of a girl. One soul had departed and another was on its way.

There was a lot of unnecessary unkindness and unpleasantness behind the scenes. Zelda la Grange writes about it in Chapter 13 of her book *Good Morning, Mr Mandela*.* In that chapter, she chronicles accurately, painfully and in detail what transpired from the moment the news broke about Madiba's passing. One of the logistical issues that we faced was making sure that his closest friends were treated with the absolute dignity they deserved. At one point, I was asked to go to Luthuli House, the ANC head office, to collect accreditation for those on the 'friends list', only to discover that just half of the people on the list had been accredited. The memorial was the next day. We had people from abroad flying to South Africa for the memorial and funeral, but no idea whether they would be accredited. On top of that, no invitations were sent out, and Madiba's friends were expected to just go to the stadium on a first-come, first-served basis and then find seating among the crowds. This included people like Archbishop Desmond Tutu! In one paragraph, Zelda writes: 'At times Josina, Basetsana and I all yelled at one another, then we cried hysterically and then would pick up the pieces and try to find order again. We knew our outbursts were safe with one another no matter what nature.' Reading that chapter brought me to tears all over again.

Five days later, it was time to bury Madiba at his home in Qunu. While he was born in the rural village of Mvezo in the Eastern Cape, Madiba chose to make the nearby village of Qunu his home because it was where he had grown up. It is a small, rural place where people still live off the land. In fact, probably not much has changed since Madiba played there as a child. The rolling hills and valleys set against a backdrop of dramatic sunsets and starry nights give the place an almost magical feel.

I accompanied Mum Graça to the ANC memorial service at Air Force Base Waterkloof, from where Tata's body was to be flown in a military plane to Qunu. I donned my full ANC Women's League regalia and sat right behind Mum. I was stocked up with water and a stash of those Lindt chocolate balls that she likes, and I held her handbag. While Mum and the family flew out from Waterkloof, I rushed to

---

* Zelda la Grange, *Good Morning, Mr Mandela* (Cape Town: Penguin Random House, 2014).

Lanseria to catch a flight to Qunu in businessman Faizal Motlekar's jet with some of the ministers. Malaika, Johanna, Rebs and Mashadi had gone to Qunu the day before, at Mum's request.

Arriving in Qunu, I encountered one of the most extraordinary scenes. All the way from the airport, over the hills and valleys as far as the eye could see, people were standing alongside the road to receive Madiba, son of the soil. Life in the villages came to a halt as thousands of men, women and children lined the streets in a simple guard of honour to welcome Nelson Rolihlahla Mandela home to his final resting place.

The following day was the funeral, and that was a huge undertaking. People had come from all over the world. Besides family and dear friends like Ahmed Kathrada, Archbishop Desmond Tutu and George Bizos, President Jacob Zuma and all the cabinet members were present, and there was a big showing of international guests, from musicians, models and actors to presidents and world-renowned ministers such as the reverends Jesse Jackson and Al Sharpton. Icons, world-shakers and history-makers all attended to say farewell and pay their last respects.

Inside a huge marquee, in front of a big portrait of Madiba, was his coffin, draped in the South African flag and flanked by ninety-five candles, one for each year of his life. It was a beautiful and moving sight. The day was a blur of emotion, but what I remember best are those candles, and the sound of children singing. Madiba loved children, and he would have loved the beautiful children's choir that came to sing farewell – *hamba kahle* – to their *Khulu*.

I continue to do what I can to promote the values that Nelson Mandela espoused and represented, and to honour him and his legacy. Since its inception in 2007, I have been on the board of the Nelson Mandela Institute for Education and Rural Development. This is one of the legacy organisations that Madiba founded – along with the Nelson Mandela Foundation, the Nelson Mandela Children's Fund, the Nelson Mandela Children's Hospital and the Mandela Rhodes Foundation – to continue his vision. It is well known that Madiba was passionate about education and children, and the institute was founded to focus on improving the quality of primary-school education for rural children. It starts with educating children in their mother tongue, the proven best practice for literacy, and then emphasising literacy and numeracy in the foundation phase. The institute, based at Madiba's alma mater of Fort Hare, is built around partnerships with schools and communities, and relies on donor funding.

It's important work and I find it most fulfilling. I was privileged to be exposed to the greatness of Nelson Mandela, to learn the meaning of true servant leadership, and to witness real humility and greatness. People all around the world continue to commemorate his immense contribution. In 2009, the United Nations officially declared 18 July, Madiba's birthday, as Nelson Mandela International Day in recognition of his dedication to serving humanity. In South Africa, we are encouraged to spend sixty-seven minutes doing something for the less fortunate on Mandela Day. This is in remembrance of the sixty-seven years he fought for social justice in our country.

We can all continue his legacy in our own way. We can all effect change and bring others along on that journey. We just have to remember to find the Mandela in us.

PART VIII

THE HUSTLE IS ON

THIRTY-TWO

THE HUSTLE IS ON

Like so many women, I balance a busy career and a busy home life. Being a working mom is hard, there's no doubt about it, and I think every working mom could attest to that. However, I'm a happy working mom. It brings me immense joy and delight, and is very fulfilling. I think I would pull my hair out if I were a lady of leisure, going off to the spa for a treatment and worrying about my nails and hair all the time. That's not who I am. I am someone who needs the stimulation and sense of achievement that a career brings.

I also know my limitations. I'm not able to do everything myself, and I'm not trying to win the trophy of Miss Superwoman and Mom of the Year. To manage this busy life, I've had to create an infrastructure that works. I fully acknowledge that I'm privileged in that I am able to have the extra help and support that makes life run somewhat smoother. We are so lucky to have Rakgadi, and when I was expecting Kgosi, Mary Singini joined the family. She is more like a daughter to us and a friend to the kids, and a beautiful and kind Malawian darling. Mary is such a delight and cares deeply about the children's well-being. Now, with the children all at school and us living quite far from their schools, we have Victor Mogale, who assists with the driving. Victor has been helping us for eight years and he is fiercely protective of the children – they call him Malome (Uncle), and he gives the two youngest lots of piggyback rides, *nogal*. He does tend to indulge the kids a tad, buying them ice cream after school, but they have an incredible connection with him. It gives me such peace of mind to know that my children are in good hands.

My executive assistant, Louise Sherriff, is amazing. She runs my work, family and travel diaries, and also helps coordinate my children's activities. Every single day she sends me my diary and the kids' diary on email and WhatsApp, and of course it's all scheduled in my Google calendar as well, so every minute of my day is well scheduled and planned properly. She tells me who's got swimming, water polo, rugby or soccer, and who's got piano lessons and when Bontle has ballet, who needs to bring fruit, vegetables and tinned food to school, and who needs to be where, at what time – the whole picture for the day. I actually don't know what I would do without Louise. She is my 'sheriff', as her surname suggests, and runs a tight ship. She takes no prisoners and worries about my health and well-being – she routinely schedules my workout sessions and holds me accountable. If meetings are running late, she graciously comes into the boardroom and reminds me that it's time for me to leave for a school commitment or gym. That lovely lady keeps me sane. She's got my back.

If I can show up for a soccer match, I do, but there are times when I can't. Early on in my mothering I really tried to be that mom who shows up everywhere and goes to everything. But with three kids who are fully engaged, it's actually not practical or possible. I've come to realise that it's okay, I don't have to go to everything, and I don't feel guilty about it any more. You might sometimes be judged by what I call the 'car-park brigade', when you're rushing off to work, suited up and not in your yoga gear, with little time to chit-chat, but that's okay. I am blessed that I work because I want to, not because I have to, and that's a true privilege considering the socio-economic status of most women in our country.

My #Tribe today is very busy, and it's not just at school. There are social arrangements, play dates and birthday parties every weekend. I try to show up where I can, and if I can't, I ask a friend if she wouldn't mind helping out. I also have #DaughtersOfMyHeart, young people I have mentored through the years and who form a very strong and solid part of our family. Those 'baby girls' truly show up for us. It's true what they say: it takes a village to raise a child. I am so fortunate to have a great community of friends and extended family. We are blessed to have people who lovingly assist us.

Romeo's parents, Mama Jenny and Papa Mpho, are very involved in their grandkids' lives. The children love to go to Dawn Park to stay with Koko and Khulu during school holidays. Our children are growing up multilingual. I speak to them in English and Sesotho; Romeo in English and isiZulu; and Rakgadi in Setswana and Sesotho. Mary, a Tumbuka from Malawi, is teaching them Chichewa. What a gift she is! Their grandparents speak to them in isiZulu and Setswana.

It was a conscious decision to first let them learn their mother tongue proficiently. It's important for every child's brain development to first learn to speak in his or her native language. Nathi started at the Montessori school down the road at three years old – I keep all the children at home for the first three years – and he only spoke Sesotho. The teachers were frustrated that he didn't understand English, but I said to them, 'Don't you worry, there is no rush, he'll pick it up along the way' – which of course he did. Now the boys are both studying isiZulu at school and doing well in it. It's a real advantage to be able to converse fluently in many of our South African languages.

All my kids start at the Glen Montessori School at age three and then go to big school at age six. I decided that they would have a Montessori grounding when I learnt that Google founders Larry Page and Sergey Brin credited their Montessori education with their success. Montessori is a method of education that is based on self-directed activity, hands-on learning and collaborative play. In Montessori classrooms, children make their own creative choices in their learning. Romeo and I made a conscious decision to give our children that foundation.

I love being a mother and I love being with my children. People often say, 'Gosh, you have so much patience,' but I just really enjoy them. I think it's because I'm a mature mom. At forty-five, I have a five-year-old. My friends' kids are in high school, some are even at varsity, and they always remind me to enjoy my children, because empty-nest syndrome is real and you miss the mess and the busyness, including the toilet paper that has run on the floor because no one cared to roll it back. My friends say they miss the empty milk cartons and the cranberry juice that you thought was there but ... *dololo* (nothing). And when you get home late and all you want is a peanut butter sandwich with tea because you can't be bothered to make a meal, then you realise ... peanut butter *dololo*, and all you want to do is cry. So I try to be fully present in every moment I have with them. I don't want to miss these special moments. I know people say it's not the quantity but the quality of time that you spend with your children, but for me, I try to do both. The quantity and the quality. And to be there consciously.

I've been highly blessed on this journey that I've always longed for, being a mother. I've been granted the privilege to raise these beautiful and precious beings. Yes, sometimes I don't get it right. Sometimes I make mistakes. Sometimes I feel frustrated because they just won't listen. And you see, I'm my mother's child as well. I don't raise brats. I'm very clear that my children will respect their elders; in fact, they will respect all people, whoever they may be, and they won't grow up to have a sense of entitlement. They will be kind, they will be considerate, they will be compassionate. I just want them to be good people. Just good people. What they choose to do with their careers, their destiny, their life's purpose, is truly up to them. But at the end of the day, if they are good and decent members of humanity, it will be well with my soul and a life well lived.

I so love that poem by Kahlil Gibran, 'On Children'. There are a few lines that really speak to me as a mother:

Your children are not your children.
They are the sons and daughters of Life's longing for itself.
They come through you but not from you,
And though they are with you, they belong not to you.
You may give them your love but not your thoughts,
For they have their own thoughts.

THIRTY-THREE

One thing I've discovered about myself is that I am a serial entrepreneur by nature. I'm not someone who sticks to one thing in perpetuity. I guess I get it from my late parents, who were serial entrepreneurs too. I love a new challenge, and I've never been afraid to go into different industries and dabble in things that pique my interest. I am not afraid to fail. Yes, I do take risks, but as an entrepreneur, over the years, I have learnt to take calculated risks.

At the same time, I believe it's important to know where your own strengths and weaknesses lie, and not try to be a jack-of-all-trades. But if you are going into a new area, always know what you know, and know what you don't know. Employ people who are smarter and sharper than you. I always surround myself with the best brains and people with skills that I don't have. I have learnt that this is one of the hallmarks of the entrepreneurs I admire and look up to.

This attitude has led me into business in industries as diverse as mining, travel, retail and property. I've been fortunate to succeed in many of these ventures, but I've had my share of failures too. The lessons I've learnt along the way have been invaluable, but I've paid some serious school fees, I can tell you that for free.

Let me take you back to 2005. I have this beautiful baby boy for whom I've been waiting for so long, and I am involved in a thriving television production company. My life is full and fulfilling. But an opportunity arises for black female–owned companies to apply for mining prospecting rights across the country.

Africa is rich in natural resources, and I've always believed that if you really want to create generational wealth, this is a space to seriously consider. So Lindiwe Leketi, Pollet Tebeila and I started Uzalile Investments, a black female–owned junior mining company. When Nathi was just a month old and still being breastfed, I left him at home and set off for Polokwane with my two partners, breast pump in hand, to apply for prospecting rights. Some of the prospecting applications were in joint venture with Sekoko Resources, owned by Pollet's husband, Tim Tebeila. Of the five we applied for, we were awarded four, three in Soutpansberg with deposits of coking coal, and one in the Waterberg area, a lucrative farm called Vetleegte with a coal resource estimate of 500 million tonnes. This was in November 2006.

Great news! Except that it's one thing to have a prospecting right and another to actually prospect and, ultimately, mine. Unless you have an investor, you can't take the next steps – exploration, indication of mining and financing capabilities, production of a bankable feasibility study, and the development and mining of the coal resource. Uzalile and Sekoko spent their own fair share in this process. For two years, we visited mining indabas and spoke to potential investors, and finally some Australian investors, Firestone Energy, came on board through Sekoko Resources and injected capital into the business so that we could do the exploration and eventually start the mining operation. We were all set to go, and so optimistic. Coal was the new gold. Eskom needed coal for their power plants and we were set to export the metallurgical coal as well. It was all set to be quite a lucrative business.

The Department of Mineral Resources and the Mining Charter are very clear that South Africans should hold the majority stake in any joint venture with international partners and investors. Moreover, the department is unequivocal in having women participate in this male-dominated industry. Long story short, the deal between Firestone and Sekoko was signed and sealed when Firestone and its partners concluded a very complicated share-swap structure on the back of their investment. Overnight, my Uzalile partners and I, by virtue of the joint venture, ended up being the minority of the minorities in our own company. Firestone Energy was now the major shareholder.

Of course, this was completely against the grain of what the department was trying to achieve, which was to make sure that women – black women in particular – could participate meaningfully in the mining space. We ended up in a protracted legal battle with Firestone that dragged on for a good five years. They, of course, had more muscle and deeper pockets than us, and, in fact, the case remains unresolved. Firestone has subsequently gone bankrupt – this is a company that was listed on both the JSE and the Australian Stock Exchange – although I've heard they are planning to resuscitate themselves on the back of the Waterberg project, which involves our property Vetleegte. So I am watching this with much interest.

Mining is a brutal industry and you need staying power, unrelenting resolve and liquidity to be in the game and stay in the game. The experience with Firestone Energy didn't necessarily deter us. We still wanted to participate in this space, so we started a new company, Pro Direct Investments. Lindiwe and I applied for prospecting rights in the Mpumalanga province. We currently have three projects on the go, two in the prospecting phase and one in full mining operation. We decided to go small scale and also to work with people who really know the industry – the best geologists, engineers, mining lawyers and site managers. So we burnt our fingers in the coal-mining space and paid some serious school fees, but we managed to regain our footing and we continue to go from strength to strength.

One thing that I found quite difficult with the Uzalile–Sekoko relationship was that we had become close family friends with the Tebeilas, to a point where I was godmother to their twins. When the coal deal collapsed, it did not only strain the professional relationships, but also the personal relationships. Our children had nothing to do with the business decisions we made and did not deserve to suffer and be dragged into the whole mess. I guess whoever came up with the saying that business and friends don't mix was onto something. Today our families are reconciled, as I believe that life is too short to hold grudges. Let go and let God.

THIRTY-FOUR

In 2004, I collaborated with three women to create PHAB Holdings (Pty) Ltd. PHAB was an acronym based on the first letter of each of our names: P for Potlako, H for Hlobisile, A for Angela and B for Basetsana. We all had different and complementary skills to bring to the business. One of the subsidiaries of the company was PHAB Properties.

Potlako Gasennelwe studied in London and has a master's degree in built environment. She also holds a bachelor's degree in interior architecture. We met through *Top Billing*, when I featured a number of the homes she had decorated. Angela Kupane, like her name suggests, was an angel, and really gifted in the area of interiors and soft furnishings. Tragically, about two years after we started the business, she was brutally murdered during a break-in at her parents' home. What a loss to us all. Hlobi de Almeida is a businesswoman, and she decided quite early on to pursue other interests, so Potlako and I ended up running the business together.

Our focus at PHAB was the acquisition, development and management of brownfields (abandoned or underused building facilities that are available for reuse), through joint partnerships with private and public stakeholders. Part of the model was gentrification in the Johannesburg CBD – to convert buildings into lofts and entry-level apartments with one or two bedrooms, geared towards young people starting their first jobs and who wanted to own property and be part of the city vibe. It was very exciting to be part of the plan to rejuvenate the CBD, and we were delighted to have Hollard partner with us.

Our first development was at 10 Anderson Street, which we named Dogon and Ashanti. It comprised 132 units that we sold off-plan. Things went very well at first – we sold the whole lot! But the timing turned out to be terrible. The 2008 financial crisis hit, and a substantial number of our buyers couldn't raise bonds. By the time we had finished the conversion and renovation, half of our sales had effectively fallen through and we had to take those units back into a rental pool. From the beginning we had problems with non-payment of rent, and by 2012 the business was really battling. Our partner, Hollard, bought our majority stake in the joint-venture company, Leungo Investments, and Potlako and I both moved on with our lives.

We still wanted to be in the property game, though, but we were not convinced that the model we had envisaged would work in the financial environment of the time. We turned our attention to Reconstruction and Development Programme (RDP) housing and won a number of tenders to build RDP houses in the Eastern Cape, Sebokeng and Hammanskraal. We established a construction company and built houses from scratch, start to finish.

Let me tell you, that business was tough! For a start, you really have to engage with the communities in which you are working, get their buy-in to come and build there, employ a certain percentage of locals, and you have to be there to manage the project. It's not the kind of business you can initially run remotely, because the reality is that if you are not there, hands-on, then you are paying wages without the project really moving forward.

Oh my goodness, I will never forget the day Potlako and I were held hostage by the labourers in Hammanskraal. The client hadn't paid, and we tried to explain that we would pay them the following week, but the labourers would have none of it. Before we knew it, one guy had locked the gate to the plant and another had blown his whistle, and in no time, the community emerged from every corner. They were all shouting, '*Yenza iFET … etsa FET.*' We understood that they wanted us to do an electronic funds transfer, an EFT, right then and there.

After trying to negotiate for what must have been three hours, it was starting to get dark. Someone in the community made a call to the police, and they basically came and rescued us. When the police arrived, the foremen who were tasked with looking after the building site claimed they had no idea where the keys to the gate were. The police eventually had to break the lock and force the gate open. After extracting us, they escorted our cars all the way to the nearest highway in order to make sure we made it home safely. The strange thing is that I can't say that Potlako and I ever felt like our lives were in danger during the incident. I think it's because I really identified with the workers. I could understand the desperation that had created the situation. We just sat on the tins of paint with our hard hats and boots and engaged with the community.

I couldn't help but think of my mother and father, and their business, Zam-Zam Construction. How proud Moeder would have been to see her daughter managing a construction project and holding her own in a crisis, together with her partner. I just became that Soweto girl who was unafraid and spoke about the reality of how difficult it is to run a business, trying to create jobs when you have no guarantee when your client is going to pay. So we said, well, we are all in this struggle together. *A luta continua!* I laugh about it now. I've been in the hustle for a long time.

That RDP construction business was male-dominated and very competitive, much like mining, but we worked at it and we found our niche in the space. What killed that business for us in the end was the corrupt tender process. We would submit our tenders, get the file in on time, all the documents in place, and then we would get short-listed. At that point, there would be a conversation along the lines of: 'You guys are looking good … If you really want this, maybe we should have an offline conversation …'

Now this just wasn't the way we did business. We were not 'brown envelope' kind of girls (people who pay bribes), and if that's what it took, we'd rather not have the work. We had worked really hard at the RDP housing model for three years and PHAB was quite successful, but if we couldn't win tenders honestly, we couldn't work in that space.

But don't you worry, honey, we were not done with the property business just yet! Around 2015, we started to look at a new business model. In those days, the Department of Public Works partnered with black-owned property companies to provide housing and office space for government departments. They called them 911s (leases for nine years and eleven months). Instead of buying these properties, the departments would take a ten-year lease. You would put up minimal collateral, and the banks would lend you money on the back of that lease. There was no problem getting the money, as the government guaranteed it, and the government would never go under, right? It was a very lucrative business model. People were making millions.

PHAB went into that space. We began to identify suitable properties around the country. We started working on a really big project in Pretoria for an intergovernmental organisation tasked with maintaining international peace and security, and developing friendly relations among nations. This was to be their South African headquarters. We had made it to the final round and were at the stage of presenting the floor plans, the look and the feel of the building, the parking access and the magnificent entrance that would greet both local and international visitors and guests. Potlako and I had both learnt an inordinate amount in the process, from coming up with a creative concept to nearing its final execution. It was valuable experience. We were very excited. It was going to be by far the biggest deal our little property company had done and we were well on our way.

We had funding for the project from one of the top four banks and were good to go, until an unfortunate situation derailed the whole business. News broke about a property mogul who had received R600 million from a bank, allegedly without following due process. Questions were asked about the legitimacy of the lease, the tender process and all the other intricacies of a transaction of that size. There were allegations of bribery, and a huge media scandal and legal case ensued.

Immediately, the department stopped issuing 911s and would only give month-to-month contracts. No bank was going to fund a business that was dependent on a month-to-month contract. It was too risky. It was like watching dominoes fall.

That was the end of our adventures in the property business. I think after running that race for the better part of a decade, we just ran out of steam. We said, you know what, we've given it our best shot, and there have been some great wins and there have been some spectacular losses. We graciously doffed our hats and bowed out like the ladies we are!

THIRTY-FIVE

O f all the things I've done in my life as a businesswoman and entrepreneur, the creation of content is my passion. It's my happy place. If you ask me what really gets me out of bed every day, it is this drive to create content.

Tswelopele Productions is still going strong after twenty-five years, and I've continued to work in that business while developing other interests. In 2009, I was part of a consortium that was formed with a view to starting a television channel. The Connect consortium came together to take advantage of the envisaged digital terrestrial television migration. This development was going to open up many more channels and would equate to an increase in capacity for content. Who was going to fill all that airtime? Well, that's what we hoped to do. The consortium's plan was to meet the anticipated growth in demand for local content by producing local channels to be carried by the existing broadcasters.

Unfortunately, digital migration was, and continues to be, delayed. It's a saga that I won't go into, but it turned out that our Connect Channel idea was premature. After formulating an entire strategy with a full scheduling slate, and making it through the various stages of adjudication, instead of being awarded a channel, we became an enterprise development entity under MultiChoice tasked with creating a block of content.

At the time, MultiChoice was looking for low-cost, high-volume content that could be produced quickly, so game shows were the perfect solution. We produced and delivered hundreds of hours of studio shows. So, while we did not get the channel we had hoped for, MultiChoice still gave us our initial breakthrough and helped us create many jobs.

Content trends started pointing towards the reality genre, with shows like *Keeping Up with the Kardashians* taking the world by storm. As a company, and with buy-in from MultiChoice, we moved in that direction, producing some innovative local formats, and the viewer numbers really started to climb.

Currently, Connect Channel produces two of the highest-rating television shows on the Mzansi Magic channel, which sits within MultiChoice's Compact Bouquet. *Our Perfect Wedding* is a reality show that follows engaged couples as they put the final touches to their dream wedding and gives viewers a front-row seat to the nuptials. What is lovely about *Our Perfect Wedding* is that it cuts across cultural differences and resonates with a broad audience. It is both inspirational and aspirational. People who never thought they would be on television are all of a sudden open to the experience because of this remarkable show. It's quite magical. I mean, who doesn't love a happy ending? I know I do!

Our other hugely successful show is called *Date My Family*. This fun and entertaining programme helps singletons find love by setting them up with a potential partner's family. It seeks to explore that age-old truth that we don't just marry a partner, we also join their family. Like *Our Perfect Wedding*, it is hugely popular with the mass market. Both shows are also currently being produced in Zambia, *Date My Family* is about to launch in Botswana and *Our Perfect Wedding Zimbabwe* is currently in production. What this tells us as a company is that our work has pan-African appeal, and this presents remarkable opportunities for skills transfer and content origination.

These two shows were real game-changers in the genre in terms of how they created a conversation on social media and, more specifically, in how they inspired 'Black Twitter' to engage in second-screening. When those shows are on air on Sunday night, Twitter is abuzz. We live in an age where people don't just engage with content on TV, they also want to have their say at the same time. You watch the show on television, and while you are watching, you get on Twitter to engage with other viewers all over the country.

Content is no longer consumed in a linear fashion, thanks to on-demand TV services such as Netflix, which have become real disruptors in the space. Viewers are also creating their own user-generated content around shows, which is a great tool for gathering data.

We don't only make shows to entertain viewers; we also produce another type of show that we call 'social intervention' or 'emotainment' reality TV. In these shows, we actually get involved in people's lives and help them by intervening in some way. These are real-life stories featuring real people with real struggles, and by involving trained psychologists and other professionals we try to assist the subjects with tangible solutions.

One such is docu-reality show *Utatakho* – a Xhosa term that means 'your father'. In black culture, it's often said that if you don't know your father and his ancestry, calamities may befall you. To avoid this, you need to find your father and perform certain ceremonies and rites. It is believed that this will greatly improve the situation. You might find a good job, for example, and have a happy and prosperous life. Of course, there are many people in South Africa who don't know the identity of their father, or whose fathers are absent, or who have never actually been able to confirm paternity.

The journey on *Utatakho* starts when someone writes in to the show with a question relating to paternity. It might be a father who believes he is being lied to about his child's paternity, or a mother who wants to be vindicated in her claim of paternity, or a child who wants to know who their father really is. So you might have a young person of twenty-five who has never known his dad but who has heard stories, or may be wondering whether this uncle who used to come around could be the one … We speak to the family and look into the history, and ultimately do a DNA test to ascertain whether or not there is a biological relationship.

This show can be incredibly painful to make and to watch. You see how people's lives have fallen apart because they don't know their parentage. Sometimes we ascertain who the father is and he just isn't interested in taking responsibility. There are times when I'm editing the show and think, 'I can't air this. It's too gut-wrenchingly painful.' Occasionally, once we've wrapped, the family will in hindsight say,

'Please don't put this on the television,' and we have to respect that. But *Utatakho* can also be incredibly beautiful and moving. Families are healed. Relationships are forged.

Another powerful and popular intervention reality show is *Please Step In*. Viewers write to us for help when they have a major family crisis. The letters are really heartbreaking: 'our son is a drug addict', 'our marriage is falling apart'. 'Please step in,' they ask us, and we do. We bring in experts, from psychologists to social workers or drug counsellors, depending on the problem, and they help the family to find a resolution. Another programme we produce for SABC3, *Saving Our Marriage*, is in a similar vein. We go into struggling couples' lives and see how we can help them pick up the pieces of their relationship.

We know we are dealing with very sensitive issues, and that's why we use professionals. When the cameras stop rolling and we've wrapped, we continue to assist the families to find resolution and peace going forward. You know, most people don't have access to therapy or a support group, or even friends in whom they can confide. They certainly can't afford a DNA test. So although we are providing content and entertainment, we are also providing a service.

People really love the reality genre. It is still hugely popular the world over. Viewers want to be entertained and get a glimpse of other people's lives. But they also want to learn; they want to be able to take away something of value from someone else's experience. So maybe when they watch some other person's struggle, they recognise something of themselves in it. They might hear a marriage counsellor's advice to a couple and think, you know what? That might help me in my marriage. This is what we mean when we say we aim to produce content that resonates with the viewer.

And it's so evident in the feedback we get on Twitter. People saying, 'I was watching *Saving Our Marriage* and you know what, wow! Now I know what's been going wrong in my marriage.' We are giving people the tools to communicate and interact better with their loved ones, and to stand a better chance of making their unions work.

Television is a very powerful medium, as it can be used to help and educate people as well as entertain. It can inspire change and raise consciousness. The majority of our people don't have the resources to change their lives. Most live below the breadline. We live in a country where teenagers think getting pregnant is a good option because then they can get a social grant. The gap between that teenage girl and me demands that I use what I have at my disposal for the greater good. I am a television producer, so how can I use this powerful medium of television to impact lives? When I'm making a tangible difference in people's lives, only then will I be fulfilling my life's purpose and my calling as a teacher.

And we are having an impact. We get thank-you letters from people who've been on our shows. Thank you for restoring my dignity, because now I know who I am, where I come from. Thank you for restoring my family, my marriage. And we get letters from viewers who have learnt from those people. That warms my heart, and I feel grateful for the opportunity to do this important work.

THIRTY-SIX

As you've probably noticed reading the story of my career, I am a big believer in collaboration. In my businesses, I am generally in partnership with someone else, who brings different skills and attributes to the project. Partnerships are not necessarily easy, and indeed can be difficult to manage. I believe in being honest with each other, and in being able to agree to disagree without disrespect. Agreeing to disagree means I might hold a different viewpoint, but I don't negate your contribution towards what we're discussing. There's an understanding that we each have so much value to add, collectively, for the greater good of the business. Working with friends is even more complex, but a business needs to transcend that level of familiarity for the desired output and vision to be realised.

I tend to partner with and employ a disproportionate number of women. This is quite deliberate. People often say that it's hard to work with women. I disagree. In both Tswelopele Productions – where I have been in partnership with Patience for twenty-five years – and Connect Channel, we employ predominantly women. It's a creative environment in which I find women work well. I have worked with women at PHAB Properties, and my partner in another company, Pro Direct, is a woman.

There's another reason, though. Women have historically been excluded and economically disadvantaged in the workplace. And a black woman has been triply disadvantaged: by marginalisation, poverty and patriarchy. As an employer and an entrepreneur, I think it's my duty to try to move the needle if I can, to bring women into my businesses, into the workplace, where equal pay for equal work is the norm and not the exception, and to nurture them to be their best selves and realise their full potential.

When I look at my own journey, I often say that I stand on the shoulders of great women, women who continue to inspire me to be the best version of myself, to be my authentic self, to push boundaries and to take other women along in the process. I think of iconic women such as Mama Winnie Madikizela-Mandela, Mama Albertina Sisulu, Auntie Ruth Mompati, Mum Graça Machel, Mrs Zanele Mbeki, Professor Thuli Madonsela, Dr Phumzile Mlambo-Ngcuka, Professor Mamokgethi Phakeng and Lindiwe Sisulu. And I think of the business-women who served as an example and inspiration, women such as Felicia Mabuza-Suttle, Wendy Appelbaum, Louisa Mojela, Irene Charnley, Nolitha Fakude and Phyllis Newhouse. I think of my early mentor Doreen Morris, who had such a huge and positive impact on my life. And of course I think of my primary role model, my mother. I stand first on the shoulders of that woman. She was a tangible role model who showed me what a woman can achieve with very little, and who demonstrated the values of partnership, courage, fortitude, resili-ence and brilliance. Even within our household, I saw how Moeder collaborated with Rakgadi to raise us and instil in us a value system. It wasn't necessarily framed as a collaboration, but they both needed each other to 'do' life and they were the best example of partnership.

And so that's my blueprint for understanding that when women work together, magic happens. I am the daughter, the sister, the aunt, the mother, the wife, the friend, the confidante and the businesswoman I am because of the women who have surrounded me and who con-tinue to surround me, and whom I consciously seek to surround me. There is a saying that you are the average of the five people with whom you spend the most time. I say you are the product of the people you hang around with, so choose them wisely.

I can't talk about collaboration and partnerships without talking about Romeo, my husband and my greatest collaborator. To be honest, I've had reservations about going into business with my husband. It can put a great deal of strain on a relationship.

Romeo and I first went into partnership in a business early on in our relationship, around 1999, and it was a disaster. Here's what happened. He had his eight to five, and I had mine, but we had this vision of working together as a team. We thought, let's venture out and supplement our incomes. We were going to get married and have children, so why not start building something for them, for the future? My mom always said you need to have something for a rainy day. This was going to be it. On his initiative, we bought a Spar in Bryanston, which was a going concern. We partnered with another couple, our good friends Ntombi and Carlos Pereira. Carlos had retail experience. We did our due diligence, but the business was a disaster. It seemed, in the end, that the books had been cooked. The sellers took us for a big, fat ride. Six months in, we had to shut the doors. (We remain very good friends with the Pereiras.)

Both the suppliers and the seller sued us. To have a business fail is a terrible thing, but when you are Basetsana and Romeo and your business fails, you end up on the front page of the Sunday papers. It was a painful experience. We were just starting out in our life together as a couple and this venture could easily have sunk us. We put everything we had into buying into that business – everything I'd saved and built since I got my first pay cheque at twenty. All the extra money Romeo had made and saved with his side gigs as a DJ on the weekends. We lost the lot. The whole lot. We have always been supportive of each other and trusted each other's decisions. But now we had lost money. There was huge disappointment, and finger-pointing and blaming, and we had to work through that.

I speak very openly about this in my seminars and in my talks and workshops. I am someone who has tried a lot of things and who has had some spectacular failures, some of which have ended up on the front pages of the newspapers. Would I venture into unknown territories today? Yes, I tell my audiences, I would, without a shadow of a doubt. With every experience, good or bad, I've grown and I've learnt so much. I can't say I picked myself up the next day after that Spar disaster – far from it – but I did do it eventually. *We* did it. We went on to do other things, other successful ventures. I like to use the term 'fail forward'.

Where I've been very fortunate as an entrepreneur is that I don't fear failure. So many people are held back by that fear. My position is, you can't know if you don't try. I don't want to live a life of regret, wondering when I'm sixty-five what my life could have been like had I tried this or that. Wondering if I could have, should have, would have. I would rather try something and fail spectacularly at it than not try at all. And that's my business philosophy. It's what I want to teach my children as they come into their own: Don't live a life of regret. Don't be afraid to fail. And if you do fail – which you will, because we all do, that's life – pick yourself up, learn your lessons and move on. Don't berate yourself. If I can leave them with this life philosophy, I think they'll be okay in this world.

Back to Romeo and me. It took a long time, but we recently started working together again! Romeo left corporate life in 2016 after a very successful twelve-year career at Vodacom, and before that at the SABC. He just felt it was time to hang up his tie. And I mean that literally, by the way. He now goes off to work in a shirt, jeans and sneakers, and occasionally a jacket for 'serious' meetings.

When he left Vodacom, Romeo was very clear on what he wanted to do. He is a telecoms specialist, and he wanted to build either a private equity or venture capital firm where he would still focus on his skill set in that space, but branch out into new, related areas. His vision was to build a pan-African, tech-focused venture capital and private equity ICT investment firm, the ecosystem of which includes infrastructure, devices, terminals, and the software and applications that run them. My guy is totally obsessed with the digital transformation of the continent.

I was very keen to be involved, given his experience and expertise, and, of course, the growth in that sector. What I do know is that this telecom and technology space is the future. The Fourth Industrial Revolution, artificial intelligence, the advent of big data, and disruptors such as Uber, Airbnb and Amazon have changed the game for all businesses, not just American businesses.

Romeo brought me in, took me under his wing, and has nurtured and taught me about this new future. It is quite daunting, working with your husband. We have had our share of fights. I'm not really used to reporting to someone; I have always been self-employed. Then there's the fact that we have very different styles of leadership and management. We both have our strengths and weaknesses.

Romeo is very structured and methodical. He literally has to have a matrix and a spreadsheet, and he checks out all the angles and all the possible outcomes, and dots every i and crosses every t. If it doesn't make complete commercial sense, he calls it. I'm more of a risk-taker. I'll say, 'Let's try it anyway, we've got nothing to lose.' Romeo will say, 'We've got everything to lose!' As a rule, he tends to stick to his areas of expertise. My portfolio is very diverse, because I like to try new things.

Sometimes I get frustrated because there are opportunities I'd like to pursue. I always look at the bright side, whereas Romeo will tell me, 'That business opportunity might look good on paper, but let me take you through the potential pitfalls.' He looks at the variables and non-variables and says, 'It's not for us; I'm not prepared to gamble on our children's future.' I guess that's what corporate teaches you. I'm just a born hustler! Romeo is very strong in his conviction that he's working for his family. He gets up every day to work for his children and their future, not for himself. So I might sulk a bit, but I can see that he's making sense.

I've learnt so much from him over the last three years. He's sharpened my business skills and has taught me to be a bit more circumspect about what I choose to get involved in. He has a razor-sharp focus; he'll see what he's focusing on right through to the finishing line. But he also knows to call it early if it's not looking good, whereas I will give it a third and even a fourth chance. One thing about that hunk of mine, he's really not fazed by what people think of him. He does what he needs to do. He has also taught me to trust my instincts about people, which I have always known will never fail me. I have given too many people too many chances, and then I come back to him crying, and he says, 'But I told you about that person.' I am learning those lessons. Age is so defining, and much like my mother, I have learnt not to suffer fools any more.

Working together has its challenges, but it's also incredible to work with someone whom you trust implicitly, admire, love and have total faith in. We both value that. I sit on the boards of the companies he's invested in, and that's given me exposure to the technology sector. If

I find myself out of my depth, I'll go home and talk it through with him and he will school me.

So that's where we are now. We've decided to partner as husband and wife in the ICT sector specifically to grow a legacy not only for our #Tribe, but also for the children of our continent through our family foundation. Romeo says it makes him happy to wake up every day and know that, every waking hour, he is out there building a legacy for his family on his own terms, and impacting lives on the continent in a tangible and meaningful way. I do like that … very much. So, yes, I love him, but I really like him too, very much so. He has an incredible work ethic.

It has been a good experience so far. I've realised that when you sit in a boardroom with your husband, you have to wear a different hat. He's not only my husband, the father of our children, my lover and my friend, he's also my business partner. I might feel, hey, he's actually not such a nice person today, but I leave that at the door and, when we go home, it's Basetsana and Romeo, husband and wife, Mom and Dad, the best of friends!

I have lived, I have loved, I have danced in the rain, I have basked in the sun, I have sung in the shower, I have cried, I have hurt, I have been in darkness and now I live in light. I celebrate each day with which I am blessed. I am fully engaged in everything I do, I take nothing for granted, I am worthy, I am present, I am whole, I am enough, I am healed and I am complete.

This is my story and the journey continues …

PAYING IT FORWARD

_____ MY JOURNEY OF HOPE _____

S omething that keeps me awake at night is South Africa's unemployment rate, which is over 27.1 per cent, but particularly the youth
unemployment rate, which is sitting at around 53 per cent.

The job market can't absorb all of us. For South Africa to be able
to move forward and be competitive, we need entrepreneurs, we need
job creators. I believe it's incumbent on those of us who can to be job
creators, to see how we can add value by being employers and bringing
as many people as we can into the mainstream of our economy.

The businesses in which I am involved employ a lot of people. The
mining business is labour intensive, as is its nature. Then we employ
about 700 people in the travel management business, Travel With Flair.
And there's a cascading effect from each individual in terms of the
effect of their employment on their families and other people. They say,
on average, that one employed person in a household feeds ten people.
Where we have the opportunity and resources to employ people, even
on a small scale, the wider impact is significant.

So job creation is important, but I'm particularly passionate about
mentoring. This past Mother's Day, I was moved to get messages and
shout-outs on Instagram, Facebook and Twitter as a 'mother of the
tribe'. These were from young men and women whom I've mentored,
acknowledging me for the impact I've had on their lives.

Very little can warm your heart more than seeing the young people
you have mentored succeed. Oh, I could tell you so many stories, but
here's one about Dr Tshidi Gule. Tshidi started writing to me when she

was in her fourth year of medicine at the University of the Witwaters-rand. She would send faxes in those days, asking me to mentor her. Those faxes kept coming, and one day I said, 'Okay, let me see this person.' I met up with Tshidi, and at that time she was at a crossroads. She wasn't sure if she really wanted to become a doctor and if she should stay another three years to complete her degree. My advice to her was: Finish what you start. She did, and a couple of years later, I went to her graduation. Long story short, she started a business called the Medispace Wellness Institute, in which I've been an angel investor for the past twelve years. Tshidi wrote a book called *Rough Diamond* about her journey with me as her mentor.

Then there's Bonang Matheba, whom I first noticed as a presenter on a music show on SABC1. She auditioned twice to be a *Top Billing* presenter – that was her dream. I liked her hunger for it. The second time round, we said yes, let's give her a chance, she has so much poten-tial. She was with us for three years, travelling the world. She reminds me of a younger version of myself – how she holds her own in front of the camera, how she's used her brand equity so brilliantly to become a household name. She is now a brand ambassador for Revlon and developing her own line of lingerie with Woolworths, as well as her own brand of bubbly. Kudos to the young person who's sharp enough to understand the moment and who takes every opportunity presented to her. I say big ups to you!

There's also Pearl Thusi, the actress, Penny Mkhize, an HR specialist, and Gugu Makhubele, an attorney. These are just some of the young women with whom I have journeyed. Another, Papama Mtwisha, is the power behind the social movement 'Africa Your Time Is Now', whose merchandise is available in Bloomingdale's online stores worldwide. Papama called me three years ago to say she had decided to leave formal employment. The conversation went something like this:

'Ma, I need to tell you something,' Papama said.

'Yeeeeees.'

'I want to leave my job and pursue the dream I've always told you about.'

'Well, what are you waiting for? What have you got to lose, child? Are you calling me because you're afraid? Follow your heart and your instincts. There are many nets to catch you if you fall. But you won't. We raised you well.'

I have known Papama since she was nineteen. My dear friend Shumikazi Dantile birthed her for me. The actress Nomzamo Mbatha is another young woman with whom I have journeyed. I've known her since she was a little brown-eyed girl, through our good friends Carlos and Ntombi Pereira. To see the many children that I have mentored through the years come into their own has been one of the most rewarding parts of my journey of life, my journey of hope. That is what mentoring is about for me, seeing young men and women realise their full potential. That is my life's purpose. There are not enough hours in the day for me to mentor all the people who contact me from around the country, asking for one-on-one mentorship. Before I had children it was easier, I could put in more hours, but the way my life is now, I engage more with people online.

Once a year, I host a full-day mentorship workshop at the Basetsana Mentorship Academy. From the requests that we receive at the office, we ask everyone to give a motivation and tell us their story, and I select fifty candidates. We get a remarkable range that includes both men and women. This year, we had a woman who was fifty-nine. I was taken aback when she applied, but she said that even though she was older than me, she believed I had something to teach her. I think that's amazing. We are never too old to learn from others.

My journey is quite limited and not that helpful to someone who wants to become, say, an attorney. So I invite friends and captains of industry to be part of the mentorship day as presenters and to take on individual responsibility for mentoring people in their field. But all of us, collectively, have so much to offer.

On the mentorship day there are practical modules – how to start a business, how to raise capital – as well as more inspirational modules. While I can't teach you what you can learn in a lecture hall at university, I think mentoring and mentorship has an important role to play and often teaches you more about life in its totality.

Believe me, this mentoring is not one-sided. I get back so much from these young people. They really keep me on my toes and up to date on what is relevant, hip, hot and happening! They give me a new perspective and fresh ideas, which is great, because I'm quite old school in many ways. I grew up so fast that I missed out on a lot of 'young people' things. I'll open up my WhatsApp and someone will have shared a meme that will keep me in stitches for days. Or there will be a new jam: 'Mommy, there's a new single that has dropped, check it out.' It's helpful for me professionally, too, because being in television and modern media I have to know what's happening in order to keep my finger on the pulse.

It pleases my heart to be an inspiration to young people, especially young women. I'm immensely proud of this new generation of smart and ambitious young women.

And then I have my fabulous friends and peers. Somizi Mhlongo is one such. We both share a passion for mentoring. We believe that 'to whom much is given, much is expected'.

Over the last twenty-five years, while living my truth, writing my own script and walking my journey, little did I know that there were young people – some of them were just tiny tots at the time of my crowning as Miss South Africa – growing up who found inspiration in my life story. Over the years, I have been privileged to meet so many amazing young men and women who have inspired me and conscientised me to take mentoring and mentorship seriously and to be intentional about paying it forward, passing on the baton and trying to make a difference. Mentorship is a symbiotic relationship and I have learnt so much from these beautiful beings. My life is richer and fuller because of having met and journeyed with them. Instead of describing my time with some of these phenomenal #DaughtersOfMyHeart – young people who have gone on to do fantastic things with their lives – I thought it would be more appropriate to ask them to write about their experiences of mentorship. Here are their stories.

* * *

Bonang Matheba
@BonangMatheba
Media personality

There are very few people in life who get the opportunity to work with those who inspire them or who are their role models. Some of my role models include Oprah Winfrey, Beyoncé Knowles, Ava DuVernay, Khanyi Dhlomo and Basetsana Kumalo. Furthermore, it is seldom that one gets the opportunity to meet a woman whose very presence helped shape your future. I have been lucky enough to experience that.

Not only did I witness Basetsana Kumalo being crowned Miss South Africa in 1994, I also saw her journey on *Top Billing*. I saw her become one of South Africa's first black female television executive producers while also being a mother, a wife and essentially an inspiration. I not only got the chance to be employed by her, I also got the opportunity to be directed and mentored by her.

Basetsana successfully managed to diversify herself from Miss South Africa into a *Top Billing* presenter and then executive producer, and she inspired my career as a media personality and multifaceted business-woman. In some ways, I have taken her life as my blueprint.

They often say 'representation matters', and Basetsana Kumalo is one of the first faces we saw on South African television that we could relate to. She therefore marks an important moment in our history. Not only does she mark a significant time in my life, but she also marks a significant time in the country's history.

Basetsana represents change, newness, forgiveness, unity and strength. She is a woman who broke through limitations and borders. In everything she does or in which she is involved, there is love and family; that is what I also try to replicate. She has paved the way and shown us, the new generation of broadcasters and businesswomen, how to pay it forward.

* * *

Dr Tshidi Gule
@drg_wellness
Medical doctor and entrepreneur in the wellness space

To be in the presence of experienced minds is a privilege every bright-eyed mentee can attest to. But to be in the presence of the kind of mentorship that energises, inspires, stretches and empowers you as a young woman forging your own path is a story very few mentees get to tell. I met Mama B fifteen years ago as a tired and passionate medical student seeking guidance on an ambitious concept I'd developed to expand the focus of South African medical programmes towards preventative and digital health. I was raw, I was scared and, back then, extremely but endearingly naive about how business worked.

We were an unexpected mentee/mentor pairing to those who didn't foresee a long and mutually inspiring relationship between a medical nerd and a broadcasting giant. Our joint passion for health innovation and seeing young minds get a chance at impacting the economy positively is what made my mentorship with Mama Bassie a special one. She saw and recognised the wild dreamer and astute medic trapped inside a very shy introvert, and through a series of conversations, took ownership of guiding the process of building my confidence in communicating and piloting my concept to various test audiences, until it was market-ready. That process took six years, but what transpired during that time, the real magic of working with her, is the lifetime of personal one-on-one lessons that have continued to inspire and shape my journey as a woman, entrepreneur and voice within wellness.

Mama Bassie's commitment to the success of young people is truly one of the most remarkable parts of her life story. Mainly because she is a consistent voice of clarity, passion, faith and excellence. I am yet to meet a woman who juggles as much as her and still embraces others with the humanity, compassion and grounded energy she exudes, day in and day out. I often say to her she is a rare gem, because she genuinely is. It is becoming extremely tough for mentors to open their arms to guide and teach in a world where values such as confidentiality, privacy and trust are easily broken. If I could pinpoint one thing that has deepened our relationship outside of our genuine enjoyment of each other's

230

company, it is our inherent understanding of the love and respect we show each other. What I share in my talks on mentorship is how easy it is for mentees to display entitlement around their mentors as 'fixers' rather than sounding boards. It is so important that every mentor is appreciated in the process and held to the values to which I hold myself. That's common decency to me.

One of my fondest memories of my mentorship journey with Mama B took place in 2015, when she sat me down for one of the toughest conversations she's ever had to hold with me. The nature of the talk confronted some tough topics – dealing with loss, human nature and 'knowing who your tribe' really is. I was in deep distress about leaving behind a comfortable and secure life as a doctor. Her candour brought an assurance that choosing the road less travelled does come with a lot of sacrifice, but that any achievement worth pursuing seldom comes without a price. It was a defining moment for me and a moment in time that deepened my appreciation of the sisterhood mindset she imparts to all her 'kids'. I've known very few mentors who are able to easily impart crucial lessons at the level of vulnerability that she does so willingly.

Watching Mama B work makes you want to work just as hard to achieve your dreams. She leads not by her words, but by setting an accessible example of success and personal mastery, something that I continue to draw great inspiration from. It is an honour for me to have someone of her incredible experience show faith in my ideas and put her money where her mouth is, knowing full well the challenges of breaking new ground and staying the course. She is a sharp-shooting mentor who displays courage in both her professional and personal environments. She suffers no fools or laziness, and has helped me navigate some of the toughest chapters of my own. The solid principles she provides are both a compass and a comfort to any young mind who dares to do what they dream. What has humbled me most about my continued journey with her is how her own journey of personal sacrifice has not deterred her from sharing her time, attention and talents with others. Being mentored by Mrs K has been a real testament to the patience, self-mastery and transcendent generosity it takes to realise your own potential, be rewarded for it and pay it forward. We rumble on a lot of issues that young women face together. But don't be fooled, there are plenty of fun times and laughs in between to fill a twelve-foot time capsule! I have grown in leaps and bounds with her next to me and I never apologise for such a rare and unforgettable experience as her mentee. I owe her my gratitude and continued resilience in business.

She is a tour de force. So many women I know both personally and otherwise have been enriched by her passion for youth, strength of character and the softness of a queen whose beauty this country just can't get enough of.

* * *

Gugulethu Makhubele
@gugu_makhubele
Admitted attorney and COO at Soaring Summits Developers

Where does one even start?

I met Ma in 2012 during my first year at the University of Pretoria. Just seeing someone like her on TV made it easier for me to see myself in areas and fields that I never thought I could access. I do not need to repeat her accolades and achievements, but for me, a young girl from a place no one knows, seeing a black woman taking up her (well-deserved) place in spaces that excluded black women was unimaginable. Yet this woman did it and continues to do it with so much ease, it just oozes out of her.

I was also too young to process just how important representation was. She normalised black excellence to a point where I realised I didn't have to beg for inclusion. Conversely, I realised that I had the ability to fight for my own place in the world.

You could only imagine my shock when this woman became a real part of my life. Outside of my dreams, outside of my vision boards and the celebrity status of uMama, this amazing woman became my mentor.

She ensured that I worked towards my goals. She was always very realistic with goal-setting, and her groundwork left me more than prepared. Mama has nurtured me, cared for me and coached me for what seems like my whole life: from cooking onions until they are 'golden brown' to presentation of self, clear enunciation and pronunciation of words during interviews, self-confidence and self-assurance, assembling a wardrobe and/or outfits, coaching me with my career and its demands, and the importance of protecting one's brand.

To be succinct, uMama has taught me fearlessness. She groomed, nurtured and fostered a drive and an ambition in me that I never really saw for myself. Her humility, her kindness and her love are all contagious. Her spirit is so generous. There is no one better fitted to teach self-love and growth. I couldn't have picked a better mentor and I am so much the better for it.

* * *

Penny Mkhize
@pennymkhize
HR specialist

I will never forget January 2008. That was the beginning of what has proven to be a most beautiful journey. I had just finished my NDIP: Human Resources and was embarking on my BTech in the same field, but part time, as my mother had told me that I needed to get a job to further my studies. My mother back in KwaZulu-Natal had told me she would only assist me with registration for the BTech and rent for January to March, then I was going to be on my own, as her job was done.

Here I was, in Pretoria in January 2008, having just returned from the holidays. I was so stressed out because I only had three months to sort out my life, meaning I had to get a job so I could pay for my studies, and I had to get that degree because a diploma would not get me very far.

Word got out to family and friends in Gauteng that I was looking for a job, and while I was job hunting, I received an email from a cousin of mine saying Sekoko Resources was looking for an HR assistant.

I immediately thought to myself, 'That job has my name written all over it.' I sent in my CV and received a response within hours with an interview date and time if I was interested.

It was 31 January 2008 when I walked into Sekoko Resources for an interview. Firstly, it was my first interview ever and, secondly, I was nervous to the point that my belly ached. I was asked to have a seat until I was called for that dreaded interview because I was early – I had to be. It was hardly five minutes when Basetsana Kumalo walked past.

Time stood still. There she was, a woman I had admired literally all my life. I stared. Our eyes met and all that would come out of my mouth was 'hi'. With a warm smile she said, 'Hello, darling' in her deep voice. I was pleasantly surprised.

She walked away and I continued to look at the receptionist for confirmation while my jaw dropped. It had been a tradition at my grandmother's house that we all watched beauty pageants together in the 1990s. We would all choose our favourites from the top ten, and if your favourite didn't make it to the top five, you would get another chance to choose. Bassie was my favourite from the word go and my aunt and I were betting on her. As young as I was, I remember it all.

My heart was racing throughout that interview. I travelled back to my flat in Pretoria. As I entered the lift, my phone rang and I knew it was Sekoko calling. Maybe they wanted me for another interview, but no, they were offering me the position and I was to start that very next Monday, 4 February. I humbly accepted. In the back of my mind I wanted to know what my idol had been doing at my new workplace.

The first thing I asked the HR manager was why Basetsana Kumalo was at Sekoko the day of my interview. I learnt that she was a director of one of Sekoko's joint venture partners, Uzalile Investments, and that I would be seeing her almost every day.

The offices at Sekoko were made of glass so you could see everyone walking past. And there she was again, walking past the HR office because her office was right at the end of the passage. She opened the door and greeted the HR manager, then she looked at me and said, 'We met last week, didn't we?' Before I could answer, she shook my hand firmly. 'Hi, I'm Basetsana Kumalo, nice to meet you.' In my head I was like, duh, I know who you are. The HR manager just had to add, 'You almost made her faint last week when she saw you.' She looked at me with a smile on her face and that was the beginning of a lifelong journey.

I still believe that my steps were ordered by God and that the only reason I got that job was so that I could meet Mama Bassie. She immediately took a liking to me. She would bring me lunch and we would share it during my lunch break. The first month I would be so nervous sitting across from her in her office, then, after cracking a few really funny jokes, I came to see her as human. Our mentorship journey started off by her wanting to know everything I was busy with at the office and really putting me to task. She would be interested in my studies and what book I should be reading that would make sense to the module I was doing at school at the time. At the office, I started being known as 'Bassie's baby'.

I left Sekoko Resources but our relationship carried on. Her wings covered me, and they grew even wider when she learnt about the hardships of my life. She wanted to see me flourish and prosper. I was her little project that she wasn't going to let go of.

On the morning of 9 September 2009, my cousin and his wife came to tell me of the sudden passing of my mother. She had been brutally murdered by her fiancé the previous night because he was jealous, and when he learnt that my mother was planning on leaving him, he ended her life as well as his own. I had to live with the reality of this murder-suicide. My world took a turn, and not for the better, for the worse.

On a random evening two weeks after the burial of my mom, I received a text: 'Hi Baby, are you ok? You've been quiet, just checking on you.' Only then did I realise Ma didn't know what had happened. I told her that I wasn't fine, and when she kept prying I immediately called her as I couldn't type what had happened – it would've been a reminder of my painful reality. I could hear her breathing on the other end and both of us said nothing for a good minute. She then said, 'You coming to see me tomorrow, right?' She carried on: 'Are you back at work? Who are you staying with right now?' The questions just kept coming. Eventually she said, 'Why didn't you tell me?' I then sobbed on the phone. 'It's okay, child, I'm here and not going anywhere,' she said.

The coming months were difficult, but Ma called me every day without fail when driving home from work. If she didn't call, she would send me a text late in the evening explaining how hectic her day was and assuring me we would talk in the morning.

Three months into mourning, I had not laughed or smiled. One particular morning, I woke up at 3 a.m., my pyjamas soaked in tears because of a dream I had had. I called Ma in the wee hours of the morning. 'Baby girl, are you okay?' she asked in a sleepy voice. No words were coming out of my mouth, all she could hear was weeping. Ma stayed up reading the Bible and singing to me until 5:30 a.m, when she eventually said, 'Child, weep no more, I am here now, I'm your mother now ... sssshhhhhhh.' I was taken aback, but I knew she meant every word.

Our relationship grew from strength to strength. She shifted from my mentor to my mother. But if you know Ma, you know mentorship is twenty-four/seven. She doesn't need to teach a class, but being around her and being fortunate to sit at her feet, you are guaranteed a lesson. It's natural for her to drop pearls of wisdom. Ma has been with me every step of the way in my career, really pushing me to reach for the stars, and sometimes it was uncomfortable but necessary.

In 2016, I was turning thirty years old and it had become evident that I had not done a ceremony called *uMemulo* (coming of age). I was stuck between a rock and a hard place as I was advised that I could not buy the livestock myself, meaning my uncle or someone in my family had to buy the cow and goats from their own pockets. It was imperative that this ceremony be done. My family in KwaZulu-Natal was consulted and my aunts said they would buy the goats, but no one came forward for the cow. If my mother had still been alive, this would've been done by her.

My heart ached because I could see that without this cow, this ceremony would not go ahead. One afternoon, I went to see Ma. She saw that I had been crying and asked what was the matter. I told her about the cow and that no one in my family was willing to bite the bullet and do this for me. She looked at me and said, 'It takes a village to raise a child, and I have been part of that village that raised you, so I'll buy the cow, baby girl, don't worry.' My family tried to oppose it, but Ma said, 'If I don't do this for this child, who will?' The silence was very loud. Little did we know how profound this gesture actually was.

It was a symbol of her 'purchasing' me. When I learnt what it meant after the *uMemulo*, and had to tell Ma, she was gobsmacked. Not that she would've changed her mind, but it's always better to know all the repercussions before getting into something.

I have been scolded, not just scolded, *really* scolded when I went astray, but she has never given up on me. When the world is certain that Ma is about to walk away from me, she reaches out her hand again and declares that I am her child and that there is no bin for children.

I have never met anyone with a heart of gold like Ma. She doesn't suffer fools, but I always tell her, 'Ma, you're a better human than me,' and I'll always love her for taking me in and raising me as her own. Ma always talks about paying it forward, but I don't know if I will ever be able to do for someone what she has done, and continues to do, for me. I cannot qualify it in monetary terms, as I'm sure it's sitting in the trillions. If only she knew, she wouldn't have greeted me in the foyer of Sekoko Resources. God knew exactly what He was doing that day.

* * *

Nomzamo Mbatha
@nomzamo_m
Actress and UNHCR Goodwill Ambassador

My late baby sister Carla and I were often packed into the back of my aunt and uncle's car to go to Romeo and Bassie's house for lunch or dinner or a Sunday Soul session. The adults would roam the garden, laughing loudly and dancing ever so jovially against the backdrop of a braai stand, a buzzing kitchen and uncle Romeo on the decks handling the music. We would run around the house, play in the swimming pool and sometimes Aunt Bassie would just wrap her arms around us and kiss our cheeks.

She was truly the picture of happiness. With the light of the world dancing in those almond-shaped eyes. Just pure joy. Sometime in 2003, this one particular Sunday trip was in the direction of Soweto. It felt different. My aunt had buckled Carla and me up in the car and was awfully quiet on the way to our destination.

We arrived in Soweto and walked through the door of the house we were visiting. Aunt Bassie was on the couch, face down and completely broken, in tears. Those eyes were without the light of the world dancing in them. My aunt sat next to her and held her as she wept. Carla and I stood and watched, knowing that something was wrong. Her father had passed away. She was holding onto his brown tweed jacket the whole time. In that moment she said something that sat in my soul for a long time. She looked up to my aunt and said, 'I found myself sitting in his closet, Ntombi. I have been smelling all of his clothes. I want to always remember his scent.'

She might not remember this particular moment, as I have never shared it with her. But this moment taught me so much about grief and loss. That a person's scent can serve as a lingering nostalgic reminder of what was. That pain demands to be felt. Two years later I lost my father and I held onto his jerseys in the same way, wanting to always remember his scent.

Whether in winning or losing, she is the very personification of liberation – everything and everyone around her finds their personal freedom too. With no apology, with zero permission. All very unconscious. Just like purpose. Graceful in every way possible, and my God does she operate from a place of truth and sincerity with integrity and fairness as her compass.

Aunt Bassie, God made sure that heaven was at a standstill when He made you. Your soul has lived for centuries and lifetimes before this and will continue to live into the next lifetime. You have never missed any of my milestones and you celebrate my success as though it is your own. You remind us to always listen to the voice within and trust our instincts.

God's purpose over our lives will be manifested in an even greater way. As you love to say, 'Shy don't pay the bills, honey!'

You are living and breathing proof of God's love for us, and gog'Moeder taught you the value of hard work and humility. From selling fruit in the township to standing on global stages. Never discouraged by social barriers.

Your footprints in the sands of history were etched from the day you were born and I am grateful to be living in your lifetime and be nestled in the bosom of your love. Forever my guide and prayer warrior.

They say family is your first line of defence, and my goodness, do you hold the fort for those you love. I'm always learning.

Thank you. For everything.

* * *

Somizi Mhlongo
@somizi
Media personality

I first met you when you entered Miss Soweto and I was like, 'There's a star right there. There is something special about this woman.' And when I got to know you, you actually inspired me.

I realised how selfless you are, how giving you are and how content you are with the space you are in, from the time that you started presenting *Top Billing* and you were not shaken when the new 'IT' girls came on board.

You actually embraced them, you created the 'IT' girls and that inspired me, and showed me how important it is to hand over the baton and how important it is to be content with your space and realise how big the pie is. Through the years I realised the importance of mentorship because we need to realise this thing is a journey, this thing is generational and we have to leave a legacy.

What is the point of being a shining star and when your star dims or when your star dies all you leave is darkness? You made sure that when your star one day dims, it won't cause darkness; it will actually cause more light, more brightness, more shine.

Your light will keep on shining through others, and I have been inspired by that and I'm very big on doing that as well. I know now that my star is still shining bright and one day it's going to dim, and when it dims, it won't switch off because there's another star that will ignite and carry it on. Mentorship is very important to me because I know that no man is an island; one and two, this pie is big enough for us to share it together. No one will be left unfulfilled or hungry.

I am a huge believer that when I win, my friends win or anyone that is inspired by me and looks up to me wins. When somebody else wins, I also win because it feels like a win to me. I am a big believer in having a circle of winners and I have always used this example that the minute you are the Beyoncé of the group all the time, there's something wrong with you.

You need to switch roles: one day you're the Beyoncé, the next day you are the Kelly, the next day you're the Michelle, and it means that Michelle learns from Kelly, Kelly learns from Beyoncé and Beyoncé also learns from Michelle, who has qualities that Beyoncé doesn't have. Beyoncé can learn tenacity, perseverance and patience from Kelly, and both Michelle and Kelly can learn work ethic, endurance, hunger and staying power from Beyoncé.

So if we can't learn from each other then we are doomed as human beings. I am a big believer in mentorship, in sharing, caring and handing over the baton, and you, my friend, you've done it very well over the years and you are still doing it. Well done to you, kudos, I love you. And *yaaasss*, here's to great reading, *yaaasss bazala* Bassie.

* * *

Pearl Thusi
@PearlThusi
Actress and media personality

I met Sis Bassie around July 2007. I was nineteen and pregnant. As excited as I was to meet her, I was nervous … What interesting thing did I have to say to a woman of her stature? I was a pregnant teenager essentially, so how did I expect her to even take me seriously?

But I had to set my insecurities aside and realise that this was a lifetime opportunity to meet one of my idols and really take in every ounce of knowledge I could from this incredible opportunity the universe had just afforded me. 'Everything happens for a reason,' I reminded myself. Still, I felt embarrassed that she'd taken some time to meet little pregnant me when she had TV shows to produce, businesses to run and a family to take care of. I am forever grateful to the person who arranged this meeting … it changed my life.

We had arranged to meet at the Palazzo hotel in Montecasino. I remember looking around and feeling so overwhelmed by the opulence around me and feeling like I didn't belong there. I saw her and carefully approached her, and finally the moment had arrived.

Her aura, her smile, her energy, her glow … I could have drowned in it. But no, it was dense with warmth, care and kindness. I floated blissfully in its strong and healing power. I enjoyed so much being drenched, and I splashed, like a child, in our conversation as it continued.

I watched the ripples spread into my spirit and create waves that crashed into my consciousness and dissolved my deepest insecurities and washed away my doubts. A deep, bottomless ocean of knowledge that keeps on giving with no concern of ever going dry … love never runs dry anyway. That day is a landmark in my life.

Dear Mother and Sister of Mine …

What I have enjoyed most about learning from you is that your kindness comes in a powerful, intangible form but is balanced with tangible practicality. Something I have carried with me and applied in what has become my own way of showing love.

As a young pregnant woman, I'd never consulted a gynaecologist – you asked me about it and I told you I hadn't found one. You arranged my first ever appointment. He then delivered my first child.

You prayed for my unborn child. You told me I was beautiful, smart and had a bright future. I remember thinking, 'If she thinks that, then it must be true.'

The first laptop I ever had was a gift from you.

Without you, I wouldn't have been able to bury my grandmother. You made sure my daughter and I were there to pay our last respects.

You let me accompany you to places and circles that grew my mind and spirit.

You let me come to your home and spend priceless time with you and your children … I watched you cook. You came to my daughter's birthday parties. I couldn't believe it.

I'll never forget walking into your home ... the fact that 'I can do this too' burnt so bright when I looked around me and saw the fruits of your hard work standing strong and proud. A young black woman with so much strength. I know what's possible because you let me see and welcomed me into a world of possibilities.

No one will ever be perfect. Not a single person on this earth will know what it is like to create or follow the perfect footsteps. That's what they say ... and if this is true – if imperfect people are the only people in this world, and you're the one God has brought my way – then I'm at least in the perfect company.

Thank you for being my star, compass and anchor. I love you so dearly. I am so proud of you. The world tried to break you, and I've seen you soldier on in the darkness and through tears. Still loving, still giving ... If only they knew they were fuelling your fires, that you control your elements with God's guidance, they might not have bothered.

You became a sister and a mother to me. I have experienced you walk the talk, first-hand.

I understand the power of mentorship through you. That giving of one's time and resources is not just an act of selflessness or Godliness, but also an act of faith. Faith in yourself, those you give to, humanity and, most importantly, God.

* * *

Papama Mtwisha
@papamar
Creative director and founder of the 'Africa Your Time Is Now' movement

I often say that my story would be incomplete without a chapter on the impact you've had on my life. Some of the priceless lessons I have learnt from you directly and indirectly are:
- My love for God is vital and should govern everything I do.
- To never get too attached to praise or criticism.
- Humility.
- Most of the life-changing books in my library are from you.

Your presence has been such a gift in my life, Ma. Knowing that I have you in my corner has made this journey a tad easier. Thank you for being my safe space to share, vent and cross-check my decisions.

There are few people I know who are as busy as you, but you have always made time to respond to my requests – no matter how big or small. Do you have any idea what that does for someone? Being reminded that you matter, and you are heard and you are seen. My world is truly a better place because you are in it.

Because of all that you are to me, I have no choice but to pay it forward. You inspire me more than you know.

I thank you from the bottom of my heart.

* * *

Harmony Katulondi
@harmonythe1
Forbes Africa 30 Under 30, creative entrepreneur, philanthropist and *Top Billing* presenter

Phenomenal! That's what I thought the first time I saw uMama Basetsana Kumalo on TV and I knew that I would one day meet her; it was inevitable. From her gracious smile, poise and intellect to her drive and ambition, it's no wonder she's achieved so much. The more she achieved, the more limitless her opportunities seemed. But it wasn't necessarily the success that drew me; it was what she did with the success that really got my attention. From her philanthropic work and successful businesses to her faith, she seemed wholesome, balancing everything with a sense of harmony, and that's what I was about. Watching her on *Top Billing* made me feel like I would one day be there, it was possible! But I didn't want to be limited by just being on TV – there is so much more to me, I have so much more to offer; from different sectors in business to different gifts, talents, ideas and philanthropic strategies … And she embodied all of this. If she could do it, so could I.

One of the most important traits of a great mentor is their ability to inspire, motivate and mentor their mentees through the way they live their lives, which is what uMama Bassie did for me – she was a mentor to me before we even met and before she even knew my name. Her actions would inspire many of the steps I took in my career. Her boldness broke the mould of the image of great entertainment, shattered the barriers of what black people can do and put faith to work, showing that with God anything is possible.

I would always see her at church, always elegant, well dressed with a chic sense of style. Her demeanour was always kind, ready to say hi to anyone who was brave enough to approach her. She was very respectful, greeting everyone the same and leaving you with kind, wise words here and there. Down to earth for someone who soared so high. And when she stepped onto the Rhema Bible Church stage, her personality was not only noticeable but also enchanting! It was clear that she was made for this and that God's hand was on her.

And then I got a message, followed by a phone call. Rhema Bible Church was having a conference with over 75 000 people attending and viewing online across the world, with an amazing line-up of great worship and international speakers, and they wanted me to be the host. If that was not enough of an honour, I was to do it alongside the oh-so-fabulous uMama Basetsana Kumalo! I was humbled. There was obviously the pressure of being able to keep up with her, but I knew God had a plan.

Then she asked to meet up. I thought it would be to discuss how we were to work together on stage, but she called me so that she could listen. If God had orchestrated this, she wanted to know who I was, to see where I was in life and the state of my heart. I told her about myself and she shared the same. I actually wished that I had recorded the session, but many of the wise words she poured into me that day and the days after will live with me forever.

I was surprised at how open and real she was with me. Telling me about the tough times she faced from helping keep her family afloat at a young age to going through some difficulties with children. 'Life happens to all of us, but we have to keep going,' she said. Which is what she did, whenever she fell due to her own choices or when life knocked her down, she would get back up, dust herself off, look unto God and keep going, something that I do to this day too.

The biggest thing that struck me about our conversation was the fact that she took the Rhema Bible Church stage/platform (and any other platform) seriously. So much so that she was going on a fast to thank God and ask for His guidance to be the best vessel and servant possible and to do His will to the best of her ability, which inspired me to do the same. 'You shouldn't take this opportunity lightly, my boy, it's a big responsibility,' she affirmed. 'Pastor Ray has done so much for this country and the church, and now has entrusted us with this conference and so has God. Don't take it lightly; in fact, don't take any platform you're given lightly.' These words echoed the wise counsel of many great people who poured into my life. She was right!

There were so many people who fought and sacrificed for her to be where she is now, and she continues to do the same for people like me to get me to where I am today and to go even further! And I will do the same for others to achieve even greater heights, because of great people like the amazing uMama Basetsana Kumalo.

Over the years, I've learnt so much from her and her life: honour God always, especially with your actions, no matter what's going on in your life. Never give up – God knows our hearts and will grant us our hearts' desires if we're faithful. Your beginning is not your end. We're all gifted with a talent that we can use to impact this world. You playing small does not serve anyone. Go out and slay!

Mama Basetsana Kumalo, thank you for setting a great example. For being an inspiration and for honouring God with your gifts. One of the things I love most about you is how you honour God and God's servant, our spiritual father Pastor Ray McCauley. You recognise his sacrifices and you serve with a beautiful heart. You respect all those around you, but you're not afraid to break boundaries and reach new heights, setting the way for us to follow. You stand on the shoulders of many people who made great sacrifices and now we stand on your shoulders, doing things the previous generation couldn't even have imagined!

I can proudly say that I'm a Forbes Africa 30 Under 30, *Top Billing* presenter, entrepreneur and philanthropist (among many other things), and it's thanks to the phenomenal people I have in my life, like you, uMama Basetsana Kumalo.

I will forever continue pushing, continue believing, continue trusting in God, continue breaking ground, continue soaring, continue leading, continue succeeding, continue winning, continue positively impacting nations, continue changing the game and continue setting new trends. Inspiring and motivating others! And I wish you all this and so much more.

EPILOGUE

I'm sitting in the family room, writing this last chapter of my story. It is a comfy, sunny room that opens onto the *stoep*. Through the window, I can see the kids playing on the jungle gym. It's a sight that always makes me happy, because when I was young, I dreamt of having children and building a big jungle gym for them in the garden. In the evenings, they watch TV in this room, and because it opens onto the kitchen, I can see them and chat to them while I'm cooking supper.

It took us nearly two years to build our dream home. We loved it from the moment we moved in – the house, the privacy and the calm that comes with being out in the country.

Walking through my home, I'm reminded of so many moments in our lives. The walls and surfaces are filled with photographs, some professional, but many taken by us and our friends and family. So many photographs – of our wedding and our travels, of our family and our children at every age and stage. One of my favourites is a frame with three photographs: Romeo holding each of our newborns. There's a whole mantelpiece reserved for our godchildren – Romeo and I have ten between us! But the most special and emotional are the many pictures of my parents and of Madiba.

There are photographs of me with some of the people I met as Miss South Africa and then as a presenter on *Top Billing*. Each takes me back to a specific moment in time. It's a real who's who: Michael Jackson, Quincy Jones, Will Smith, Sol Kerzner, Hugh Masekela, Walter Sisulu, King Mswati III of Swaziland, Wesley Snipes, Luther

Vandross, Blair Underwood, Mama Winnie Madikizela-Mandela, President Thabo Mbeki, President Jacob Zuma, the Bee Gees, Samuel L. Jackson, Kenny Lattimore and – *oh dahling!* – Patsy, or I should say Joanna Lumley, from *Absolutely Fabulous*. There are pictures of Mama Miriam Makeba, Oprah, Sade, Mariah Carey, Jean-Claude van Damme, James Earl Jones, Al Jarreau and Gloria Estefan. And there are so many more … Who would have thought that a girl from a little four-roomed house in Soweto would find herself in such esteemed company?

Looking at these photographs brings me into a space of reflection and gratitude for the blessed life I've lived and the people I have met, known and loved.

When you go into the kitchen, that's where you see the real talent! The children's drawings and artworks that they bring home. I always put those on the fridge. I want my kids to feel a sense of pride and achievement from their own efforts, and to see that hard work pays off. There are school certificates acknowledging their interests and talents, from marimba band and soccer to Kgosi's Mathletics. There's even a pen licence – that was a big moment, I tell you. No more writing in pencil for Nathi! He sorts out our house gadgets now.

When I'm cooking, I sometimes stop to read the prayer that I have stuck up on a cupboard door:

> Lord bless my kitchen, and the food I prepare,
> with grateful thanks and loving care.
> We bow our heads in gratitude,
> for the joyful blessing of our food.
> Bless all who share the food you provide with happiness and peace
> And forever, thy love.

If you were to go upstairs, you might find some unofficial artworks from my young Picassos. Yes, they have drawn on the walls. And yes, at the time it makes you mad, but at the end of the day a wall is just a wall. You can repaint it. This is a home, after all.

My story is coming to a close, for now. It has been a nostalgic and heart-warming experience, going back over my life. I've remembered incidents and people I thought I'd forgotten, my memory jogged by the yellowing press clippings and photographs in my archives. I've cried, thinking of the painful times, the loss of my beloved parents and of my unborn children. I've laughed, remembering the fun times I have had. I've revisited the choices I've made, the good and the bad. And the most important one: marrying Romeo! Writing this memoir has been a cathartic and healing experience for me.

Overall, I have to say, there's very little I would change. I will continue to dance to the rhythm of my own beat. I will continue to laugh, to live fully and to love.

When I look at my life, all forty-five years of it, I feel like I'm just at the beginning of my journey. There's so much more I want to do. I'm inspired to be an even better wife, mother, sister, aunt, friend and mentor. The entrepreneur in me isn't ready to rest, not by a long shot!

I have done what I set out to do. To tell my story and my truth, in my own words. When my children and grandchildren read this book, they will hear my voice. Thank you for sharing this journey with me.

Wishing you love and light on your own journey,

Basetsana

ACKNOWLEDGEMENTS

To God be the glory for carrying me through the last forty-five years. Through it all, my faith has carried me. Getting a manuscript ready for publication is not easy, but more challenging is remembering who to thank, not only for bringing the book to realisation, but also for featuring in my life and thus providing material for this book. My heartfelt gratitude to all those who have helped bring *Bassie – My Journey of Hope* to life in so many different ways. To my two angels in heaven, my mother and father, *Ke a leboga ndiyabulela*.

This book was inspired by my children. Thank you, Nkosinathi, Kgositsile and Bontle ba Morena, you are my greatest gifts and my highest calling, and this book is my gift to you. Thank you for choosing me to be your mother. To the love of my life, Romeo, thank you for standing by me and walking this journey of writing this book with me. Your honest and constructive critique has been most appreciated, even though at times it was hard to hear. You are such an amazing man; thank you for being my biggest supporter. To my siblings, I love you deeply.

Advocate Thuli Madonsela, my sheer admiration for you, for what you stand for and for what you believe in has restored my hope in humanity. You are a moral compass whom many of us look to for direction. Dr Phumzile Mlambo-Ngcuka, words cannot begin to describe how sincerely grateful I am that you took the time to read my memoir and pen such deep, profound and beautiful thoughts – they evoked a deeper consciousness in me. You have always been a shining example of a woman who lifts others as they rise. Thank you for believing in me. Thank you both for honouring me by writing the forewords. I am truly grateful.

To Mum Graça Machel, you inspire me to do better. When I grow up, I want to be like you. I love you, Mum.

To my dear Louise Sherriff, my brilliant executive assistant, I couldn't have done it without you. You knew what a priority this project was to me, and you became the 'sheriff' and made sure everything worked around it. To my authentic friend and legal eagle Jack Phalane of Fluxmans Attorneys, thank you for always being there and making sure I dot the i's and cross the t's. I can confidently say that you have my back.

The Penguin Random House publishing team, you have made the experience of writing this book remarkable. I would particularly like to thank my publisher, Marlene Fryer, and managing editor, Ronel Richter-Herbert, for putting Penguin Random House resources behind this book – you are amazing. Melt Myburgh, you believed in the book from our very first meeting – you are such a gem, thank you. My editor, Bronwen Maynier, thank you for your diligence; my proofreader, Dane Wallace, thank you for your perfectionism. Surita Joubert, Talita van Graan and Amanda van Rhyn, thank you for your enthusiasm, energy and the brilliance you brought to the project.

To my glam squad that worked on the cover shoot: creative director Papama Mtwisha, photographer Sibusiso Sibanyoni, hair stylist Ade Ogunneye and make-up artist Lomso Kwinana, thank you for bringing your creative geniuses to the fore. It was so much fun doing the shoot with you. I think the cover came out beautifully.

A special thanks to all those who helped bring this book to life in so many other ways: Kate Sidley, Kopano Gelman, Doreen Morris, G.G. Alcock, Josina Machel, Zelda la Grange and Dr Tshidi Gule – my deepest gratitude to you for your time and contribution.

Savita Mbuli, Jill Grogor, Thato Matuka, Ofentse Matuka, Dr Mpho Ndou, Rudy Rashama, Yele Agunbiade and Philip Sowah, you have made this labour of love come alive in such a beautiful way. Thank you so very much. It's been absolutely delightful to work with you on the launch event. Sandton City mall, thank you for hosting the launch of the book.

Rakgadi Agnes Mofokeng, Mary Singini, Victor Mogale, Mandla Ncube, what would I do without you? You are the blessing that the Lord bestowed upon our family. Thank you for loving #TheTribe and for looking after them when duty calls. Without you I would not be able to fulfil the roles of being a wife, a mother and a professional. You daily help me straddle the world of being a working mom, a caring mom and a present mom. I can never thank you enough. May the Lord remember each of you, and your families, by name. To my spiritual father Pastor Ray McCauley, what a gift you have been to my life and the kingdom. You and Zelda mean so much to me and my family. Thank you for your unwavering love.

To my business partners Patience Stevens of Tswelopele Productions (Pty) Ltd, Clifford Elk of Connect Channel (Pty) Ltd), Lindiwe Leketi of Pro Direct Investments (Pty) Ltd, and Johanna Mukoki, Robert Wilke and Tibor Zsadanyi of Travel With Flair (Pty) Ltd, thank you for your understanding when I needed to go on a writing retreat and you kept the ships sailing.

To the extraordinary women in my life who have been a great sister-hood, you know your fine selves by name. My girlfriends, my mentors, daughters of my heart, you make this journey of life so beautiful – thank you for your love, loyalty, laughter and the fun times.

To each and every person who deemed it worthy to purchase my memoir, thank you. It is my sincere hope that this book will inspire you in some way, to count your blessings and indeed write your own story.

May the blessings of the Lord be upon you always.